The Future for the Global Securities Market

Legal and Regulatory Aspects

The Future for the Global Securities Market

Legal and Regulatory Aspects

Edited by
FIDELIS ODITAH
Barrister; Travers Smith Braithwaite Lecturer in Corporate Finance Law, University of Oxford, and Fellow of Merton College

CLARENDON PRESS . OXFORD
1996

Oxford University Press, Walton Street, Oxford OX2 6DP
Oxford New York
Athens Auckland Bangkok Bombay
Calcutta Cape Town Dar es Salaam Delhi
Florence Hong Kong Istanbul Karachi
Kuala Lumpur Madras Madrid Melbourne
Mexico City Nairobi Paris Singapore
Taipei Tokyo Toronto
and associated companies in
Berlin Ibadan

Published in the United States
by Oxford University Press Inc., New York

British Library Cataloguing in Publication Data
Data available

Library of Congress Cataloging in Publication Data
The future for the global securities market : legal and regulatory aspects / [edited by] Fidelis Oditah.
p. cm.
Includes Index.
1. Securities. 2. Capital market—Law and legislation.
3. Financial institutions—Law and legislation. I. Oditah, Fidelis.
K1114.F87 1996 346'.092—dc20 [342.692] 95–26851
ISBN 0–19–826219–1

1 3 5 7 9 10 8 6 4 2

Typeset by Hope Services (Abingdon) Ltd.
Printed in Great Britain
on acid-free paper by
Biddles Ltd.,
Guildford & King's Lynn

Foreword

The papers contained in this book were originally prepared for presentation at a Colloquium in Oxford in September 1995 organised by the Norton Rose M5 Group and they are of great value. The contributors are distinguished, and come from many different fields and from several countries. The papers discuss many of the different facets of the global financial markets. Thus they explain how a global offering can be achieved. Conflicts of laws problems are identified and discussed. The nature of rights arising from dealings in securities in the Euroclear and Cedel settlement systems are analyzed. Securitisation is explained. The regulation of the financial markets from the point of view of the United States, the United Kingdom and France is examined. The papers look to the future to see what progress is being made towards cooperation between regulators. The liability of dealers in derivatives is discussed.

These papers are very timely. In the last ten years or so there have been major changes. In 1986 Professor Tamar Frankel wrote:

> The current developments show a multitude of practices in international trading. Large brokerage firms have developed their own around the clock trading techniques, while they simultaneously trade through stock exchanges and organisations or broker-dealers. In other words, there is no clear emerging pattern of trading or institutional organisation. Right now, anything and everything goes, so long as it works. Since we are at the beginning of the era of international securities markets, we may expect a period of experimentation and perhaps the emergence of a number of dominant patterns and institutions that will continue to develop side by side.[1]

The papers in this book show some of the progress that has been made in the last ten years. But the process of development is a continuing one in response to changing needs. One example may be given. In February 1995, Baring Brothers & Co. Ltd., a leading merchant bank, went into administration. The speed and manner of its collapse gave rise to much concern from the point of view of regulators of the banking and securities industries all over the world. This concern led in May 1995 to the Windsor Declaration, an agreement on cooperation in certain specific areas between regulators from sixteen different countries. This and other recent events may mark the beginning of a new era of cooperation on an international basis in the field of regulation of global financial markets. To use Professor Frankel's words, a new 'dominant pattern' may be emerging in this field of international cooperation in specific areas.

What the papers contained in this book cannot reflect is the lively debate that took place at the Colloquium itself. It was generally agreed that the global market only exists in the sense that the principal domestic markets co-operate with each other and that the diversity of legal and economic structures makes convergence difficult. Beyond that there was much debate: should there be more or less regulation?

[1] Introduction to a symposium on the Internationalization of the Securities Markets (1986) 4 Boston Univ. Int. L.J.1,2.

how extensive is systemic risk? does the global market lead to the diminution of the rights and protection of investors? should regulators be prepared to accept financial statements prepared in accordance with accounting standards applying in the home state of an overseas issuer as an alternative to requiring compliance with the more stringent accounting standards applying in their own jurisdiction? There is much to be gained from informed debate. We have no doubt that these papers will provide as firm a basis for discussion of issues arising from the future evolution of the global securities market as they did for the debates at Oxford on 14th and 15th September 1995.

Royal Courts of Justice
London
14 November, 1995

Andrew Morritt
Mary Arden

Editor's Preface

This book is the product of a Colloquium held by the Norton Rose M5 Group of independent legal practices and the Oxford University Law Faculty at St John's College, Oxford, on 14 and 15 September 1995. Its theme—The Future for the Global Securities Markets—is very important and topical. Securities markets worldwide are going through a period of unprecedented change and growth. Cross-border securities transactions both in the primary and secondary markets as well as the range of financial products have increased dramatically in the last decade. The change and growth has created more choice and risk for investors, increased the breadth and depth of securities markets and given issuers unparalleled access to a global investor base. It has also enabled practices developed in one jurisdiction to be adapted and exported elsewhere. It is now possible to talk about 'global' offering of securities. Several factors have driven and shaped these developments, including: the deregulation of many national economies in terms of abolition of exchange controls and liberalisation of capital flows; advances in information technology; the rise of institutional investors particularly pension funds; privatisations; the increasing internationalisation of investments; and the increasing competition for business and influence between different securities markets. These factors have brought about increasing integration and convergence of securities markets in different parts of the world. However, the integration and convergence of different securities markets has not yet resulted in the emergence of a truly single 'global' securities market.

This is largely because in virtually every jurisdiction (with the possible exception of Member States of the European Union), the regulation of public distribution of securities as well as the financial intermediaries through whom second-hand securities are bought and sold on organised markets is territorial, and shows insignificant deference to the laws and practices of other jurisdictions. Reciprocity is not a strong feature of securities regulation worldwide with the result that securities regulation is fragmented. This, by itself, is unremarkable: legislation and its enforcement are inherently territorial. Most securities laws impose penal consequences for violations and, with insignificant exceptions, no country enforces the penal laws of another. The problem is how to adapt national securities regulation to the increasingly cross-border nature of securities transactions. The challenges which the existing fragmentation of the regulation of the emerging 'global' securities market pose for cross-border securities transactions include the following: first, how issuers in one jurisdiction can access the securities market in another; second, how licensed financial intermediaries in one jurisdiction can carry on business and effect customer orders in another without becoming subject to the licensing and other laws of the other jurisdiction; and, finally, how territorial enforcement of securities legislation can contain transnational securities transactions. There is, in addition, legal uncertainty arising from the identification of the applicable law. Even where there are choices of law agreements, these frequently have to yield to mandatory rules of different countries, even though the objective of securities regulation in all jurisdictions is investor protection primarily through mandatory disclosure requirements.

Some of these challenges are being tackled. In the European Union, for example, the implementation of the Public Offers Prospectus Directive, the various Mutual Recognition of Offer Documents Directives and the Investment Services Directive, represent a significant step towards thc creation of a single European securities market. It is now possible for an issuer in Denmark who has prepared a public offer prospectus approved by the Danish Competent Authority to use the same prospectus for a public distribution of securities anywhere in the European Union without having to prepare separate ones for each of the markets in which it proposes to make a public distribution. Also from 1 January 1996, a financial intermediary in one Member State can carry on investment business anywhere in the European Union on the basis of its home-state authorisation. These developments have significantly opened up and liberalised the European securities markets, but are only a small step towards the creation of a truly global securities market. Other securities markets, particularly the United States, Canada and Japan, need to respond to developments within the European Union by lowering the significant barriers which impede access to their markets. Regional cooperation, such as exists between the United States and the Canadian provinces, is welcome but insufficient. Liberalisation of national securities regulations which creates safe harbours for sales to qualified institutional investors, such as United States' Rule 144A and Regulation S, are a step in the right direction but discriminate against retail investors and do not address the significant barrier to cross-border securities transactions which the United States' Accounting Rules (US GAAP) impose. In this regard, the agreement entered into between the International Organisation of Securities Commissions (IOSCO) and the International Accounting Standards Committee (IASC) enabling, from the end of 1999, financial statements of issuers making a cross-border securities offering to be presented in accordance with a single set of internationally accepted accounting principles, is welcome. When the agreement comes into force it would obviate the need to adapt financial statements to the (sometimes conflicting) accounting requirements of different jurisdictions. There is therefore evidence that at least some of the impediments to cross-border securities transactions are being discussed and addressed. However, much is left to be done.

The chapters in this book explore some of the issues arising from cross-border securities transactions. The book is divided into two parts: comparative legal problems and market regulation, and hopefully contributes to a better understanding of the issues which arise from the increasingly cross-border nature of securities transactions. Both the Colloquium and this book would not have been possible but for the assistance of a number of individuals. I would like to thank Peter Smith, the Chief Executive of the Norton Rose M5 Group, for assisting with the organisation of the Colloquium and proof-reading some of the papers, his secretary Emma Guest, Professor Roy Goode, the contributors for keeping to a very tight deadline for the submission of their papers, Lord Justice Morritt and Mrs Justice Arden for chairing the working sessions at the Colloquium and writing the foreword to this book. Finally, I am grateful to the editorial staff of the Oxford University Press, particularly Richard Hart and Margaret Shade, for the speed and enthusiasm with which they handled the publication of this book and for preparing the tables and index.

Fidelis Oditah

Gray's Inn
21 December 1995

Contents

List of Contributors

Bernard Asher, Chairman, HSBC Investment Bank Limited

Jeffery Barratt, Norton Rose, London

Daniel Braverman, Cleary, Gottlieb, Steen & Hamilton, London

James Cheek III, Senior Partner, Bass Berry & Sims, Adjunct Professor of Law, Vanderbilt Law School

Fiona Christie, Manager, New Issues, Cedel Bank

Margaret Coltman, Norton Rose, London

Christopher Cruickshank, Principal Administrator, DG XV, European Commission

Herdeep Dosanjh, UK Legal Counsel, Cedel Bank

Roy Goode, Norton Rose Professor of English Law, University of Oxford

Edward F. Greene, Cleary, Gottlieb, Steen & Hamilton, London

Hans van Houtte, University of Leuven, Stibbe Simont Monahan Duhot, Brussels

John Kay, Chairman of London Economics, Visiting Professor of Economics at the London Business School

Edmund Kitch, Joseph M. Hartfield Professor of Law, University of Virginia

Fidelis Oditah, Barrister; Travers Smith Braithwaite Lecturer in Corporate Finance Law, University of Oxford, and Fellow of Merton College

Michael Perry, Executive Director and Group Compliance Officer, UBS

Calin Rovinescu, Stikeman, Elliott, London

Simon Sackman, Norton Rose, London

Jennifer Schneck, Cleary, Gottlieb, Steen & Hamilton, London

Hal Scott, Nomura Professor of International Financial Systems, Harvard Law School

Wayne Smith, Head of Non-French Securities, Société des Bourses Françaises

Gilles Thieffry, Norton Rose, London

Andrew Whittaker, Head of Trading Markets Policy, Securities and Investments Board

Table of Conventions

Table of E.C. Directives

Table of Statutes

Table of Statutory Instruments and Regulations

Table of Cases

Abbreviations

ADB	African Development Bank
ADR	American Depository Receipt
BCCI	Bank of Credit and Commerce International
BIS	Bank for International Settlements
BMTN	French medium-term notes
CA 1985	Companies Act 1985
CAD	Capital Adequacy Directive
CBV	Conseil des Bourses de Valeurs
CDC	Caisse de Dépôts et Consignations
Cedel	Centrale de Livraison de Valeurs Mobilières
CFTC	Commodity Futures Trading Commission
CME	Chicago Mercantile Exchange
COB	Commission des Opérations de Bourse
CSD	Central securities depository
Draft NP 43	Draft national policy statement of the Canadian securities regulators
DTC	Depository Trust Company
DTI	Department of Trade and Industry
DVP	Delivery versus payment
ECA	Export Credit Agency
EEA	European Economic Area
EGAT	Electricity Generating Authority of Thailand
EGCO	Electricity Generating Company Limited
EIB	European Investment Bank
EPIC	Entreprise Publique à Caractére Industriel et Commercial
EU	European Union
FCPA	Foreign Corrupt Practices Act
FHA	Federal Housing Administration
FHLBB	Federal Home Loan Bank Board
FRS 5	Financial Reporting Standards 5
FSA	Financial Services Act 1986
GAAP	Generally Accepted Accounting Principles
GAS	Groupements d'actionnaires stables
GATS	General Agreement on Trade in Services
GDR	Global Depository Receipt
IASC	International Accounting Standards Committee
IBCA	International Bank Credit Agency
ICSD	International central securities depository
IMRO	Investment Management Regulatory Organisation

IOSCO	International Organisation of Securities Commissions
IPE	International Petroleum Exchange
IPMA	International Primary Market Association
IPP	Independent Power Project
ISD	Investment Services Directive
ISDA	International Securities Dealers Association
ISDA	International Swaps and Derivatives Association
ISM	International Securities Market
ISMA	International Securities Markets Association
ITS	Intermarket trading system
LCE	London Commodities Exchange
LDT	Leveraged derivatives trade
LIBA	London Investment Banks Association
LIFFE	London International Financial Futures Exchange
LME	London Metals Exchange
LSE	London Stock Exchange
MFN	Most favoured nation
MGB	Morgan Guaranty Brussels
MGT	Morgan Guaranty Trust
MJDS	Multijurisdictional disclosure system
MOF	Multiple option facility
MS	Member States
NASD	National Association of Securities Dealers
NYSE	New York Stock Exchange
OECD	Organization for Economic Cooperation and Development
OSA	Ontario Securities Act
OSC	Ontario Securities Commission
OTC	Over the counter
PIA	Personal Investment Authority
POS	Public Offers of Securities Regulations 1995
PRC	Peoples' Republic of China
QIB	Qualified institutional buyers
QSA	Quebec Securities Act
QSC	Quebec Securities Commission
RUF	Revolving underwriting facility
SBF	Société des Bourses Françaises
SCSC	State Council Securities Commission
SEC	Securities and Exchange Commission
SFA	Securities and Futures Authority
SIB	Securities and Investments Board
SICOVAM	French central securities depository
SRO	Self Regulatory Organisation
UCC	Uniform Commercial Code
UNIPEC	United Petroleum and Chemicals Co. Ltd.

PART I

Comparative Legal Problems and Solutions

1

The Development of a Global Securities Market

BERNARD ASHER

I propose to consider this topic in two parts. In the first part of this Chapter, I would like to look at the various developments that are taking place in equity and bond markets.

In the second part, I will focus specifically on the global equity new issue market in order to highlight some of the legal and procedural hurdles which still need to be addressed in creating a truly global market.

DEMAND FOR A GLOBAL CAPITAL MARKET

The rapid shift to a global securities market is a result of two major trends that accelerated through the 1980's and are set to continue into the next century. The first is a significant increase in the *demand* for a global securities market. The key source of this demand is the pool of institutional assets which have grown exponentially and have diversified internationally. The second is *deregulation* which has opened up the world's economies and securities markets, increasing the breadth and depth of investment opportunities.

Pension Fund Growth

The expected growth in the global pension fund industry is staggering. According to the InterSec Research Group, a US pension consultant, global pension funds will top $11.2 trillion in assets by the end of 1999, an increase of 59% from the $7 trillion at the end of last year (see Appendix 1, below). International investments will form the largest part of that growth, more than doubling to $1.7 trillion from $788 billion last year. To put this in perspective, the international growth represents a 464% increase from $302 billion invested outside domestic markets at the end of 1989.

Much of the increased commitment to overseas investment has and will continue to come from the major pension markets, given their dominant size. The US, Japan and UK pension funds, for example, accounted for 80% of total global pension assets last year, with total assets of $5.7 trillion. US pension assets alone ($3.76 trillion) accounted for 53% of global pension assets. These assets are set to grow sharply, particularly as a result of changing legislation covering state funds in Europe. In addition, as a result of ageing populations in the Western economies, there will be a rapid rise in the private provision of pensions forcing individuals to invest in markets for the first time.

But it is not so much the growth of pension fund assets that is creating the global market place, rather the decision to diversify pension assets overseas. A geographically diversified portfolio has a superior risk/return profile to single country portfolios. It is widely agreed amongst the actuarial profession that a 30% diversification to overseas assets gives the maximum benefit of risk reduction, irrespective of base country. Of the major pension industries in the world, only the UK is near to this target at 28%.

While InterSec expect British pension funds to keep overseas investments at around 28% of assets, they expect a significant move into foreign markets by US and Japanese funds. US pension funds have more than doubled their international investments over the past five years. These investments are expected to increase further from 8% of assets in 1994 to 12.5% by the end of 1999. This would increase overseas funds to $725 billion from $300 billion, 19.3% compound growth rate during the period.

In Japan, foreign investment has contracted because of the combined effect of the collapse of the local equity market and the weakness of the US Dollar. Overseas investment by Japanese institutions is expected to triple to $252 billion from $85 billion last year over a five-year period ending 1999. A surge in foreign investment by Japanese public pension funds, triggered by the liberalisation of pension rules by the Japanese government, will be a major factor in the funds flow into international investments.

DEREGULATION AND SUPPLY

Privatisations and New Issues

The process of deregulation has been led by a massive wave of privatisations and international equity offerings over the last ten years. The trend towards privatisation both boosts the liquidity and market capitalisation in individual markets as well as raising the scope for cross-border investment.

The UK's success with its privatisation programme has encouraged state sell-offs elsewhere in the world. The increase in shares of privatised corporations around the world has raised the liquidity of the global capital market and the interest by investors in them. The deliberate under pricing of most issues has helped the markets' willingness to accept privatisation issues. Privatisation, which involves international distribution, is intensifying the development of the global market. The process includes a wide marketing effort to investment institutions. As an example, my bank was a lead manager for the sale of shares in Telefonica de Espana outside Spain, part of an operation involving presentations to over 500 institutions in 25 cities, in 11 countries.

Moreover, the trend towards privatisation is not restricted to the major economies. Despite the collapse last year in the Mexican market, the enthusiasm for privatisation issues from Latin America, Asia and Africa has been undiminished, while investors' long term belief in these markets remains intact. In 1994 governments from emerging markets raised a total of $17.6 billion, about $2 billion more than in 1993.

Global Industries

Privatisation has led to an increasing tendency for investors to look at the world in terms of large global industries and to compare stock valuations across markets. Privatisation has given the world markets large telecommunications and electric utilities to trade in and compare, while deregulation and the increase in world trade has put them, and other industries such as steel, mining, pharmaceuticals and oil, into competition with each other, in what were once their own protected markets. It is, therefore, increasingly possible to compare Thyssen with British Steel or Roche with Eli Lilly and view them as competing investment alternatives. This focus on global industries is, of course, also making it easier for large multi-national companies to raise both debt and equity on stock markets across the world, rather than concentrating on the market where their main listings lie.

International Debt Finance

In addition to the growth in the international equity markets, there has been a significant expansion in the sources of international debt finance. For example, total net issues of Euronotes and international bonds soared by 45% between 1993 and 1994. Announcements of new Euro-securities surged to $197.2 billion last year. Despite the rise in world interest rates in 1994, announcements of international bond issues were still equal to $372 billion last year.

Derivatives[1]

The growth of financial derivative instruments has benefited global markets by providing liquidity to institutional investors and facilitating portfolio construction. A major shift between countries can be made cheaply and

[1] Hal Scott, infra, chapter 17, considers the liability of derivatives traders under United States law.

quickly through the futures markets, without having to sell the underlying securities.

Infrastructure for a Global Market

Improvements in infrastructure, the regulatory environment and information technology are rapidly being put into place in order to facilitate the increasing free flow of capital around the world. This is essential if the trends of the last fifteen years are to be continued.

Accounting Standards

A key barrier to the development of a global capital market is the multitude of different accounting standards. That has meant accounts prepared in one country are frequently difficult for investors in another market to comprehend. Eliminating such barriers will stimulate capital flows through the improvement in investor confidence.

In July 1995, an agreement between IOSCO, the International Organisation of Securities Commissions, and the International Accounting Standards Committee (IASC) was a significant step towards creating a unified global accounting standard. It is hoped that by 1999, companies preparing their accounts according to IASC rules will be able to list their shares on any of the world's capital markets. More importantly, they will be able to list their shares in the US, gaining more immediate access to the world's biggest capital market, without adapting to stringent US rules. Unlisted American Depositary Receipts (ADRs) have, until now, been the only way most non-US companies have of tapping the US market.

Access to New Markets

Governments have played a key role in the development of a global securities market by opening up their markets to foreign investors. The most important development was the wholesale removal of exchange controls in the 1970's and 1980's. The process of liberalisation continues.

Authorities in a number of countries continue to deregulate their domestic bond markets and facilitate access by domestic companies to Eurobond financing. Measures taken in domestic markets have generally been designed to improve efficiency, liquidity and cost-effectiveness for resident issuers and to make the markets more attractive to foreign investors. For example, in Italy the stamp duty on the regulated trading of government bonds was removed; in Portugal the 20% withholding tax imposed on foreign holders of government bonds was abolished and non-residents are allowed to issue on the domestic market without requiring official permission; in Switzerland the authorisation requirement for foreign issuers was lifted in February 1995. In

Japan there have been widespread initiatives to remove the restrictions on foreign issues of Euro-yen bonds while about $200 billion of public pension funds have been opened up to foreign investment advisers.

Other developments in the regulatory environment include:

Capital Requirements for market operators (brokers, banks, etc) are being stepped up in many countries. The norm is to use Bank of International Settlement guidelines (India and South Africa are the latest examples of this). This encourages major international investors.

Listing Qualifications increasingly seek to meet international criteria in terms of financial history, share capital structure and liquidity etc, though efforts have been made to create simpler qualifications for small companies.

Compliance with new insider trading and market manipulation rules is being enforced.

Market operatives are being required to pass professional exams to ensure compliance with best practices, and thereby helping to create universal professional standards and greater transparency.

Membership of exchanges is increasingly being opened up to foreign participants.

Technology

The technological revolution, aided by information services such as Reuters and Bloomberg, is rapidly improving the dissemination of financial news and the exchange of information around the world. Other developments in CD Roms and interactive communications systems will also facilitate international communications for financial services.

Screen-based trading systems are not only leading to the demise of traditional trading floors, but also opening up the possibility of direct access to markets from overseas locations. For example, this year a new electronic trading system is being introduced on the Chicago Mercantile Exchange (CME). The Globex system has been developed in conjunction with Reuters. The CME has heralded the advance of Globex as the benchmark for the industry, and has made an effort to sign up other exchanges in a bid to turn Globex into an industry-wide network. The LIFFE electronic system, APT, has so far been used to extend the trading day on the London Futures Exchange. Although only currently used for an hour and a half a day, it is likely to be extended to replace the floor system.

At the end of 1993, a new electronic trading system, 'Bridge', was established between Cedel and Euroclear thereby eliminating a time delay between the delivery of securities and payment for them. With the move to electronic overnight processing, Cedel can settle trades with Euroclear on the same day.

Such developments will clearly contribute to improving the access of exchanges to investors around the world, as well as to providing global 24 hour trading. They will also bring considerable savings in transaction costs as well as improving processing speed and accuracy and market liquidity.

Improved Settlement and Custody

An important factor that promises to ensure the continued growth of international investment is the increasingly sophisticated custodian and settlements practices. Improving standards are being fuelled by international regulatory drives and technological advances. In the UK the move to a five-day settlement halves the previous settlement period. The ultimate aim in the UK is for same-day settlement but that is dependent on the operation of paperless trading. Swifter settlements in the UK are part of a world-wide trend stimulated by the desire to reduce the risk of failed trades and by the rapidly growing number of securities in issue. (The new settlement period in the UK moves it more in line with other leading financial centres. The US runs a five-day selling settlement; Japan three days; France three days and Germany two days, while the situation in emerging markets is tougher.) There are likely to be more improvements in the future. Taiwan, for example, settles on a T+1 basis now.

Coupled with improved settlement practices, the growth of custodial and settlement agency facilities is increasingly being restructured and dominated by a handful of global banks, such as HSBC, which have the international reach and technological capability to handle the massive increase in this business. The benefits of such concentration include greater efficiency, security and lower costs. To institutional investors, however, the greatest benefit is the knowledge that even in some of the world's more exotic emerging markets, their trades will be settled.

Global Depository Receipts[2]

The success of American Depositary Receipts (ADRs) in encouraging international companies to raise capital from US stock markets is well known. They enable companies to access foreign capital while giving US investors an ability to settle trades and receive dividends in their home market and currency. Global Depositary Receipts (GDRs) are a new form of this type of instrument, increasing the potential for raising capital and liquidity. Typically, GDRs are issued to facilitate a London or other European listing, but priced in dollars in conjunction with a local equity issue. The convenience of trading GDRs is popular with investors and will therefore grow in importance. This may, in part, substitute for trading on local exchanges, as has been the case in Latin America. If that continues to happen, the fear of losing trading business to off-shore exchanges can only spur local stock markets in developing countries to reforms that make their markets more attractive for international investors.

[2] For further analysis of GDRs, see Sackman and Coltman, infra, pp. 22–3.

THE GLOBAL EQUITY NEW ISSUE MARKET—PRACTICAL AND LEGAL PROBLEMS

Introduction

I would now like to focus specifically on the global equity new issue market to illustrate some of the practical and legal problems which still need to be addressed in creating a truly global market.

International equity issues, particularly large privatisation offers, often have the biggest single impact in creating a global market for a security. The aim is simply to generate as much investor demand as possible, as widely as possible, in a limited offer period.

These issues provide a large ripple effect through widespread investor interest. This spills over into other stocks and can internationalise the stock market as a whole. They also clearly show the inter-action of banks, lawyers, regulators and governments.

Regulators and governments lay down rules for investment and to protect investors. Depending on how this is done, it can do much to encourage, or slow down, the globalisation process.

Bankers and brokers want to encourage the global flows between issuers and investors in new issues and secondary trading. Like marriage-brokers, they need lawyers to check and legitimise their activity.

I have discussed how privatisations and international equity issues have intensified the development of a global securities market. They provide a great opportunity to internationalise portfolios and spread a shareholding base. But they also offer a fair chance of spreading investor unhappiness, and even lawsuits, across several jurisdictions at once—if something goes wrong.

The lawyers' role

What therefore do the lead managers of international equity issues, which are marketed across a range of countries, look for from their lawyers?

The question is best answered by considering the investment banker's needs. Take two of those needs. One, compliance with securities laws on the offering of stock in different countries. The other, ensuring the right level of information on the issuer and the issue is provided to investors—to avoid any comeback.

As we know in the UK, the second can be a matter of interpretation at the time of the offering, as much as of legal wording.

Both needs—compliance and adequate information—are clearly crucial in allowing global issues to happen. Lead managers take advice from their lawyers at every stage of the transaction. But when the lawyers say:-

We will need to consult local lawyers whether it is possible to market the stock there in that way

or

We will need to revise the offering memorandum or the selling agreements to reflect the different rules in each of these countries

or

We can't be entirely precise here—it may or may not be doable,

they are saying in effect that this international issue may not be marketed on a fully global basis. The lead manager and issuer may decide not to take the potential risk or may decide that the extra documentation is excessive for the likely extra orders.

The clearer the legal advice and the fewer the local exceptions, the easier it becomes to market "global issues".

Governments and regulators

Much depends on the way regulators and governments act. In the country of the issuer, governments can:–

- fix exchange controls;
- restrict overseas ownership of stocks;
- set foreign quotas;
- limit ownership to certain classes of shares;
- demand foreigners fulfil complicated registration requirements as investors.

This means there may be few global stocks in a portfolio—but a large number of stocks with restrictions.

Fortunately, today, governments need to privatise and to attract large inward portfolio investment. As a result, they have often agreed major changes in the rules in a remarkably short time in the run-up to privatisation issues in particular.

In the countries of the potential investors, regulators have a legitimate concern to protect. But securities laws designed particularly with retail investors in mind can obstruct global issues. These are often principally marketed to the growing groups of professional institutional investors in that country.

Requirements for further globalisation

As a banker I would make three requests of governments and regulators in this area to push globalisation further. Lawyers may be able to help.

First, continue liberalising. To take an example, more shares should be opened up to foreign ownership. Some investors hold GDRs or ADRs, not out of preference, but because they are not allowed to own the underlying ordinary shares. Others do not hold GDRs because movement in the premium or discount against the underlying stock represents an unacceptable additional investment risk.

There are surprisingly few "global securities". GDRs and ADRs are probably the nearest thing so far, other than for some New York-listed blue chips. They are very convenient and have contributed enormously to globalising investment.

But can a stock held in different form by local and international investors really be called a "global security"?

Second, harmonise securities regulations and legal documentation for new issues across markets as much as possible. For example, it is good news that Canada will now accept compliance with US private placement rules as compliance with its own rules.

Third, separate retail regulations from professional. Make easier the rules for marketing issues to professional institutions. It is clear that they are powering the growth in global investment. But so far, it is still a relatively small group—maybe as few as 500 institutions worldwide.

THE LEGAL AND PRACTICAL HURDLES

The Investment Case

Investors need to be persuaded of the investment arguments to subscribe. Depending on whether they are "top-down" or "value-driven", they will focus on the case:-

- for that country (the macro-economic and political factors)
- for that industry sector
- for that stock (the company's strategy, the strength of its management, its financial condition, its earnings prospects).

Global issues, therefore, require a big cross-border marketing exercise, and

in the case of institutions the use of detailed brokers' research reports can be vital in attracting demand. However the reports are restricted in their content, timing and distribution by local laws.

"Content" restrictions in research can prohibit

profit estimates or formal recommendations.

"Timing" restrictions can require

research to be distributed at least 30 days before publication of the preliminary prospectus ("blackout period") or prohibit publication for at least 40 days after completion of the issue.

"Distribution" restrictions may prohibit or constrain sales in particular countries.

For example, we received contradictory advice from two major New York law firms as to whether we could distribute research to US QIBs in relation to a Mexican new issue we lead-managed in 1994.

This interpretation of these rules is not constant. A US law firm may insist on a more restrictive black-out period for research than a European lawyer, even for the non-US tranche of an issue.

One US law firm may permit distribution of the research to Qualifying Institutions in the US, others would not.

Investor presentations and one-to-one meetings are another key element, but different lawyers may give differing opinions on the content of the presentation and by how much, if at all, it may give information which is not in the offering memorandum. In the US we must remember never to give copies of the presentation to investors.

Fund managers receive a battering or buttering up from equity sales teams in various financial centres during the marketing. Again, what the salesman or woman can say depends on the local rules.

Marketing restrictions may stipulate, for example,

the maximum number of investors who can be marketed to within the definition of a private placement or
where the salesman/woman is located.

Marketing to retail investors involves different weapons:-

- advertising and publicity campaigns (complete with health warnings)
- press briefings for journalists (some jurisdictions such as the US may restrict these too)
- Share shops and retail banking outlets (in the domestic market).

The Legal Documentation

The offering memorandum (including the listing particulars) is, of course, in the eyes of the lawyers the only selling document for the issue. Several questions arise:–

- the place or places of listing, and what that means for listing requirements and the amount of disclosure;
- striking the right balance between the issuer, who may be concerned at disclosing valuable commercial information, and the investor's legitimate interest;

- reconciling domestic and international stock exchange demands. Oddly, in some markets the local requirement can sometimes be greater. For example, a Polish listing document may need a profit forecast which our international lawyers would prefer not to see in an international prospectus!
- the underwriting agreements need to reconcile international practice, which has become much more standardised, with local requirements;
- some governments see the law chosen to govern underwriting agreements as a potential problem in privatisation offerings. Whilst English and US law usually prevails in international issues, the French for example in privatisation issues require the application of French law
- the accounts may need re-casting to US GAAP, UK GAAP or other international standards.

Much has been done to standardise documents, such as legal opinions, but more would still be welcome.

Stock Exchange Listings

The first question is whether to seek a listing on an international exchange, as well as on the domestic market.

Is it needed to persuade investors to buy the stock at all? Disclosure requirements may not be sufficient in a local listing. The local market may lack liquidity or transparency. In the case of the half a billion US$ issue HSBC lead-managed for Ashanti Goldfields of Ghana, this decision was clear-cut. We listed on London.

It may be required to get a higher price or wider spread of investors. Or for corporate reasons of long-term strategy or prestige.

However, different listings imply—at least currently—different initial listing requirements and continuing obligations for the company.

The success of SEAQ International has shown that a formal international listing is often less important for investors than liquidity and transparency in trading—assuming a minimum level of information disclosure on the local stock exchange!

The Stock Exchange in London has encouraged international issues to trade on SEAQ-I by becoming much more flexible in its definition of a "recognised investment exchange".

We have taken advantage of this flexibility in lead-managing, for example, some of the first international issues for Mexican, Indian and Hungarian companies.

Several listings may mean that it is the company which has to become global, rather than the investors! Companies have de-listed from Tokyo, for example, because additional reporting requirements and costs were not justified by shareholdings.

Assessment of Geographic Demand

A global issue may not mean demand is equally widespread.

That will depend on:–

- the company and country of issue
- local factors (such as currency fluctuations for the Japanese)
- local perception of the sector (for example, a local property slump will affect demand for a property issue from another country)
- the size of the issue.

Whether, and how to market the issue in the US is always a key question—maybe not at all, or by private placement to Qualifying Institutions (through Rule 144A) or full SEC registration.

The anticipated additional demand must justify the extra work, time, cost and documentation—as well as the unquantifiable risk of the markets moving against the issue in the meantime.

To take an extreme example, in 1994 we did the first ever international "bought deal" for an Indian company, Great Eastern Shipping. Despite our obvious preference for speed, we decided to include a Rule 144A private placing in the US which required extra documentation, because we believed that a wider placing would assist the after-market.

The Form of Security

A large international issue may consist of three different forms of stock.

Firstly, local stock sold globally—priced, traded and settled locally, even between international holders. This offers a single global security but a global issue in this form alone may "repatriate" itself sooner or later.

Secondly, local stock traded internationally (for example European or other international shares traded on SEAQ International).

Thirdly, stock re-packaged into international form as ADRs or GDRs. These are priced in US dollars and settled offshore through DTC in New York, Cedel or Euroclear in Europe.

A large global issue may still consist of all three of the above, issued simultaneously to suit different investors.

Even an issue of a single form of stock—a single Global Depository Receipt issue worldwide—may need, for US legal reasons, to consist of an American Master GDR and a European Master GDR, one held in New York in DTC and the other in Euroclear or Cedel. Because if the issue is not registered with the SEC there will be a need to ensure stock is kept separate so it will not end up where it shouldn't.

Trading

Liquidity is a key concern of global fund managers. Their requirement is to obtain a firm bid or offer in the stock, in reasonable size, at once.

A real global security should be traded in several international financial centres in different time zones, as well as in the local market.

Investors in a global new issue want to know which banks and brokers will trade it, in what size, with what bid-offer spread, and where.

As another banker put it, the lesson of emerging markets is that "It is hard to emerge in an emergency"!

Settlement

The back office may sound boring but it can save—or cost—investors or brokers lots of money!

The main questions to be addressed are:–

Is the stock to settle only in the domestic market (is that an efficient market place?).

- If it will settle offshore too, how easily can settlement take place between the different locations?
- Do different settlement periods need to be reconciled?
- Will separate settlements help or hinder liquidity in the stock?

Offer Timetables

Global issues must reconcile differing offer periods in different markets. This is especially important between any local offer period and the international book-building.

The differing timetable may reflect a minimum period for the Offer for Sale in the local market or different underwriting mechanisms.

Pricing

Global offers tend to highlight differing pricing objectives—and sometimes pricing mechanisms—which must be reconciled.

The open book-building process seeks to do this but must also take account of other priorities, e.g. discounts for the local retail investors.

The more markets in which an issue is sold, the more scope for allegations of short-selling by institutions or ramping of the underlying price by the issuer or vendor.

Detailed procedures, involving considerable disclosure by investors and traders of their activity before and during the offer period, have now been developed. Government vendors have been a prime mover in this area.

Stabilisation

Global issues can create huge flows of stock in the immediate after-market, requiring stabilisation. International and domestic regulations must be reconciled.

After-market

Global shares can flow back home even after a successful offering. Serious attention is needed to the after-market. There must be:-

- an ongoing investor relations programme by the company;
- ongoing broking coverage with research and sales support from a range of houses;
- a formal commitment to market-making by several international houses;
- and finally—a continuing prospect of a high return for the investor.

Appendix 1

Table Showing Total World Pension Assets

The table below shows total public and private pension funds' assets country by country, in billions of dollars. The figures in brackets show the percentage of assets invested abroad. As with all forecasts in the financial industry, the five year numbers should be considered as indicative.

Country	*1989*	*(abroad)*	*1994*	*(abroad)*	*1999(e)*	*(abroad)*
United States	2,425	(3.7%)	3760	(8.0%)	5936	(12.2%)
Japan	513	(8.4%)	1118	(7.6%)	1750	(14.4%)
United Kingdom	453	(22.7%)	775	(28.0%)	116	(28.0%)
Canada	181	(6.4%)	238	(17.2%)	381	(19.2%)
Netherlands	202	(11.5%)	264	(18.9%)	361	(22.9%)
Switzerland	133	(4.3%)	191	(12.6%)	343	(15.5%)
Germany	84	(4.5%)	124	(3.2%)	177	(5.1%)
Australia	42	(17.5%)	82	(15.9%)	166	(20.5%)
Other	305	(4.3%)	501	(11.0%)	1005	(16.2%)
Total	4338	(7.0%)	7053	(11.2%)	11236	(15.1%)

Source: InterSec Research Corp.

Appendix 2

Table Showing the Total of Securities Issues in the G5 Countries Since 1993

US $ MN		*1993*			*1994*		*'94Q4*	*1995QI*	
	Equities	*Bonds*	*Total*	*Equities*	*Bonds*	*Total*	*Equities*	*Bonds*	*Total*
Germany	11800	441791	453591	17980	383195	401175	3056	104742	1077
France	42421	92817	135238	48246	72572	120818	16316	17972	3428
Japan	11468	1116762	1128230	N/A	1161046	N/A	N/A	317172	N/A
UK	24465	91260	115725	21569	54127	75696	2817	11161	1397
US	114200	1432700	1546900	66100	1145100	1211200	11600	323200	334800

Source: OECD, Fin. Stats.

2

Legal Aspects of a Global Securities Market

SIMON SACKMAN and MARGARET COLTMAN

Introduction

Although the world is becoming a global market place for securities, this does not mean that there is, or indeed will be, a single capital market. Instead, what we now have is a collection of capital markets, which are becoming increasingly integrated and global in scope, with an increasing amount of freedom of movement between the markets. The global market has over recent years undergone a period of unprecedented change, fuelled by increasing demands from institutional investors, particularly in the US, by a growing wave of privatisation and by improvements in technology, which now make it possible to access markets, in real time, from anywhere in the world. Deregulation has been another important factor, not least the relaxation of exchange controls in the early 1980s.

For many countries, particularly the emerging markets, the development of a securities market which will attract cross-border investment is of fundamental importance to their economic development. What these markets must recognise, however, is that if they are to attract investment, certain key safeguards must be met. First, adequate standards of investor protection are required in relation to offerings of securities. Secondly, investors need to be able to deal and to settle dealings in a timely and efficient manner. Investors also need to be confident that market manipulation is inhibited and that the institutions through which they deal are reputable and are operating on a sound basis. Even in the more sophisticated securities markets, such as the US and the UK, where these standards have long been recognised as minimum requirements, an international offering gives rise to legal issues concerning the interplay of the applicable laws and requires the co-ordination of different practices, as well as an acknowledgement on the part of the regulators that their insistence on compliance with local regulation by foreign issuers may be inhibiting the development of their market and prejudicing the interests of local investors.

The globalisation of the securities market also means that where a particular practice has been used successfully in one jurisdiction, there will be demand for it to be used elsewhere, to the same effect. In addition, investors who are driven by a search for high returns and spreading of risks create a demand for new and innovative financial products. The challenge for the practitioners and regulators operating in the global market place is to recognise this fact and to encourage innovation and risk-taking, whilst at the same time seeking to maintain the fundamental safeguards.

Key Requirements

Protection of Investors

Potential investors in securities offerings, whether debt or equity, expect certain minimum standards to be adhered to, in order to ensure that they may make an informed investment decision. Where the securities are listed on a major stock exchange, those standards will be prescribed to a large extent by the relevant local legal and regulatory framework.

For example, investors acquiring shares pursuant to public offers which are listed in the US or the UK have for many years been able to do so confident in the knowledge that the prospectus must conform to the disclosure standards prescribed by the relevant legislation and stock exchange rules. Broadly speaking, these standards require the prospectus to contain such information as is required in order to enable potential investors to make an informed assessment of the offering company and its securities.[1] Adequate disclosure will mean that those responsible for the prospectus will avoid legal liability for non-disclosure and will also be an important component of the selling process.

Both countries also regulate the publication of material which is used to market a securities issue. In the UK, for example, an investment advertisement must be issued, or approved for issue, by a person who has been authorised under the Financial Services Act to carry on investment business in the UK.[2] That person is then required to ensure that the advertisement is fair and not misleading to potential investors.[3]

[1] For example, Section 146(1) of the UK Financial Services Act 1986 requires the following: 'In addition to the information specified by listing rules or required by the competent authority as a condition of the admission of any securities to the Official List any listing particulars submitted to the competent authority under section 144 above shall contain all such information as investors and their professional advisers would reasonably require, and reasonably expect to find there, for the purpose of making an informed assessment of:

(a) the assets and liabilities, financial position, profits and losses, and prospects of the issuer of the securities; and

(b) the right attaching to those securities'.

[2] Section 57(1) of the Financial Services Act 1986 provides that, subject to certain exceptions, 'no person other than an authorised person shall issue or cause to be issued an investment advertisement in the United Kingdom unless its contents have been approved by an authorised person'.

[3] Rule 5–9(1) of the Conduct of Business Rules of the Securities and Futures Authority provides that:

'Where a firm issues or approves an investment advertisement, it must:

Of course, not all investors require the same degree of protection, and there are therefore exceptions to this requirement. For example, an investment advertisement can be distributed without such authorisation to persons who are sufficiently expert to understand the risks involved.[4] By making an important distinction between the retail and non-retail investor, this exemption permits the distribution of brokers' research and of pathfinder prospectuses to professional investors in the UK whose support will be crucial to the successful marketing of a new issue.

In some cases, the rules of a domestic market may be unduly restrictive for an overseas issuer. For example, in the US the requirement of the Securities and Exchange Commission (SEC) for foreign issuers to either prepare financial information in accordance with, or to reconcile such information to, US Generally Accepted Accounting Principles (US GAAP) has been found to be unduly burdensome, particularly in terms of cost. Daimler Benz faced a number of difficulties when arranging an introduction on the New York Stock Exchange (NYSE) and is still the only German company with an NYSE listing.[5] The SEC has now enacted certain changes to streamline registration and reporting requirements for US and foreign companies, including changes which relax accounting rules for foreign issuers.[6]

The recent agreement between the International Organisation of Securities Commissions (IOSCO) and the International Accounting Standards Committee (IASC) to develop a set of accounting standards by mid-1999 for companies seeking a listing in global markets and for the raising of cross-border capital is another important step in the right direction, although the target date may prove to be ambitious. It is understood that the NYSE has been pressing for freedom to accept IASC standards.[7] The German government, pushed by German businesses eager to raise capital in the international markets, has also said that it will accept the use of international standards for those multinational companies seeking a foreign listing.[8]

In many cases, concerns about inadequate disclosure standards, particularly where the home market is an emerging market, can be overcome by the fact that the securities are registered with the SEC or listed on a major European Stock Exchange. Even here, however, disclosure can still give rise to sensitive

(a) apply appropriate expertise; and

(b) be able to show that it believes on reasonable grounds that the advertisement is fair and not misleading.'

[4] Article 11 of the Financial Services Act 1986 (Investment Advertisements) (Exemptions) Order 1995 (SI 1995 No. 1266).

[5] As of June 16th 1995.

[6] SEC Release Nos. 33–7117, 34–35093, International Series Release No. 757; Release Nos. 33–7118, 34–35094, IC–20766, International Series Release No. 758: Release Nos. 33–7119, 34–35095, International Series Release No. 758; Release No. 33–7120, International Series Release No. 760, 13th December, 1994.

[7] Financial Times 12th July 1995.

[8] Financial Times 11th July 1995.

issues. For example, a government's desire to achieve a successful privatisation issue in an emerging market must be balanced against a need to present to potential investors in the offering circular a fair assessment of the degree of risk associated with investing in that country's market. The fact that a change of government may lead to re-nationalisation may be an important political risk factor to disclose to prospective investors, however unattractive this may appear to be to the government as the principal sponsor of the issue.

Investors must also be satisfied that they can retain their shares notwithstanding local regulatory limits on foreign ownership. This issue was highlighted recently with the Qantas global offering where the foreign ownership limits on the holding of shares in the Australian airline were breached, with the result that certain foreign investors were required to sell-down to below the threshold limit. The sponsors of the offering attracted criticism for failing to address this issue in advance.[9]

Dealings and Settlement[9a]

The development of the global securities market has also brought with it concerns on the part of investors as to their ability to deal on a timely basis in securities with which they are familiar, to be confident that the trades which they have carried out will be settled and that they can receive income on their securities in a currency with which they are familiar. The US market's response to these issues in relation to securities in overseas companies was to create the American Depositary Receipt (ADR). This is now increasingly used on a global basis, in the form of a Global Depositary Receipt (GDR) to facilitate offerings, particularly in emerging market securities.

A GDR is a means of packaging a company's shares into a 'unit' which, because it is not a share, can be traded and settled in the international markets without having to comply with the laws of the country of incorporation of the issuer of the underlying shares as to changes in ownership. On issue, GDRs are usually represented by a single certificate known as a Master Global Depositary Receipt. This is issued by the bank acting as a depository of the shares concerned and represents the relevant number of underlying shares held by the bank. It is evidence of ownership of the company's shares and persons credited with interests in the GDRs may, following the issue of the Master Global Depositary Receipt, request that they be issued with individual Global Depositary Receipts representing their specific interests. These individual GDRs can then be traded as a negotiable instrument.

A GDR is to all intents and purposes the same as an ADR. It operates in the same way as an ADR and is recognised in the US markets as a famil-

[9] IFR 1096 August 26th 1995.

[9a] For a detailed consideration of the practical elements of settlement and custody, see Christie and Dosanjh, infra, p. 131 ff; and for a penetrating legal analysis of the nature and transfer of rights in dematerialised and immobilised securities, see Goode, infra, p. 107 ff.

iar instrument. Moreover, a GDR is normally denominated in US dollars and therefore enables international investors to hold securities in a currency with which they are familiar. Dividends received in the local currency are converted into US dollars, albeit at a cost to the holders of the GDRs.

Another important advantage of GDRs is that they facilitate the transfer of beneficial ownership. Whereas a holder of foreign registered securities may be required to follow unfamiliar or inconvenient transfer procedures and send the certificates abroad for transfers, ownership of GDRs may be transferred on the books of the depository or through the clearing systems of The Depositary Trust Company (DTC), Euroclear and Cedel.

However, GDRs are not without their problems. Where they are held through the DTC, Euroclear and Cedel systems, they are held by participants on behalf of clients and in practice it is often difficult for the issuer to find out who has the beneficial interest in its shares.

Exercise by beneficial owners of their voting rights within the normal timetable of shareholder meetings is a cumbersome process and a holder who is particularly keen to vote on any given matter may need to withdraw his GDR from the deposit programme in order to be able to do so.

In addition to these practical considerations, there are some important legal issues which need to be considered in relation to GDRs and similar instruments. For example, the precise legal nature of the interest held by investors in the pool of securities which are the subject of the Deposit Agreement needs to be characterised and the method by which ownership and security rights may be created and perfected needs to be addressed.

Inhibition of Market Manipulation

The UK Securities and Investments Board (SIB) recently identified three basic criteria which are required to achieve and retain investor confidence in an open market. First, market users must be confident that they will be treated equitably when they deal; no one group of participants should be able to use the market to the disadvantage of another. Secondly, there must be confidence in the price formation process and, thirdly, there must be continuing confidence that all reasonable steps will be taken to maintain safeguards against market abuse and that, if abuse does occur, it will be discovered and punished.[10]

It is important in this context that markets should require the timely disclosure of information by issuers. In the UK, for example, a company must notify the Company Announcements Office without delay of any major new developments in its sphere of activity which are not public knowledge and which may lead to substantial moves in the price of its shares.[11] Companies

[10] Preface to the Report by the SIB on Regulation of the United Kingdom Equity Markets—June 1995 (SIB Report).

[11] Rule 9.1 of the Listing Rules of the London Stock Exchange.

with a primary listing elsewhere and a secondary listing on the London Stock Exchange are also required to comply with an equivalent requirement.[12]

Even if an overseas company is not listed on the London Stock Exchange, its shares may be eligible for trading on the London Stock Exchange's International Equity Market. This market is for members of the Exchange to trade in equities issued by companies incorporated outside the UK and listed on approved overseas exchanges. In order for these exchanges to be approved, they must have listing requirements and company news dissemination arrangements which are broadly equivalent to those utilised by the London Stock Exchange.[13] Even if an exchange does not meet the normal criteria for access to SEAQ International, for example because it is a developing market, a security listed by or quoted under the rules of such a market may still appear on SEAQ International in what is known as the developing market sector. In this case, the proponent must still satisfy the London Stock Exchange that the issuer has effective arrangements in place to allow for timely disclosure of company announcements to at least its local exchange.[14]

The prohibition of insider trading is another important factor which contributes to the maintenance of an open and transparent market, as is the regulation of disclosure of substantial shareholdings. These requirements, and many other matters relevant to market integrity, are regulated by statute in the UK.[15] In addition, the SIB has recently published two draft standards which address further issues of market integrity[16] and has also reached agreement with the London Stock Exchange which will result in a significant increase in post-trade transparency from the beginning of next year.[17]

Financial Institutions

Issuers need to feel confident that the institutions through which they are dealing are operating in accordance with sound financial principles and within a suitable regulatory framework. The collapse of Barings has served to demonstrate that, even in the most sophisticated of financial markets, there is a need to ensure that institutions which are entrusted with assets by

[12] Rule 17.22 of the Listing Rules of the London Stock Exchange.

[13] Section Two—London Stock Exchange Guide to the International Equity Market—August 1994.

[14] Section Two—London Stock Exchange Guide to the International Equity Market—'Developing Markets sector'.

[15] See for example the provisions of Part V of the Criminal Justice Act 1993—Insider Dealing—and Part VI of the Companies Act 1985—Disclosure of Interests in Shares.

[16] 'The Overall Standard of Equity Market Integrity'—Appendix 2, SIB Report and 'Standards of Market Integrity—Standard 2: Market Maker Privileges and Obligations'—Appendix 3, SIB Report.

[17] Preface to the SIB Report.

investors should be required to operate in accordance with procedures which safeguard those assets.

In the UK, the operation of financial institutions is prescribed by the regulatory structure which was put in place under the terms of the Financial Services Act 1986 (FSA). The FSA requires that any investment business must be conducted by persons who are authorised to do so and that the supervision of this investment business is to be in the hands of the SIB, which also supervises the activities of the UK recognised investment exchanges, such as the London Stock Exchange, as well as the clearing houses for equity transactions.

The Chairman of the SIB recently acknowledged that the rate of change in the financial services industry, and the increasingly international nature of the business, demand an equivalent response from regulators. He commented:

> 'Only by improving still further the level of co-ordination and co-operation between regulators will the challenge be successfully met. The need for such an approach is beyond dispute. The question people will rightly ask is whether we can make it happen.'[18]

There is clear evidence that the regulators are seeking to make it happen. For example, in November 1994, the SIB set up the 'London and Global Markets Group', bringing together recognised bodies, government, the Bank of England, practitioners and academics to identify the key medium-term trends in international securities markets and to address the relevant regulatory issues.[19] More recently, the US SEC made a joint announcement with the SIB to the effect that it had agreed with two international integrated securities houses that they would undergo a trial of closer supervision and monitoring by these regulatory authorities with a view to testing information flows within multi-national, multiple business institutions. It is apparent from the report of the Board of Banking Supervision on the collapse of Barings that the huge losses sustained by Barings Futures Singapore went undetected until a few days before Barings had to be placed in administration in London.

The SIB and the Commodity Futures Trading Commission of the US also issued a declaration earlier this year, known as the 'Windsor Declaration', that they aimed to increase co-operation between market authorities to improve the supervision of futures exchanges. The authorities agreed to promote an increase in surveillance of market exposures and to ensure customer positions can be ring fenced from proprietary positions. The work will be taken forward under the auspices of IOSCO.

These examples of multinational collaboration, involving the major

[18] Andrew Large 'Modern piracy and other challenges' Financial Times 18th July 1995.
[19] Paragraph 3.42, SIB report.

markets and creating a protective framework, are all examples of a movement towards a multinational regulatory framework which will impact on the operation of the global securities market.

Co-ordination

A global offering gives rise to a need to co-ordinate different market practices which are commonplace in different jurisdictions; it will also result in legal issues concerning the impact of the various applicable laws to the particular offering in question.

Due Diligence

One area where practical co-ordination is required concerns the differing approaches in the US and the UK to the investigation process which is carried out as part of the offering procedure. This process, which is commonly called 'due diligence', has a number of purposes. It provides those who are responsible for ensuring that the offering circular contains adequate disclosure with a defence against liability, it enables information to be obtained for the purpose of preparing the offering circular, and, not least, it enables the lead managers to be satisfied that they have addressed any issues which may impact adversely on the success of the offering, and, by implication, their own commercial reputations.

Although these purposes will be common in both the US and the UK, the conduct of a due diligence exercise will vary from jurisdiction to jurisdiction, reflecting differences in the legal approach. To a US lawyer, due diligence will involve a detailed review of relevant documents and issues and detailed question and answer sessions of management but will not require the production of a written report which is kept as a long term record of what has been done. In the US, the litigious climate means that any written materials which have been created during the due diligence process are destroyed after the process has been completed!

In contrast, to the UK lawyer, due diligence involves not only the production of a detailed report written by the lawyers on relevant legal issues, but will also encompass the preparation of a Long Form Accountants' Report—a document which has for many years been an integral part of the domestic UK flotation process but which is not commonly used in the US new issue market. In addition, a UK offering will also involve the production of a detailed record of verification of the offering circular. It is difficult to see how, in the UK, a sponsor of a new issue would be able to demonstrate to the regulatory authorities or in a Court that it had adequately performed its duties in the absence of such written reports.

The nature and conduct of the due diligence exercise is also relevant in the context of the provision of a '10b–5' disclosure opinion to the US lead managers.[20] This opinion is required to protect the US lead managers from charges of negligence which they might face if there were material misstatements or omissions in the selling prospectus. Provided the lead managers can show that they have done what is reasonably necessary to confirm that there is no material omission from a prospectus, they will have the benefit of the defence.

Notwithstanding recent developments in the US which suggest that a 10b–5 opinion may no longer be a requirement on a private placement, for example, under Rule 144A,[21] the production of the 10b–5 opinion is a key issue in a global offering with a US tranche. US lead managers are unlikely to accept a 10b–5 opinion from anyone other than a lawyer qualified in the US securities laws who is familiar with the relevant standard and legal framework, although competitive pressures mean that this issue is subject to some debate. However, considerations of cost mean that, in practice, US lead managers are prepared to accept a 10b–5 opinion which relies in part on the due diligence efforts of non-US counsel, particularly where the due diligence has been carried out in a language other than English. In addition, non-US counsel may give an opinion which reflects a disclosure standard based on their own legal system. What is important, in this case, is to ensure that the local counsel are made fully aware of what is expected of them at an early stage in the process.

The standard to which due diligence is to be conducted is an issue which needs to be addressed at an early stage in the offering process. This will be affected by various factors, including the nature of the issuer, the type of security comprised in the offering and the jurisdictions in which the issue is to be sold. An offering of debt securities by a highly rated issuer based in a major market will require a different approach to due diligence compared with an offering of GDRs in respect of a newly-privatised entity based in an emerging market. In practice, a due diligence exercise should be conducted in accordance with the highest level recognised as appropriate in the various jurisdictions in which the securities are to be sold.

Marketing

Careful co-ordination of marketing activities is also required where securities are offered in more than one jurisdiction. For example, while brokers' research materials can be distributed in the UK, albeit within reasonably well-defined parameters, the distribution of such materials in connection with the same offering in the US will not be permitted in the same manner. In a global offering which includes a Rule 144A offering[22] in the US, particular care must be

[20] Rule 10b–5 of the US Securities Exchange Act of 1934.

[21] US Supreme Court decision in Gustafson v. Alloyd Co., Inc.—28th February 1995.

[22] Rule 144A of the US Securities Act of 1933. For a more detailed analysis, see Rovinescu and Thieffry, infra, at pp. 51–7.

taken not to make directed selling efforts in the US (such as press conferences or the circulation of press releases) since this could lead to the SEC requiring a cooling-off period to be imposed, resulting in a delay in the offering.

Innovation and Competition

Innovation

The globalisation of the securities market has resulted in the export and adaptation of successful practices from one market to another. An interesting example of this is the increasing use of the US bookbuilding process in equity offerings originating outside the US. The principle behind bookbuilding is that shares can be marketed during the bookbuilding period without fixing the price. The global bookrunner obtains non-binding expressions of interest in which potential investors indicate the number of shares they are prepared to take at varying prices, usually within an indicated range. The offer is not underwritten until just before the commencement of trading and immediately after the price is fixed at the end of the bookbuilding period. This contrasts with the more traditional UK style offers for sale where the price is fixed at the outset and the issue is underwritten for an offer period of some two to three weeks. For many years, the major UK privatisations were structured on the same basis as UK domestic securities offerings, with a group of primary underwriters committing to take up shares, in return for an underwriting commission.

The first UK privatisation which used the bookbuilding procedure was the second BT offer,[23] and the procedure has been used for a number of UK based global offerings since BT2.[24] The principal advantage of bookbuilding compared with the more traditional UK style of underwriting is that the price can be matched more accurately with demand, thereby limiting underpricing and reducing the possibility of an underwriting 'stick'. Competition between investors is encouraged, creating price tension, and it is also possible to use the process to ensure a broad spread of investors and to favour those perceived to be long-term investors.

Increasingly, financial products are tailored to the requirements of potential investors. For example, the difficulties encountered by Qantas in maintaining its overseas shareholder base within the prescribed limits recently provided an opportunity for Macquarie Bank in Australia to create an innovative debt security, known as a QanMac, which provided overseas investors with an opportunity to acquire a security which had the characteristics of a Qantas share, in terms of price and yield, but which was not subject to the same regulatory restrictions, since it was not considered to give the foreign investors a direct shareholding in Qantas.[25]

[23] December 1991. [24] For example, Wellcome, BT3 and National Power/PowerGen.
[25] Financial Times 31st August 1995.

The massive funding requirements for infrastructure projects, particularly in South East Asia, have caused potential funders to look to securitisation as a possible new way of meeting the funding requirements, but not without raising some complex and difficult issues on matters such as risk assessment and the liabilities of trustees.

Choice of law issues have also meant that legal structures which have been commonplace in one jurisdiction have had to be adapted in order to operate under the laws of another jurisdiction. For example, Deposit Agreements, governed by English law, and used in connection with GDR programmes, have been modelled on the structures of New York law ADR programme Deposit Agreements.

Competition

The development of the global market has seen an increasing amount of competition between different jurisdictions for the provision of facilities to accommodate the new financial products. For example, in 1994 the London Stock Exchange responded to competitive pressures from the Luxembourg Stock Exchange by agreeing to admit GDRs to listing on the Official List.[26] The global offering by Ashanti Goldfields Company Limited involved the first ever GDR listing on the London Stock Exchange and this has been followed by a number of other GDR London listings, including listings of companies based in India, Korea and Taiwan.

The London Stock Exchange's SEAQ International has been extremely successful in providing a facility for trading in international securities. In 1993, international turnover exceeded domestic turnover in London for the first time and this continued into 1994. London traded over twice the amount of international shares compared to the NYSE in that year.[27]

The SEC's relaxation of a number of its rules in order to accommodate registration by foreign issuers is another example of the impact of competitive pressures. The US has long been recognised as having probably the most rigorous disclosure standards in the world and the SEC has been concerned to redress the balance and to attract the foreign issuers whose securities are currently being listed elsewhere.

Summary

The demands set by both the investors of capital as well as those who require it mean that the global securities market is set to continue to expand at a significant rate. Although there will always be investors who are prepared to take risks with a view to achieving commensurate rewards, the majority of investors will seek to avoid those markets where their interests

[26] Amendment No. 1 to the Listing Rules 18th March 1994 (effective 10th March 1994).
[27] London Stock Exchange statistics.

cannot be safeguarded, preferring instead to invest in those markets where they can feel confident that they will be adequately protected both in terms of the securities they acquire and the manner through which they hold and deal in them. There has been a marked acceleration in the response of regulators to this requirement, particularly since the Barings collapse.

The real challenge is to ensure that the protections are maintained in an environment which does not stifle innovation and risk-taking, so that as the global market evolves, it continues to accommodate those new products and services which investors demand.

3

Cross-Border Marketing

CALIN ROVINESCU AND GILLES THIEFFRY[1]

INTRODUCTION

The recent globalisation of the securities markets has enabled issuers to raise capital outside their own countries. According to the International Financing Review, in 1985, US$4.3 billion in international equity issues were completed worldwide. This market grew to US$20.9 billion in 1987 and US$22.5 billion in 1992. By 1994, the total value of all issues into the US market alone came to US$55.97 billion. Such international capital raising exercises require coordination on the part of the different financial intermediaries involved in the placement of securities as well as compliance with the various marketing requirements in the different jurisdictions where such securities are placed, in view of the potential liabilities arising out of such placements.

Irrespective of the different regulations applying to the offering, the coordination of the placement of the securities will typically be undertaken by a financial institution acting as global coordinator. The cross-border marketing effort will be controlled by marketing arrangements. Such arrangements may either be informal or formal in the form of an orderly marketing agreement. Broadly speaking, such arrangements will establish the respective roles of the different members of the syndicates (or of the different regional syndicates) and can sometimes be fairly detailed and include the specific names of certain institutional investors to be approached by the respective managers; this is relevant when deciding whether a specific investor falls into one geographic syndicate or another (e.g. the relevant test may be the place of incorporation of the investor in any specific region or alternatively its actual place of business). In addition to specific contractual marketing restrictions, formal orderly marketing agreements sometimes specify the different selling restrictions imposed by local securities laws. These restrictions often apply to the information which can be distributed in the context of an offering.

[1] Gilles Thieffry wishes to express his gratitude for the help provided by David Lewis of Norton Rose.

This Chapter adopts a case study approach to investigate and give a broad overview of different European and North American regulations applying to cross-border marketing. The case envisaged is that of a Danish company effecting a combined global offering comprising a primary offer by the issuer together with a secondary offer by the principal shareholder. The company (the 'Issuer') will raise new capital, and the principal shareholder will sell a block of its existing securities, by way of a Danish public offering and an international placement. A leading international financial institution will be appointed as global coordinator for the placement. The international placement will itself be divided into different tranches. Such subdivisions vary widely from one transaction to another having regard to the volume of shares placed, the interest in the Issuer in different countries, the placement capabilities of the respective managers and the current situation in the relevant markets. The case study assumes the fairly common feature of an international offering divided between a 'home country' tranche, 'North American' tranche and a 'rest of the world' tranche. As the Danish public offering will have to meet the specific requirements of Danish law, the global coordinator will have to address three major issues:

(i) Which documents (reports and prospectus) can be used by the respective members of the syndicate in the different jurisdictions for the purpose of marketing the securities; this will largely be dictated by whether or not the placement is a private or a public offering in the relevant jurisdiction;
(ii) By whom and to whom can such documents be distributed; and
(iii) What type of liability can arise as a result of such marketing activities.

It is worth remembering that, whilst the contractual relationship between the Issuer and the managers for the international placement, as well as the agreements among managers, may be governed by one set of laws (usually English or New York law), any liability (civil or otherwise) arising out of a breach of regulations in the marketing or placement of the securities in a particular jurisdiction will be governed by the laws of such jurisdiction and not the law of contract which does not bind investors or potential investors. In other words the 'lex contractus' is not the most relevant for the purpose of this paper, but the 'lex loci delicti' is where our attention lies. Moreover, even in the context of the agreement between the Issuer and the managers, the governing law clause may be overridden by the law of one of the managers' jurisdictions (see for example the comments relating to France at pp. 48–9 below).

It is also interesting to note that the issues raised by marketing activities on a cross-border basis are not, as many people think, a brand new phenomenon. 'Global offerings' were quite commonplace at the end of the 19th century.[2] As a result some case law, mostly in England, was developed as it was already recognised that 'The representation of one, unless . . . some repudiation of the position be clearly and unambiguously made, is the representation of all . . . If it can be shown that a material representation which is not true is contained in the prospectus . . . and the shareholder comes within a reasonable time, and under proper circumstances, to be released from that contract, the Courts are bound to release him from it'.[3]

This Chapter will limit itself to cross-border marketing activities before any sales are consummated including 'conditioning' potential purchasers. Whereas the prospectus is regarded as the 'statutory' marketing document in a transaction, analysts' research reports, marketing memoranda and road shows are clearly the most practical elements in the marketing of an international offering so far as financiers are concerned.

For ease of reference, this paper is divided into two parts, the first giving an overview of different European jurisdictions and the second dealing with North America.

PART I—EUROPE

UNITED KINGDOM

Analysts' Reports

The first issue to be considered with regard to analysts' reports is whether or not such reports were produced by one of the co-managers and, if so, how those reports can be used. If an analyst's report is prepared by a financial institution which has no connection with the offering, the only requirement will be that it must be issued or distributed by an authorised person as defined under the Financial Services Act 1986 (FSA)[4] and will typically only be distributed to persons of a kind described in Article 11(3) of The Financial Services Act 1986 (Investment Advertisements) (Exemptions)

[2] The 20th century concept of 'globalisation' is closer to the concept of ouverture of certain capital markets to foreign issuers, subject to adjustment to the local rules. The 19th century capital markets were more global than nowadays. In 1870, lead-manager Rothschild 'globally' offered £12,000,000 5% Bonds due 1951 for the Imperial Government of Russia. These Bonds were offered and listed in London, Paris, Frankfurt, Amsterdam and Berlin.

In 1888 Cleveland and Canton Railway Company 'globally' offered one of the first partly paid mortgage backed bonds ($2,000,000 first mortgage 5% Gold Bonds due 1917). Dent, Palmer & Co. lead managed this issue which was listed in New York, Boston and London. Due diligence was already a question as the prospectus used for the placement indicates 'A member of the firm of Messrs. Dent, Palmer & Co. has recently personally inspected the line, and reported very favourably for it.'

[3] Mair v Rio Grande Rubber Estates Limited [1913] AC 853 at 868–9, per Lord Shaw, which cites previous authorities on false prospectuses.

[4] Sections 7–34 (inclusive) of the Financial Services Act 1986.

Order 1995.[5] Generally, members of the public are not permitted to receive such materials.

If the analyst's report is prepared by one of the financial institutions involved in the offering certain recommendations need to be followed. First, the analyst in charge of producing the analyst's report should not be involved in the preparation of the prospectus and, in more general terms, should be supplied with the same information as is provided to analysts working for other financial institutions not involved in the offering. A strict Chinese wall needs to be in place between the analyst and the team in charge of executing the offering on behalf of the Issuer and the selling shareholder. In addition, the analyst's report should clearly state the role that the financial institution will play in the forthcoming offering. It is advisable to refrain from producing such reports during the twelve weeks prior to or subsequent to the launch of such placement where a prospectus or listing particulars for a listing on the London Stock Exchange is involved. This cooling off period, though not imposed by law is regarded by many practitioners as a safe rule to avoid doubts under section 154 FSA as to whether the report constitutes an advertisement. Where no London listing is involved this period is often reduced in practice, but care still needs to be taken to ensure that the report does not constitute an unauthorised 'investment advertisement' within section 57(2)FSA.

[5] Under Article 11(3) of SI 1995 No. 1266: 'A person falls within this paragraph if he is either:

(a) an authorised person; or

(b) an exempted person; or

(c) a person who is acting in the course of a business or employment which involves the dissemination of information concerning investments or activities of the kind described in Part II of Schedule I to the Act through newspapers, journals, magazines or other periodical publications or by way of sound broadcasting or television; or

(d) a government, local authority or public authority within the meaning of Note 1 to paragraph 3 of Schedule 1 to the Act; or

(e) a body corporate or an unincorporated association which either:

(i) if it is a body corporate and has more than 20 members or is the subsidiary of a holding company which has more than 20 members, it, or any of its holding companies or subsidiaries, has a called up share capital or net assets of not less than £500,000; or

(ii) if it is a body corporate other than one described in sub-paragraph (e)(i) above, it or any of its holding companies or subsidiaries has a called up share capital or net assets of not less than £5 million; or

(iii) if it is an unincorporated association, it has net assets of not less than £5 million; or

(f) a person who holds a permission granted under paragraph 23 of Schedule 1 to the Act; or

(g) a person acting in his capacity as a director, officer or employee of a person of a kind described above in this paragraph being a person whose responsibilities, when acting in that capacity, involve him engaging in activities which fall within Part II of Schedule 1 to the Act or which would fall within that Part were it not for the provisions of Part III of that Schedule; or

(h) any trustee of a trust where the aggregate value of the cash and investments which form part of the trust's assets (before deducting the amount of its liabilities) is £10 million or more or has been £10 million or more at any time during the previous two years.'

Prospectus

On 19th June, 1995, the United Kingdom implemented the EC Public Offers Directive[6] and gave effect to certain remaining provisions of the EC Listing Particulars Directive.[7] The prospectus used in the context of the Danish domestic public offering will be unlikely to satisfy the requirements of international investors as regards the financial information to be provided, which will typically need to relate to standards familiar to an international investor base and, in any event, will need to be in English. The Issuer will therefore have to produce an international prospectus in the English language whose content will cover more detailed information than the placement documents used domestically in Denmark. The distribution and the use of such prospectus in the UK will therefore need to comply with the Public Offers of Securities Regulations 1995 (the POS Regulations[8]).

In addition the Issuer may decide to seek a listing on the London Stock Exchange. The reasons for doing so would include the wish to raise the Issuer's profile on the international markets. In order to analyse the relevant applicable UK rules, it is necessary to determine whether a listing on the London Stock Exchange will be sought or not and whether the placement will constitute a UK public offering.

Where application is being made for the admission of the securities to the London Stock Exchange, it is Part IV of the FSA which will determine whether a prospectus or listing particulars must be published in relation to the offering to the public in the UK. Part IV of the FSA is the primary prospectus regime for initial public offerings in the UK of companies wherever incorporated seeking admission to the Official List of the London Stock Exchange.

Under the new prospectus regime, if the securities 'are to be offered to the public in the United Kingdom for the first time before admission' to the Official List of the London Stock Exchange a 'prospectus' will be required, unless one of the exemptions referred to at pages 37–8 below applies in which event 'listing particulars' will normally be required.

If the securities are to be admitted to the Official List of the London Stock Exchange, but are not 'offered to the public' (e.g. in the case of an introduction where there is no public offering or where there is deemed not to be a public offer by reason of one of the exemptions applying), it will still

[6] Council Directive 89/298/EEC, which was intended to harmonise EC laws on prospectuses for public offers of securities.

[7] Council Directive 80/390/EEC.

[8] Public Offers of Securities Regulations 1995 (SI 1995 No. 1537). For a helpful overview see Chris Bates 'The New UK Prospectus Rules' in Butterworths Journal of International Banking and Financial Law, July/August 1995 pp. 296–303.

be necessary to publish listing particulars in compliance with Part IV FSA and the Listing Rules.[9]

Part II of the POS Regulations is the primary prospectus regime for initial public offerings in the UK of companies wherever incorporated which do not seek admission to the Official List of the London Stock Exchange (including where application is made to trade securities on the Unlisted Securities Market or on the new Alternative Investment Market).

Offers to the public in the United Kingdom

Prior to 19th June 1995, where an application had been made to the London Stock Exchange for securities to be admitted to the Official List, Part IV of the FSA applied and under the Listing Rules it was necessary to prepare listing particulars and to register and publish them.[10]

Part IV of the FSA dealing with listed securities has been amended by the insertion of section 142 (7A) to incorporate a new definition of 'offering shares to the public'; the same definition is contained in Regulation 5 of the POS Regulations dealing with unlisted securities, so that there is consistency in approach. 'A person offers securities if, as principal:

(i) he makes an offer which, if accepted, would give rise to a contract for their issue or sale (which for this purpose includes any disposal for valuable consideration) by him or by another person with whom he has made arrangements for their issue or sale; or
(ii) he invites a person to make such an offer,

but not otherwise; and except where the context otherwise requires, 'offer' and 'offeror' shall be construed accordingly'. Offers of securities of both UK and foreign issuers are therefore covered including invitations to treat.

It is clear that the prospectus regime covering both listed and unlisted securities now applies to offers of any variety made to the public in any form, so that offers made orally, or by any other unwritten means (for example electronically or through screen-based dealing and information systems) are now subject to the regulation. Oral offers are therefore now

[9] The Listing Rules of the London Stock Exchange, known as the Yellow Book, contain the rules governing London listings.

[10] SI 1986 No. 2246 provided that Part III and Schedule 3 Companies Act 1985 (CA 1985) should not apply and that no prospectus would be involved where the securities concerned were listed or the subject of an application for listing in accordance with Part IV FSA. However, in relation to unlisted securities, the prospectus provisions under Part III and Schedule 3 CA 1985 reflected a document based regime; every prospectus issued by or on behalf of a company offering shares to the public required to be registered with the Registrar of Companies. Because the regime was document based and because of the limited scope of the professionals only exemption in section 79(2) CA 1985, the practice developed of making professionals only offers by means of information memoranda which contained information but no invitation, combined with an oral offer of the securities by means of a telephone placing.

caught unless an express exemption applies.[11] The requirement for a prospectus depends on there being a public offer, irrespective of the form of that offer.

It should be noted that in order for a prospectus to be required it must be an offer 'in the United Kingdom' and under the new regime it is only necessary therefore to look at the offering in the UK (any form of overseas marketing not being relevant).

Exemptions from the requirement to publish a UK prospectus

Schedule 11A FSA (listed securities) and Regulation 7 POS Regulations (unlisted securities) contain almost identical exemptions which, if applicable, result in the relevant offer of securities being deemed not to be 'an offer to the public'. As a consequence, if the exemptions apply a prospectus will not be required in the case of securities to be listed on the London Stock Exchange but listing particulars will be required, and in the case of unlisted securities, a prospectus under the POS Regulations will not be required but the document may nevertheless constitute an 'investment advertisement' under section 57 FSA (unless one of the exemptions in section 58 applies—e.g. distribution only to Article 11 (3) persons).

In applying these exemptions only the UK element of the offer in question need be taken into account; most (but not all) of the exemptions may be relied on in combination or cumulatively, with the effect that an offer that falls partly in one exemption and partly in another can be treated as exempt (paragraph 4 Schedule 11A and Regulation 7(3))—consequently a prospectus is avoided if for example a cash placing or retail offer is restricted to 50 non-professionals provided the placees above 50 in number are within the professionals exemption.

Particularly in view of the criminal penalties in Regulation 16 for failure to comply with the requirement to publish a prospectus, these exemptions are likely to be of considerable importance in practice.

The principal exemptions include:

- two separate exemptions for 'professionals offers'

(a) offers to persons (i) whose ordinary activities involve them in acquiring, holding, managing or disposing of investments (as principal or agent) for the purposes of their businesses, or (ii) who it is reasonable to expect will acquire, hold, manage or dispose of investments (as principal or agent) for the purposes of their businesses; or are otherwise offered to persons in the context of their trades, professions or occupations. This exemption is much wider than the previous

[11] e.g. one of the professionals exemptions or the euro-securities exemption in the new Schedule 11A FSA or in Regulation 7 of the POS Regulations.

professionals exemption in section 79(2) Companies Act 1985 and clearly now extends to corporate treasury activities and pension fund trustees;

(b) offers to a 'restricted circle of persons' whom the offeror reasonably believes to be sufficiently knowledgeable to understand the risks involved in accepting the offer.

- offers to no more than 50 persons. It should be noted that this exemption relates to the number of offerees (probably including persons indirectly approached through intermediaries) and not to the number of resultant investors;
- offer in connection with a bona fide invitation to enter into an underwriting agreement. This exemption will cover normal underwriting and sub-underwriting arrangements but not a direct placing and probably not the solicitation of euromarket underwriting commitments where traditionally the managers resell the securities as principal;
- where the securities offered are 'euro-securities' and are not the subject of advertising likely to come to the attention of persons who are not professionally experienced in matters relating to investment. 'Euro-securities' are defined as meaning investments which (i) are to be underwritten and distributed by a syndicate at least two of the members of which have their registered offices in different countries or territories, (ii) are to be offered on a significant scale in one or more countries or territories other than that of the issuer and (iii) may be acquired pursuant to the offer only through a credit institution or other financial institution (as defined). For this exemption to apply the securities must be underwritten and distributed by a syndicate with at least two members from different countries.

Road shows and pathfinders

Although under the new regime the form and content requirements for prospectuses and listing particulars are almost the same, it is important to determine into which category the documentation falls. Under section 156B FSA it is now a criminal offence to offer securities to the public in the UK before the time of publication of a prospectus; it is therefore important in the case of listed securities to determine whether a prospectus is required. Under the old regime, once an application had been made for listing the prospectus provisions in the Companies Act 1985 ceased to apply and there were few restrictions in practice on solicitations and pre-marketing. Under the new regime it is necessary to ensure that any pre-marketing, warming up of investors or other type of solicitation to the extent that it takes place in the UK before the publication of the prospectus (where one is required) does not amount to 'an offer to the public in the UK for the first time'.

Hence, pathfinder documents and red herrings should not constitute 'offers' and any other material distributed during road shows similarly should not constitute 'offers'. If the offering is taking place by using the bookbuilding method, it will be important that the bookbuilding process only involves non-binding indications of interest which do not constitute 'offers' or invitations to treat.

It is also possible that as a result of selling and distribution restrictions the pre-marketing material will fall within one of the exemptions referred to above so that it is not treated as an 'offer to the public' (e.g. under one of the professionals exemptions).

The pre-marketing documentation may constitute an 'investment advertisement' within section 57(2) FSA, but the need for approval by an authorised person will be avoided if distribution is restricted to Article 11(3) persons. Similarly, the prohibition in section 56 FSA on cold calling will be avoided by restricting distribution to professionals or others as permitted by the Common Unsolicited Calls Regulations. The advertising restrictions imposed in the case of offerings of listed securities by section 154 FSA (e.g. mini-prospectuses) continue to apply.

As regards securities which are not to be admitted to the Official List of the London Stock Exchange, the same rules on investment advertisements and cold calling will apply as apply to listed securities; hence distribution will normally be limited to Article 11(3) persons. If a prospectus under the POS Regulations is required (e.g. because none of the exemptions referred to above apply) the offeror must publish the prospectus by making it available to the public free of charge at an address in the UK while the offer remains open.[12] Any advertisement, notice, poster or document announcing the offer which is issued to the public in the UK (e.g. pre-marketing material) must state that a prospectus has been or will be published and must give an address in the UK from which the prospectus can be obtained.[13] In contrast to the previous regime, there is no obligation to distribute copies of the prospectus to investors with or without a form of application and there is no prohibition on the distribution of other offering materials (e.g. mini-prospectuses) once the prospectus has been prepared and filed with the registrar of companies.

Some documentation may constitute both a prospectus and listing particulars (e.g. a retail offer to the public and a simultaneous placing to professional investors). This confusing position is the subject of discussion between legal practitioners and the London Stock Exchange and it is hoped that in due course the Exchange will allow a single document to be approved for all purposes, thus giving Issuers and managers the chance to pre-market securities before they decide under which category they wish to

[12] Reg 4(1) POS Regulations.

[13] Reg 12 POS Regulations.

proceed. In the meantime it is most important that Issuers and lead managers decide on their marketing and selling strategy in advance before the application for listing so as to avoid any risk of selling securities to the public (outside one of the exemptions) prior to the publication of a prospectus.

Use of the Danish prospectus in the United Kingdom

In certain circumstances the Issuer may be able to use an English translation of the Danish prospectus prepared for the Danish domestic public offering to obtain a London listing and/or use such prospectus in a UK public offering. The mutual recognition provisions of the Public Offers Directive, enabling recognition of certain prospectuses approved in other European Union/European Economic Area member states as prospectuses for the purpose of a public offer in the UK have been implemented by amendments to the Listing Rules. Under the Listing Rules a document issued by an overseas company and approved by a competent authority of another member state will qualify as listing particulars in the UK provided the relevant provisions are satisfied. In addition new paragraph 17.72 of the Listing Rules provides for the mutual recognition of a qualifying document as a prospectus where application is made for admission to listing of securities of an overseas company which are to be offered to the public in the United Kingdom for the first time before admission. In each case the London Stock Exchange must give written confirmation that the qualifying document satisfies the requirements for mutual inward recognition either as listing particulars or as a prospectus.

Schedule 4 of the POS Regulations provides both (i) for the recognition for the purposes of Part IV of the FSA of prospectuses and listing particulars approved in other member states (inward recognition by 'recognised European documents') and (ii) for the recognition for the purposes of Part II of the POS Regulations of prospectuses approved in other member states (inward recognition by 'recognised prospectuses'). Recognised European documents (whether constituting listing particulars or a prospectus) need to comply with Chapter 17 of the Listing Rules although the London Stock Exchange has no right to refuse it provided it complies with the requirements. Part IV of the FSA applies to a recognised European document as it applies to listing particulars or a prospectus.

Part II of POS Regulations applies to a 'recognised prospectus' approved in another member state. In addition the provisions of Companies Act 1985 (other than section 83) will apply to a recognised prospectus; and a recognised prospectus is deemed to comply with section 97(3) and section 693(1)(a) and (d) Companies Act 1985.

Potential liabilities

Potential liabilities relating to the distribution of information

The distribution in the UK of information constituting an 'investment advertisement' by an unauthorised person or of information the contents of which have not been approved by an authorised person carries stiff penalties unless the exceptions referred to in section 58 apply. Under section 57(3) FSA on conviction on indictment, a person may be liable to imprisonment for a term not exceeding two years or to a fine or to both, or on summary conviction, to imprisonment for a term not exceeding six months or to a fine not exceeding the statutory maximum or to both.

Section 58 FSA provides that the restrictions on advertising in section 57 do not apply where one of the Exemption Orders[14] applies or where the advertisement receives approval by the London Stock Exchange under section 154 FSA or where the advertisement consists of, or any part of, listing particulars or of a prospectus approved in accordance with the Listing Rules.

The Exemption Orders provide a number of exceptions including advertisements issued to professionals[15] (being persons sufficiently expert to understand the risks involved) and other categories of persons.

If the Issuer distributes a prospectus or listing particulars in accordance with Part IV FSA or distributes a prospectus in accordance with Part II POS Regulations, section 57 FSA will not be applicable. If the pre-marketing or marketing material or offering documentation does not fall within the above categories, it would be normal to restrict distribution to persons falling within the definition of Article 11(3). Although any authorised institution (e.g. most UK financial intermediaries) may distribute information to persons who do not fall within the definition of Article 11(3), they may thereby incur liability because they will be breaching the rules of the self-regulating organisation of which they are a member (e.g. the Securities and Futures Authority) and in addition may be liable in damages to private investors who suffer loss under section 62 SFA.

Misleading information in the prospectus

In the case of a prospectus or listing particulars relating to listed securities, the persons responsible for misstatements and omissions are the persons referred to in section 152 FSA.

In the case of a prospectus for unlisted securities prepared under the POS Regulations, the persons responsible under Regulation 13 are the Issuer;

[14] The Financial Services Act 1986 (Investment Advertisements) (Exemptions) Order 1995 (SI 1995 No. 1266) and The Financial Services Act 1986 (Investment Advertisements) (Exemptions) (No. 2) Order 1995 (SI 1995 No. 1536).

[15] Article 11(3) The Financial Services Act 1986 (Investment Advertisements) (Exemptions) Order 1995 (SI 1995 No. 1266).

each person who is a director of the Issuer at the time the prospectus is published; each person who has authorised himself to be named in the prospectus as a director or as having agreed to becoming a director immediately or at a future time; each person who accepts and is stated in the prospectus as accepting responsibility for any part of the prospectus; and each person not falling within any of the above who has authorised the contents of or any part of the prospectus. These five categories are the same as those applying under section 152(1) FSA. In addition there are two categories which reflect the persons referred to in section 152(4), namely the 'offeror' of the securities, where he is not the Issuer, as in our case study, the selling principal shareholder. Where the offeror is a body corporate but is not the Issuer and is not making the offer in association with the Issuer, each person who is a director of that body corporate at the time the prospectus is published is also responsible. Therefore, in our case study, the selling shareholder's directors would not be liable as the offer is made in association with the Issuer. Due to an oversight, under paragraph 10 of Schedule 1 POS Regulations the responsibility statement in a prospectus where an offeror is not the Issuer needs to be given individually by the directors of the offeror rather than by the offeror alone; hence where, for example, an institutional shareholder is selling shares as part of an offering of a non-London listed company (i.e. whether or not in association with the Issuer) it would seem that its directors will need to take responsibility for the prospectus. A directors' statement regarding the accuracy of a POS prospectus is also required; this must be made by the directors of the offeror rather than the directors of the Issuer where the offeror is not the Issuer or, it seems, by both sets of directors where a separate offeror is offering existing securities and the Issuer is offering new securities under the same offer.

A financial institution (e.g. underwriter, broker, sponsor) acting as agent rather than as principal is not an 'offeror' for these purposes. Where a combination of new and existing securities is offered under a single public offer, without an intermediary acting as principal, the Issuer and the vendors will be joint offerors with joint responsibility for the POS prospectus or prospectus of listed securities.

Section 150 FSA provides that the persons responsible for a prospectus or listing particulars should be liable to pay compensation to any person who has acquired any of the securities in question and suffered loss in respect of them as a result of any untrue or misleading statement or the omission of any matter required by section 146. The rules for exemption from liability to pay compensation are set out in section 151. Similar provisions are contained in Regulations 14 and 15 POS Regulations. As a consequence liability for listing particulars and for a prospectus (whether for listed or unlisted securities) are brought into line. The change is of limited practical significance in relation to civil liability; more important is that in the case of unlisted securities there is no longer an express criminal sanction for untrue statements in a prospectus (as there used to be under the old prospectus regime—section 70 Companies Act 1985). Instead, the more general criminal sanctions in section 47 FSA will apply. Regulation 16 POS Regulations provides a criminal offence where a prospectus is not published in breach of Regulation 4(1) or is not delivered to the Registrar of Companies in breach of Regulation 4(2) or where an advertisement is published in breach of Regulation 12.

Additionally, there may be a tortious liability if there has been any misrepresentation, innocent, fraudulent or negligent, which has induced an investor to enter into a contract for the purchase of relevant securities. Such a liability could result under English law in damages or rescission of the contract for purchase.

Common law liability

In addition to the statutory recourse, an investor might be able to recover damages in tort from the directors of the Issuer and/or the financial institution involved in the drafting of a misleading prospectus. Such an action would be for fraudulent or negligent misrepresentation and, if established, for fraudulent conspiracy to defraud.[16]

Selling Restrictions

If the securities of the Issuer are not to be offered to the public in the UK and no prospectus is produced, the distribution of the pre-marketing documentation should be restricted to Article 11(3) persons. In the absence of an offer to the public in the UK, securities of the Issuer should only be offered or sold to persons falling under one of the exemptions referred to at pages 37–8 above.

GERMANY

Analysts' Reports—Prospectuses

Analysts' reports and prospectuses can be distributed to a limited number of persons who, as part of their profession, occupation or business,

[16] Both the old and new directors were partners to the issue of the prospectus to the public. They knew that statements in the prospectus were untrue and misleading. There was evidence that the prospectus invited people in the plaintiff's position to subscribe for the company's issue of debenture stock. The old directors authorised the issue and were aware of the misstatements and could not have reasonably believed that the valuation was competent. . . . As to the conspiracy allegation [against the financial intermediary], it was an alternative to the cause of action for fraudulent misrepresentation, and so could only be an alternative way of getting the same damages under another head of tort. Clark & Others v Urquhart and Stacey & Others v Urquhart [1930] AC 28.

purchase or sell securities for their own account or the account of others (i.e. offer to institutional investors or financial intermediaries). Any distribution of documents other than to these persons for the purpose of allocating shares to German residents triggers an obligation to produce a prospectus, as such activities would be deemed to constitute a public offering in Germany.

Persons authorised to distribute and receive information

In the context of a non-public offering, German law does not require that the information provided to German institutional investors or financial intermediaries be distributed by German authorised institutions. Likewise, the recipient of the information can be any institution usually investing or transacting in securities.

The use of the Danish prospectus in Germany

Should the Issuer decide to make a public offering in Germany, it would use the EC Directives mentioned at page 49 below. A listing in Frankfurt could also be sought based on the Listing Particulars Directive.[17] Proof that listing was granted in Denmark and a sales prospectus (Verkaufsprospekt) in German would then be prepared.[18]

Potential liabilities

Irrespective of where the information comes from, the German Börsengesetz provides for strict liability with regard to information provided to German residents. In accordance with the said statute a person can be punished by imprisonment of up to three years or fined if the person uses fraudulent means to manipulate the exchange or market price of commodities or securities or makes inaccurate statements in a prospectus or public information item intended to cause subscriptions to, or purchases of or sales of, securities; provided, however, that the person has an intention to derive gain for himself or a third party. Obviously, these liabilities are in addition to common law recourses.

Selling restrictions

Should the Issuer decide not to proceed with a German public offer, the managers can only approach a limited number of institutional investors and undertake not to engage in public advertisements (*öffentliche Werbung*).

[17] 17.§ 40 and 18 of Gesetz zur Anderung and Börsengesetzes.

[18] Prof. Dr. Heinz-Dieter Ausmann-Petra Buck. Europäisches Capitamarketrechts EWS. Heft 71/1990 pp. 220–1.

FRANCE[18a]

Analysts' Reports and Prospectuses

Distribution of any information in France without the prior approval of the French *Commission des Opérations de Bourse* (the COB) is strictly forbidden unless the placement is effected by way of private placement.

Private Placements defined

The present guidelines of the COB as to what constitutes a private placement are as follows:

- The investors approached must all be banks, financial institutions, stockbrokers, insurance companies or financial intermediaries as defined by applicable French law;
- The number of investors contacted must not exceed three hundred;[19]
- The investors contacted must all be existing contacts of the offeror (i.e. contacts of a member of the syndicate or one of its affiliates);
- Placees must be investing for their own account and not for the account of their clients or with a view to on-selling to their clients;
- The selling material may only be mailed at the request of the placee and should be provided solely for the purpose of providing information in respect of the securities and the mechanics of the offering;
- The documents should not constitute an invitation to purchase the securities and the documents distributed should clearly state that they have not been approved by the COB and that the information contained cannot be distributed to the public in France or used in connection with an offer to subscribe or sell the securities in France;
- An application form or a subscription letter should not be attached to the offering materials;
- The offer should be structured so that the initiative to purchase originates from the placees (i.e. the distributor should not offer to sell); and
- No publicity articles and other PR exercises should appear in the French press or be made available to the French public (non-French newspapers in circulation in France do not fall into that category).

It is however quite important to stress that the above are only guidelines from the COB. As far as French law is concerned the definition of a private placement is given in the negative. In other words to qualify as a private

[18a] For a detailed examination of public offers of securities in France, see Wayne H. Smith, infra, Chapter 12.

[19] Réglement no. 92–02 de la Commission des Opérations de Bourse homologué par arrêté du 3 mars (Journal Officiel 15 mars 1992, p. 3745): instruction d'application au réglement no. 92–02 (suppl. Bulletin COB no. 256, 1992).

placement, the placement should not constitute a public offer (*Appel Publique á l'Epargne*). It is therefore important to bear in mind the French definition of a public offer.

Public Offer

French law establishes a presumption of public offer when an Issuer or principal shareholder sells securities through financial institutions acting as managers who do not know beforehand the names of the potential investors and the placement uses the dissemination of some information about the issuer to potential investors. This is irrespective of the number or quality of the investors and the means by which the information is provided (analyst report, prospectus, road shows). This presumption of public offer is set out in Article 72 of the Company Law of 1966.[20] Although this article only applies, strictly speaking, to French companies, it is regarded as defining the notion of public offering under French law. Compliance with the COB guidelines is not in itself sufficient to rebut the presumption of a public offer and, therefore, the normal practice in global offerings has been for the manager responsible for placing the securities in France to request from the COB that they confirm that the placement contemplated in France will be a private placement and that therefore no French prospectus will be required (*Note d'information*). In our case, the best advice for the lead manager would be to request from the COB confirmation that the placement envisaged is a private placement, whilst confirming to the COB that the placement will comply with the guidelines mentioned above. Based on such a confirmation and compliance with the COB guidelines, the presumption of public offer governed by company law could be rebutted before a tribunal. If the placement were to be considered as a public offer, only authorised intermediaries would be allowed to distribute the information to the public, such information to be cleared by the COB.[21]

The use of the Danish prospectus in France

If the Issuer decides to use the Danish prospectus to either get the shares listed on the Paris Stock Exchange and/or make a public offer of such shares, French wording would need to be prepared and approved by the COB.

If the Issuer decides to request a listing on the Paris Stock Exchange, the EC Admission Directive implemented in France in 1992 and, accordingly, the requirements set out in that directive will apply. Due to the French implementation of the EC Mutual Recognition Directive the Issuer will be able to benefit from mutual recognition for an offering in France:

[20] Gilles Endreo, Pierre Clermontel 'Placement Privé et Appel Publique á l'Epargne' Revue de Droit Bancaire, mai/juin 1992, p. 91–100.

[21] Intermédiaire habilité.

(i) if it has its registered office in the EU (which is the case of the Issuer) and then only if the Listing Particulars Directive and the EC Accounts Directives have been implemented in the relevant member state. All documents submitted to the Paris Stock Exchange must be translated into French;

(ii) likewise, only a public offer prospectus issued by a company with its registered office in the EC will be recognised as listing particulars in France, if such prospectus is drawn up in accordance with the Listing Particulars Directive and approved by a competent authority at the time of the public offer, and if the request for listing is made at the same time in France and in the member state of the above-mentioned competent authority, or if the request for listing in that member state was requested within three months of the public offer. However, by making a public offer in France, the Issuer may subject itself to the application of the French language law of 1994.

Persons authorised to distribute and receive the information

Provided that the requirements of a private placement described above are met, no specific requirements are imposed.

Potential liabilities

Violation of the offering rules set by French law and enforced by the COB gives rise to personal criminal liabilities, fines and potentially can render the transactions contemplated void.

In 1993, the COB referred two matters to the State prosecutor (*Procureur de la République*) for potential criminal action on financial intermediaries who marketed and offered to the public shares not listed on the Paris Stock Exchange, while at the same time issuing public warnings in the French press as to the illegal activities of brokers promoting non approved securities to the French public.[22] In addition, misleading information contained in a prospectus may give rise to potential action to annul a contract for misrepresentation (*dol*).

Selling Restrictions

If the Issuer decides not to place its shares with the public in France, then it would have to require each manager not to offer or sell the shares to the

[22] Rapport au Président de la République—Commission des Opérations de Bourse—1993, p.186. The two cases referred to related to (1) the marketing by Grimaldi Hofmann et Cie of shares of a Canadian company and (2) the non approved offer of shares in Transamerican Petroleum Corporation.

public in France nor to distribute any information related to the placement to the public.

The 1994 law on the use of the French language

In 1994, the French parliament passed a law on the use of the French language (known as *Loi Toubon* after the name of the Minister of Culture who promoted this legislation).[23] The purpose of this law is to protect the use of the French language. The Loi Toubon provides that all State Entities, agencies or any entity performing a public service[24] may only enter into contracts drafted in French (other versions of the same contracts may exist, however the French version must be a governing version and this is irrespective of the governing law). Violation of the Loi Toubon prevents a party from relying on provisions prejudicing the other party and which are not written in French. This law is part of the French Public Order, and therefore overrides a governing law clause.[25]

Article 5 provides an exception for public institutions engaging in industrial or commercial activities and whose contracts are performed entirely outside France.

It is worth remembering that several French financial institutions perform a public service or are public entities. This is the case notably of the *Caisse de Dépôts et Consignations* (CDC) and the *Caisse Nationale de Crédit Agricole*. Although both institutions engage in industrial or commercial activities (and their status is similar to an EPIC[26]), the performance of the contracts they enter into in an international offering does not wholly take place outside France.

In our case, one could argue that should the offering be a private placement, substantially all of the performance of the relevant contracts will take place outside France. Although substantially does not mean wholly, a court

[23] Loi no. 94–665 du 4 août 1994 relative á l'emploi de la langue française. Journal Officiel de la République Française.

[24] Art 5.—Quels qu'en soient l'objet et les formes, les contrats auxquels une personne morale de droit public ou une personne privée exécutant une mission de service publique sont parties sont rédigés en langue française. Ils ne peuvent contenir ni expression ni terme étrangers lorsqu'il existe une expression ou un terme français de même sens approuvés dans les conditions prévues par les dispositions réglementaires relatives á l'enrichissement de la langue française.

Ces dispositions ne sont pas applicables aux contrats conclus par une personne morale de droit public gérant des activités à caractére industriel et commercial et à exècuter intégralement hors du territoire national.

Les contrats visés au présent article conclus avec un ou plusieurs cocontractants étrangers peuvent comporter, outre la rédaction en français, une ou plusieurs versions en langue trangére pouvant également faire foi.

Une partie à un contrat conclu en violation du premier alinéa ne pourra se prévaloir d'une disposition en langue étrangére qui porterait préjudice à la partie à laquelle elle est opposée.

[25] Article 20.

[26] Entreprise Publique à Caractére Industriel et Commercial (EPIC).

could decide that a public entity such as CDC could validly enter into an English language agreement (however one must stress that no case law supports such a view). It is fairly clear that, should the placement be a French public offer, French agreements (subscription agreement, agreement among managers) would need to be drawn up in French as otherwise certain French financial institutions could escape their obligations as a result of the Loi Toubon.[27]

EUROPEAN LAW

As mentioned earlier, the implementation in the United Kingdom of the POS Regulations 1995 in June 1995 is a welcome, albeit late step in the pursuit of some sort of unity of regulation throughout the European Community. The Regulations are the fruit of the Public Offers Directive,[28] the object of which is to promote the creation of a truly European Capital Market through the implementation of a uniform policy in relation to transferable securities in member countries.

The scope of the Directive, in theory at least, extends to our Danish offering as it requires that all Member States ensure that a prospectus is published where transferable securities are offered to the public. 'Transferable Securities' is defined as being shares in companies, other transferable securities equivalent to shares in companies, debt securities having a maturity of at least one year or their equivalent and any other transferable security giving the right to acquire any such transferable securities by subscription or exchange.[29]

In Member States which provide for the scrutiny of public offering prospectuses, such as the UK and Denmark, it is possible for a person wishing to make an offer to the public in one Member State to apply for a listing in a second Member State and to prepare a prospectus the contents, procedures for scrutiny and distribution of which are determined in accordance with the relevant listing rules in the State of listing.[30] Where a prospectus is prepared in this manner, notices, advertisements and documents announcing the public offer must be sent to the relevant stock exchange or competent authority in advance, and any and all of these items must state where the prospectus is to be published.[31]

This is related to a most important provision in the Directive, that

[27] See 'Mandatory Use of French in Financing Agreements'. Antoine Besse, IFLR February 1995, p. 2—Les Contraintes de la Loi Toubon. Marie Pisanté—Frédérique Dupuis-Toubol. Expertise, Octobre 1994 pp. 348–54.

[28] EC Public Offers Directive (89/298/EEC)—17th April, 1989.

[29] EC Public Offers Directive—Article 3(e).

[30] EC Public Offers Directive—Article 8(1).

[31] EC Public Offers Directive—Article 10(1).

concerning mutual recognition.[32] This states that if an approved prospectus for a public offering of the same transferable securities is made in two or more Member States, simultaneously, or within a short period of time, the prospectus, subject to translation if required, must be recognised as complying with the laws of the other Member States without being subject to any sort of approval there and without those States being able to require that any further information is needed.

PART II—NORTH AMERICA

PRIVATE PLACEMENTS IN THE UNITED STATES AND CANADA

Securities legislation in the United States and most provinces in Canada requires registration of all offers to sell and solicitations of offers to buy securities in these countries, unless a specific exemption is provided.[33] The phrase 'offer to sell' is broadly construed in these jurisdictions and includes certain marketing activities including publication of information and statements and publicity efforts, made in advance of a proposed financing which have the effect of conditioning the market or arousing interest in an issuer or in its securities. This section of this Chapter will review the private placement regimes in each of the United States and Canada as well as outline permitted and problematic crossborder marketing in the context of a global equity offering.

In the United States, a private placement must meet two thresholds to avoid the need for registration—the issuer must sell in a transaction that does not involve a 'public' offering and precautions must be taken by the issuer to ensure that subsequent trades in these restricted securities are either again exempt or are made outside the United States. In Canada, the principle exemptions from the requirement to file a prospectus are in respect of sales to institutional or sophisticated purchasers, sales of exempt securities and sales of securities having a minimum threshold acquisition cost.

In both countries, significant restrictions on marketing exist as a condition to the availability of the private placement exemption. Therefore, in evaluating the relative advantages and disadvantages of a registered public offering as compared with an unregistered private one, the Issuer will

[32] EC Public Offers Directive—Article 21.

[33] The 'closed system' requires that a prospectus/registration statement in prescribed form must be filed with and cleared by the relevant securities regulator in respect of all distributions of securities, whether primary or secondary sales, retail or institutional placements, unless an exemption is available. The US and the Canadian provinces of Ontario, Quebec, Alberta, British Columbia, Nova Scotia, Newfoundland and Saskatchewan all have closed systems. The principal exemption in the US is at Section 4(2) of the US Securities Act, in respect of transactions not involving any public offering.

undoubtedly have considered marketing, in addition to the more obvious considerations relating to timing, cost, extent of required disclosure and liability.

UNITED STATES

Rule 144A/Regulation S

The global equity offering in the case under study will not be registered with the SEC. Like most recent private offerings by foreign issuers the Issuer and the selling shareholder have selected a Rule 144A[34] offering in the United States as opposed to a conventional private placement. A Rule 144A Offering can only be made to a designated class of professional investors; however there is no maximum number of offerees and the Rule does not require investor letters. Moreover, these offerings permit a much higher profile marketing programme and may include roadshows. To all intents and purposes the offering document used is similar to a prospectus which would be used in a SEC registered offering, except that there is no required clearance by the SEC. More importantly, conventional (i.e. non-144A) private placements lack the same potential for an unrestricted US secondary market among qualified institutional buyers (QIBs).[35]

The technique employed for US securities law purposes is to combine the exemption in Rule 144A (for shares sold in the US) with Regulation S[36] (for

[34] See Securities Act release no.6862 (April 23, 1990) (Rule 144A adopting release). Rule 144A permits immediate unregistered resales of restricted securities to qualified institutional buyers (QIBs). The rule defines this term by listing categories of institutional and other investors and prescribing a qualification test based on size of the buyer's portfolio. The only classes of securities that are not eligible for resale under rule 144A are securities that are of the same class as securities already listed on a US national securities exchange or quoted in Nasdaq and securities of mutual funds, unit and investment trusts and face amount certificate companies that are or are required to be registered under the Investment Companies Act. Rule 144A contains no specific procedures to ensure that resales are confined to QIBs but sellers or persons acting on their behalf must take reasonable steps to ensure that the buyer is aware that the seller is relying on this exemption.

[35] A QIB is an entity coming within an extensive list of buyers set forth in the Rule, including certain banks, saving and loan associations, insurance companies, investment companies, governmental and private employee benefit plans, certain trusts, registered investment advisors, registered dealers, corporations and others.

QIBs generally must have over 100 million dollars in invested assets (except in the case of dealers, $10,000,000). There are several thousand QIBs in the United States. As QIBs may freely trade these restricted securities among themselves, a formalised market has been set up. In conjunction with Rule 144A, the SEC approved a proposal by the National Association of Securities Dealers to establish a new trading system known as PORTAL for trading restricted securities eligible for resale under Rule 144A. While only QIBs may participate in the PORTAL system, they may also resell their securities under other available exemptions.

[36] See 'Offshore Offers and Sales', Securities Act Release no. 6863 (April 24, 1990). Regulation S comprises four Rules: Rules 901, 902, 903 and 904. The primary enquiry under Regulation S is whether the offer and sale of securities occurs 'outside the United States'. If

shares sold outside the US). Regulation S was adopted by the SEC to clarify, particularly in the context of global offerings, the applicability of the registration requirements of the US Securities Act of 1933 (the US Securities Act) to transactions occurring outside the territorial boundaries of the United States.[37] Regulation S has been used in conjunction with Rule 144A to attract foreign issuers to the United States and to create an active trading market for such securities. Simply put, Rule 144A allows for the immediate sale by an underwriter of the Issuer's Securities to QIBs and Regulation S allows those investors who have purchased under Rule 144A to effect an unregistered public resale in the Issuer's home country or elsewhere outside the US. Conjunctively, Regulation S may be relied upon by the Issuer to sell its securities offshore to such parties as foreign institutions or to US broker/dealer affiliates located overseas and, using Rule 144A, such parties could promptly resell the securities to QIBs in the United States.

While the marketing restrictions of both the private placement exemption and the safe harbour provisions of Regulation S should be adhered to in the context of this global offering, permitted marketing efforts in connection with the US private placement (e.g., US roadshows involving only QIBs, distribution to QIBs of offering materials) will not constitute improper activities for purposes of Regulation S.

US Marketing Activities[38]

In the context of the case under study, the Issuer, the selling shareholder and the lead managers will have custom-designed a marketing programme for the United States that will differ substantially from what is permitted in Europe. Although Rule 144A does not expressly prohibit general solicitation, practitioners and the SEC have adopted certain guidelines because of the interaction with Regulation S and the prohibition against general solicitation in Regulation D (safe harbour for private offerings). Accordingly, no general solicitation or advertising regarding the Offering should be made in the United States by the Issuer, the selling shareholder or persons acting on their behalf (including prospective syndicate members) and no offers or

such is the case, within the meaning of rule 901, the registration provisions of section 5 of the Securities Act of 1933 are not applicable. Regulation S provides two non-exclusive safe harbour provisions in rules 903 and 904. The general conditions applicable require that the offer or sale is made in an 'offshore transaction' and no 'directed selling efforts' take place in the United States in connection with the distribution or resale of the securities.

[37] See Marc I. Steinberg and Daryl L. Lansdale Jr., Regulation S and Rule 144A: Creating a Workable Fiction in an Expanding Global Securities Market, The International Lawyer, Vol. 29 No. 1, p. 43.

[38] Portions of this section dealing with US Marketing Activities have been excerpted from a paper on publicity for Reg. S/Rule 144A Offerings dated May 6, 1994 by Cleary, Gottlieb, Steen & Hamilton.

sales in the United States should be made except to QIBs. Roadshows that involve only QIBs (provided they are not invited by general solicitation) are permitted as is dissemination of offering materials destined only for QIBs.

The key constraint is that no 'directed selling efforts' may be made in the United States. Directed selling efforts include any activity that could reasonably be expected to have the effect of conditioning the market in the United States for the securities of the Issuer. Specifically, placing advertisements with television or radio stations reaching the United States or in publications that have a general circulation in the United States (even if they are foreign publications), mailing printed material to US investors or conducting promotional seminars in the United States are considered directed selling efforts.[39] Even speeches at US conferences or statements at press conferences at which the Offering is mentioned could constitute general solicitations or general advertising.

Press conferences may be held outside the United States in accordance with local market practice, and US journalists need not be barred from attending. If a press conference is to be held in Europe, only information relating to the non-US offering can be made available; there should be no reference to the Rule 144A placement. If there are any questions about whether shares will be offered in the United States, the response should be that the possible inclusion of the United States as part of the international tranches is under consideration.

Press releases that may be distributed to publications with a 'general circulation in the United States', a term which includes, for example, the US edition of the Financial Times, should be cleared in advance with US counsel. No press release, regardless of where distributed, should refer to the Rule 144A placement. Advertisements may be placed in publications that do not have a general circulation in the United States, but no advertisements should be placed in publications that have such a circulation.

Contacts or meetings with US securities analysts should not be initiated. In the event that the Issuer does have discussions with any US securities analyst, the Offering should not be mentioned.

If publicity concerning the Issuer (including research reports) which would come within the meaning of an 'offer to sell' or 'directed selling efforts' is distributed in the United States, other than pursuant to a safe

[39] (Rule 902). Certain types of advertising are expressly excluded from the definition of directed selling efforts, including advertisements that are required under either US or foreign law and 'tombstone' advertisements meeting specific statutory requirements which are placed in publications that have less than 20% of their total circulation in the United States. The SEC has also stated that while limited activities directed at a single investor may constitute solicitation this would not be considered to be a directed selling effort because of its limited effect. Moreover, the SEC has stated that Regulation S 'is not intended to limit or interfere with news stories or other bona fide journalistic activities or otherwise hinder the flow of normal corporate news regarding foreign issuers'.

harbour, or if adequate precautions are not taken to prevent publicity distributed outside the United States from being carried into the United States by others, there is a risk that the marketing activities constitute an illegal offer and the SEC could order a 'cooling-off' period so as to allow the effect of such publicity to dissipate. Although this remedy is rarely invoked by the SEC, were such a cooling-off period to be ordered, it could severely damage the success of the Offering. In addition, if such publicity contains any material misstatement of fact or omits to state a material fact necessary to make statements in such publicity not misleading, and if such publicity is distributed in or carried into the United Sates, an investor might seek damages against the Issuer, the selling shareholder and any participating syndicate member in the US.

US Blackout Period

The Issuer's behaviour is most closely monitored during the so-called 'Blackout Period'. In the US, the Blackout Period begins on the date prospective syndicate members are invited to participate in the offering and ends on the later of 40 days after the first date the shares are offered for sale or upon completion of the distribution. Although no reasonable procedures (short of eliminating all marketing activities) can eliminate completely the risk that the exemptions conferred by Rule 144A and Regulation S will be lost (or that the distribution would lead to legal liability in the United States), such risks can be reduced to a prudent level if certain prescribed procedures are followed. It is common practice for the Issuer, selling shareholder and prospective syndicate members (and their respective affiliates) in global equity offerings similar to the case under study, to follow a series of rules prescribed by counsel when dealing with offering materials, including in particular research reports, even where such materials and reports are intended to be distributed only outside the United States.

US Research Reports

The only research reports regarding the Issuer which may be disseminated in the United Sates during the Blackout Period are research reports which (i) are distributed with reasonable regularity in the normal course of business (such as, for example, in the case of a seasoned reporting company in the US) or (ii) include similar information, opinions or recommendations with respect to a substantial number of companies in the Issuer's industry, or contain a comprehensive list of securities currently recommended by the broker or dealer preparing the report.[40]

[40] Rule 139(A) and 139(B) of the US Securities Act. The second safe harbour (Rule 139(B)) is more restrictive in that it requires that the similar information with respect to other

Research reports should be prepared and delivered only in physical form and should not be included in any electronic retrieval system. In addition, they must not be distributed at any US roadshow or to the US press at any time during the Blackout Period.

The SEC deems that a research report has been distributed with 'reasonable regularity' if it contains information, an opinion or a recommendation concerning a company with respect to which a broker or dealer in the normal course of business is currently publishing research. Therefore, no prospective syndicate member may distribute any research reports in the United States or to US persons during the Blackout Period, unless such syndicate member is currently publishing research with respect to the company.

In addition, research reports that (i) contain an improved recommendation or earnings *forecast* or (ii) are directed at particular *customers* may be regarded as solicitations or illegal inducements to purchase under Rule 10b-6 of the US Securities Exchange Act of 1934, as amended (the 1934 Act). To avoid potential violations of Rule 10b-6, the distribution in the United States or to US Persons of research reports directed at particular customers should be suspended for several weeks prior to the US pricing.

Any research report prepared for distribution in the United States in compliance with these restrictions will contain a legend in large type usually on the front or inside front cover which includes language substantially to the effect that the research report does not constitute an offer and is circulated for information only.

Distribution of Marketing Materials and Research Reports Outside the United States

As discussed above, no 'directed selling efforts'[41] can be made in the United States and the SEC is sensitive to publicity and marketing undertaken elsewhere in the world. It is therefore common to restrict the activities of US brokers (and their US affiliates) outside the United States. For example, they should agree to not distribute any marketing materials relating to the Rule 144A placement outside the US during the US Blackout Period. If a US bank were the lead manager of the North American tranche but only a

companies in the same industry and that is not accorded less space or prominence than that given to the Issuer and an opinion or recommendation at least as favourable on the Issuer must have appeared in the last publication of such broker/dealer prior to the offering.

With respect to foreign issuers that are coming into the US for the first time the SEC has amended Rule 139 to permit a broker/dealer to prepare a research report in reliance on Rule 139A if the subject foreign issuer has securities registered on a 'designated offshore securities market' (as defined in Regulation S) for at least twelve months and either meets Form F-3's public float requirement or is offering investment grade securities.

[41] 'Directed selling efforts' is defined to include any activity undertaken for the purpose of, or that could reasonably be expected to have the effect of, conditioning the market in the United States.

syndicate member of the European bank led 'rest of the world' tranche, that bank's European affiliate would be precluded from distributing in Denmark, the UK or anywhere else any marketing materials relating to the US private placement even if such distribution was permitted in the given country.

The adopting release issued in connection with Regulation S explains that 'a sales communication' with persons who are not 'US persons'[42] is not precluded by the prohibition against 'directed selling efforts'. Any Non-US Broker (and any non-US affiliates of any US Broker) could, for instance, distribute research reports to non-US persons anywhere in the world other than the United States, provided any such distribution is accompanied by procedures designed to ensure that such reports will not flow into the United States during the US Blackout Period. If any reasonable doubt exists regarding a recipient's US status, a syndicate member must refrain from sending a research report to that person unless the research report could be otherwise disseminated within the United States. The 'flowback' requirement means that syndicate members must conduct some investigation before distributing these. Finally, research reports should not be sent to the press or other media.

It is also typical that research reports prepared for distribution outside the United States contain a legend in large type on the front or inside cover which, in addition to the similar disclaimer mentioned above, would provide that the document may not be taken or transmitted into the United States or distributed to any US person.

There is a risk, however, that the SEC could conclude that the distribution of marketing materials to US persons outside the United States (even by non-US Brokers and non-US affiliates of US Brokers) under certain circumstances constitutes 'conditioning the market' in the United States. For this reason, European syndicate members which are not participating in the US portion of the Offering but are affiliated with US syndicate members should be particularly careful. In addition, although Regulation S provides that offers and sales of securities to 'US investors' residing abroad will not preclude reliance on the Regulation S safe harbour, offers and sales to US persons outside the United States are not permitted under all circumstances.

Rule 144A Offering Memorandum and Potential Liability

The absence of specifically mandated disclosures in a Rule 144A offering document affords more flexibility as to format. The private placement mem-

[42] Section 902(o) of Regulation S includes in the definition of a 'US person', among other persons, (i) any natural person resident in the United States, (ii) any partnership or corporation organised or incorporated under the laws of the United States, (iii) any trust of which any trustee is a US person, and (iv) any agency or branch of a foreign entity located in the United States.

orandum is not, as such, required to meet the disclosure standards of Section 10(a) of the Securities Act. However, it does fall within the definition of 'prospectus' in Section 2(10) of that Act and therefore the Issuer or selling security holder must in any event include all material disclosure regarding the Issuer and the Offering.

This flexibility in the preparation of the Offering Memorandum does not affect the applicability of the anti-fraud provisions such as sections 12 and 17 of the Securities Act and Rule 10b-5 under the Exchange Act. These provisions allow investors to effectively sue for damages where they have been furnished with incorrect and misleading information and apply not just to a registered public offering but also to the issuance of securities in a private placement.

Section 12(2) of the Securities Act imposes liability on any person who offers or sells a security by means of a prospectus or oral communication which includes a material misstatement or omission. Liability therefore attaches to disclosure documents used in private placements and generally a plaintiff is not required to prove causation to succeed. This civil liability, however, attaches only to sellers and therefore would insulate the Issuer in respect of the shares that are sold by the selling security holder unless somehow the Issuer under the underwriting arrangements has agreed to indemnify the selling security holder in respect of any misrepresentation. While Section 12(2) of the US Securities Act is silent as to extraterritorial application, the US federal courts have formulated two tests to determine whether a foreign plaintiff may claim under the US anti-fraud provisions.[43] These are discussed in greater detail under 'Canada—the Blanket Ruling' below.

The SEC staff will not respond to questions with respect to the adequacy of the information provided pursuant to Rule 144A. Such information must be reasonably current in relation to the date of resale and, with regard to foreign private issuers, the required information will be presumed to be 'reasonably current' if it meets the timing requirements of the Issuer's home country or principal trading market.

CANADA

The Exempt Market

Unlike the United States, where securities trading is regulated principally at the federal level, securities trading in Canada falls within the regulatory jurisdiction of the provinces. There is no federal securities commission or

[43] See for example, Alfadda v. Fenn, 935 F.2d 475 (2d Cir); Consolidated Goldfields Inc. v. Minorco S.A., 871 F.2d 252 (2d Cir 1989).

federal statute regulating Canadian capital markets. As a result, the laws of the province in which a transaction occurs are determinative.

While each of the ten provinces and two territories of Canada has its own securities legislation, a large degree of uniformity exists between the laws of such jurisdictions and compliance with the requirements prevailing in the provinces of Ontario and Quebec will, with limited exceptions, result in compliance with the securities legislation of the other provinces and territories of Canada. The analysis in this paper is, except where noted otherwise, restricted to the laws of the provinces of Ontario and Quebec.

Foreign issuers and dealers can enter the highly active private placement market in Canada quite easily. Ontario maintains a special category of international dealers for foreign based dealers and underwriters who undertake limited Canadian activities such as assisting institutional trading in issues primarily offered abroad. International equity offerings are typically made on a private placement basis in Ontario and Quebec relying on either the exemptions available for distributions to 'exempt purchasers' (principally Canadian banks, provincial or federal loan and trust corporations, insurance companies, any government of Canada, municipal corporations and certain other designated purchasers); or distributions (without advertisement) of securities with an aggregate acquisition cost per purchaser of C$150,000 (provided the purchaser is purchasing as principal).[44] Neither Ontario nor Quebec regulate the specific content of offering memoranda used for these private placements, other than to require confirmation of certain statutory rights of action available to purchasers. Most foreign issuers merely sticker or 'wrap' their domestic documents to comply with the Canadian provisions.

The OSC Blanket Ruling

Recent international equity offerings[45] which included a Canadian tranche were facilitated significantly by the publication on 1st December 1993 by the

[44] Section 72(1)(d) Ontario Securities Act as modified by Section 27(1) of the Regulations, Section 51, Quebec Securities Act. The C$150,000 minimum purchase exemption is not available for corporations, partnerships, syndicates or other forms of unincorporated organisations created solely to fall within the minimum threshold exemption. If shares are sold in Ontario under this exemption to an investor which is neither a corporation nor an individual, a statutory declaration is required that each member of the partnership, syndicate or other unincorporated entity contributed at least C$150,000 for the shares. Any sales to portfolio managers on behalf of managed accounts where the amount allocated to an individual account is less than C$150,000 will not qualify for this exemption. In order to undertake such sales, a so-called 'sprinkling order' is routinely sought from the regulators.

[45] The following European issuers have included Canada in their recent international equity offerings: Usinor Sacilor, Rauma OY, Nynex, Clariant Ltd., Powergen plc/National Power plc, Granges AB, SGS-Thomson Microelectronics N.V., Telewest Communications plc, Kalmar Industries AB, Autoliv AB, Societe Generale Union des Assurances de Paris (UAP), Societe Nationale Elf Acquataine (ELF), Credit Locale de France and British Telecommunications plc.

Ontario Securities Commission (OSC) of a blanket ruling (now a Rule[46]) relating to offerings by international issuers in Ontario. The effect of the Rule was to provide relief from certain provisions of the Securities Act (Ontario) and the accompanying regulations, policy statements and rules prescribing content requirements in offering documents where the offering document used in connection with the private placement in Ontario consists of a US prospectus or private placement memorandum used in connection with a simultaneous SEC registered offering or exempt private placement in accordance with US law, as the case may be.

For both of these types of offerings, in the case of a non-US issuer, it is a precondition to reliance upon the Rule that the 'substantive preparation' of the US prospectus or offering circular involve the use of 'instrumentalities of interstate commerce' in the United States or other significant conduct in the United States.

In several provinces of Canada, including Ontario, the private placement exemption is only available if the Issuer (or selling shareholder, if applicable) provides purchasers with a contractual right of action for damages or rescission exercisable against the Issuer in the event the Offering Memorandum delivered to purchasers contains a misrepresentation. This requirement is imposed to ensure that purchasers in private placements enjoy contractual rights against the seller of securities which at least partially correspond to the statutory rights the purchasers would have enjoyed if the securities were offered pursuant to a prospectus. Liability under the contractual right of action is strict, i.e. there would be no defence to the issuer of reasonable care or due diligence. The usual practice in past privatisations and global equity offerings had been to apply to each of the Canadian securities regulators in the provinces in which the offer is being made for waivers of this requirement and, in some provinces (e.g., Saskatchewan and Nova Scotia), the application of statutory rights of action against the seller and/or issuer for misrepresentations in the relevant offering memoranda. In previous international offerings which had been extended into Canada some issuers and selling shareholders expressed resistance on both legal and logistical grounds to providing a contractual right of action and in the past, the Commission on application has granted full or partial relief from this requirement on a case-by-case basis.

As a result of the Rule a contractual right of action need not be provided to Ontario purchasers if the offering document delivered to such purchasers comprises inter alia an offering memorandum used in a Rule 144A offering (if certain other conditions are met). The OSC received opinions of Canadian and US counsel which stated that Ontario purchasers purchasing securities under inter alia a Rule 144A offering document would have the

[46] The Blanket Ruling is at (1993) 16 O.S.C.B. 5931. Pursuant to 5.1(s) of the Ontario Securities Act, this has become a rule.

benefit of the US civil liability remedies which were deemed to be substantially equivalent in terms of scope, damages, defences and limitations to the remedies which an Ontario purchaser would receive had it been given a contractual right of action. The basis of the opinion upon which the OSC relied was that the elements of a cause of action under Section 12(2) of the US Securities Act would be available in the event of a misrepresentation in the private placement memorandum as the fraudulent material (the memorandum) was prepared for use primarily in the United States, thereby creating a nexus to the United States. This would constitute fraudulent conduct occurring in the United States regardless of where the document was actually prepared.[47] The opinion therefore concluded that the Canadian investor would be able to obtain a judgment for damages under the US rules. Accordingly, this blanket ruling was granted by the OSC on the basis that, since investors in Ontario would be able to rely upon the civil liability provisions of the US federal securities legislation if the offering memorandum contained a misrepresentation, the contractual right of action was unnecessary. As the blanket ruling is limited to Ontario, discretionary relief from applicable requirements to provide rights of action for damages or rescission will still need to be dealt with on an ad hoc basis in other provinces. The grounds for seeking such relief in the other provinces would be the same as those underlying the blanket ruling in Ontario.

Staff of the OSC have, however, recently published a notice[48] impacting on certain international equity offerings into Ontario made in conjunction with a concurrent Rule 144A US private placement as a result of the US Supreme Court decision in the Gustafson case.[49] In the Gustafson case the court noted that the civil liability provisions of Section 12(2) of the US Securities Act do not extend to a private contract but only to a 'prospectus' as defined in the US Securities Act. As such, the case casts doubts as to whether an Ontario purchaser would indeed be able to rely upon US remedies equivalent to the contractual right of action. It now appears that US counsel would not be willing to provide the opinion that Section 12(2) liability under the US Securities Act would be available to Ontario investors in a private placement made in reliance on a Rule 144A offering document.

In the past, Staff of the OSC have expressed the view that where any of the key representations underlying a ruling are materially incorrect, the ruling generally should not be relied upon. Although it is not clear that any change in law resulting from the Gustafson decision has the effect of making the representations underlying the Rule materially incorrect, the Notice

[47] The cases cited in support of this position were: Continental Grain (Australia) Pty. Ltd. v. Pacific Oilseeds, Inc., 592 F.2d 409 (8th Cir. 1979), Grunenthal GmbH v. Hotz, 712 F.2d 421 (9th Cir. 1983) and SEC v. Kasser, 548 F.2d 109 (3rd Cir. 1977).

[48] (1995) 18 O.S.C.B. 1350, 24 March 1995.

[49] Gustafson et al v. Alloyd Co. Inc. et al (February 28, 1985) 1995 WL 76941 (US).

states that caution should be exercised before the Rule is relied upon in circumstances where securities are offered to Ontario purchasers by way of a Rule 144A private placement memorandum. The Notice also states that it may be appropriate to incorporate additional disclosure into offering documents concerning the possibility that certain US remedies may be unavailable to Ontario purchasers.

There is little guidance in the Notice as to the appropriateness of continuing to rely upon the Rule; however, until the OSC revokes all or part of it, it is open to parties such as the Issuer in the case study to rely upon it to market the Offering in Canada with appropriate additional disclosure.

Resale Restrictions

As in the case of 'restricted securities' in the United States, the Canadian 'closed system' securities statutes impose resale restrictions on securities which were initially sold pursuant to certain specified prospectus exemptions, including the private placement exemption. Shares sold in Ontario on an exempt basis, are subject to indefinite hold periods unless the Issuer becomes a reporting issuer.[50] Thereafter the hold period would run from between 6 months, 12 months or 18 months in Ontario (and from between 6 and 12 months in Quebec) depending on satisfaction of certain earnings tests and whether the securities are listed or posted for trading on a recognized stock exchange (Montreal Exchange or The Toronto Stock Exchange). Trades within Canada could only be made during the hold period in reliance upon further exemptions from applicable prospectus requirements.

For securities subject to Canadian resale restrictions listed only on foreign stock exchanges, it is common for the securities to be sold on a foreign exchange regardless of the restrictions even though this may be considered to violate the resale restrictions (depending in part on the extent of activity in Canada in furtherance of the sale). Issuers have obtained exemption orders expressly permitting resales on foreign exchanges following various exempt trades. However, with respect to the application of such resale restrictions to trades occurring outside of Canada, the Canadian securities regulatory authorities generally do not seek to regulate trades in securities where it is reasonable to expect that such securities will be acquired by non-residents and come to rest outside of Canada and where no question arises of bringing the capital markets of the provinces into disrepute.

An express exemption from the resale restrictions exists in Ontario where, pursuant to another OSC blanket ruling (dated 26 April 1994) the shares

[50] An issuer becomes a reporting issuer through listing securities on a recognised stock exchange in Ontario or Quebec, as the case may be, or filing a prospectus under the applicable provincial securities legislation (e.g., Section 1 OSA, Section 68 QSA).

acquired in a private placement could be resold on a stock exchange outside of Canada such as, for example, the London Stock Exchange if conditions are met.[51]

Disclosure Document

There is no requirement that a disclosure document be used in connection with a private placement in Ontario unless there is advertising associated with it. If a Rule 144A circular is used, the usual practice is to 'wrap' the Canadian disclosure requirements around the US disclosure document. In Ontario, as discussed, if the Rule is complied with, there is no need to provide a contractual right of action to investors for damages or rescission in respect of misrepresentations. In Quebec, no contractual rights need be provided to qualified purchasers.

A statement that the issuer intends to seek listing on a stock exchange is prohibited. The relevant rules in Ontario and Quebec state that no person with the intention of effecting a trade in a security shall, except with the written permission of the Director, make any written or oral representation that such security will be listed or that application therefor has been or will be made. To avoid a contravention of these provisions, it is necessary to delete such statements from the offering documents or obtain the written permission of the OSC and QSC.

The policy of Canadian securities regulation is to restrict the use of future oriented financial information in Canadian offering documents. There is generally no issue as to inclusion of such statements where the disclosure document being 'wrapped' is a US disclosure document as the restrictions in the US Securities Act on the inclusion of such material are more stringent, generally speaking, than the Canadian rules.

Certain disclosure is required as to exchange rates between non-US foreign currency and the Canadian dollar, hyperinflationary effects (cumulative inflation of over 100% over last three financial years), withholding taxes and exchange controls where financial information is presented in the offering document in a non-US foreign currency. Accordingly, the Canadian wrapper must include Canadian dollar exchange rate disclosure as appropriate including in each case a five year exchange rate history including year-end, average annual exchange rates and average rates for the periods

[51] (1994) 17 O.S.C.B. 1978. The conditions are the following:
(a) the issuer is not a reporting issuer in Ontario;
(b) at the time of the trade, Ontario residents represent less than 10% of the total number of holders of the shares in question and hold less than 10% of the shares outstanding;
(c) the trade is made in accordance with the rules of the foreign stock exchange in compliance with laws of the relevant jurisdiction; and
(d) all disclosure material relating to the issuer furnished to shareholders outside Canada is, at the relevant time, also being furnished to shareholders resident in Ontario.

for which and at which, as the case may be, financial information is presented. In addition, disclosure as to the withholding tax in the applicable foreign jurisdiction applicable to Canadian residents and any foreign exchange controls must be included.

Finally, if a distribution is made by a registered dealer or a registered international dealer in securities of a 'related issuer' or 'connected issuer', certain disclosure must be provided to prospective purchasers in Canada regarding such relationship.

Advertising, Marketing and Media Contact

Certain of the prospectus exemptions in Ontario and Quebec depend upon or require in effect that there be no advertising, marketing or media contact in connection with the Offering in Canada.

A draft national policy statement of the Canadian securities regulators[52] (Draft NP 43) broadly defines 'advertisement' to include all methods and forms of communication, including media coverage, which promote or could reasonably be expected to promote the purchase and sale of securities. This draft policy has been quite controversial and to date has not been adopted in any of the provinces; however it is generally recommended that the following guidelines be followed:

- No advertising material (including brochures, circulars, letters, advertisements, notices or other communications) other than the Offering Memorandum which could be construed as promoting the Offering should be distributed in Canada.
- The Issuer must take appropriate precautions to ensure that media coverage (including interviews) which could reasonably be considered to be in furtherance of the offering of the Issuer's shares in Canada does not take place.[53] Advertising, marketing and media contact may however occur for other purposes such as:
  - to comply with the Issuer's continuous disclosure obligations under applicable securities laws (including, for example, the continuous disclosure requirements of the London Stock Exchange);
  - customary advertisement of products and services for commercial purposes;

[52] (1994) 17 O.S.C.B. 5133 + [1995 NP 43].

[53] The Issuer can respond to and meet with non-Canadian analysts or journalists in accordance with their prior respective practices so long as any information provided is factual and they receive creditable assurances that such analysts or journalists will not distribute in Canada (including to any branch or affiliate of their organisations in Canada) the information provided. Representatives may also meet with the Canadian/syndicate numbers in-house analysts on the understanding that information provided to them will be used solely to market the Companies' shares to prospective investors who may purchase in reliance upon exemptions from applicable prospectus and registration requirements in Canada.

  - continuing to make announcements to the press with respect to factual business and financial developments (for example, new appointments, acquisitions, disposals or other events of interest to the business community in which the Issuer operates);
  - answering unsolicited enquiries concerning factual information from shareholders, financial analysts, the press and others having a legitimate interest in such information, although specific enquiries with respect to the offering of the Issuer's shares in Canada should not be commented upon;
  - continuing to hold shareholders' meetings as scheduled and answering shareholders' enquiries relating to factual matters.
- In Ontario, it would be permissible for representatives of the Issuer to meet with qualified purchasers to promote the Offering in Canada; however, it would be advisable to restrict these contacts to institutional roadshows. Such contacts are in certain instances prohibited in Quebec unless made in the company of or through a Canadian manager registered to engage in such activities. In all cases, attendees of the meeting should be provided with a copy of the offering document.
- No opinions with respect to the value of the Companies, their securities or assets should be published.
- There should be no advertisements relating to the offering in Canadian magazines or newspapers, in the North American or international editions of British publications such as The Financial Times or The Economist or in international publications such as The Wall Street Journal.
- Except insofar as may be required by the Issuer's applicable continuous disclosure obligations, persons connected with the offering (i.e. the selling shareholder, the Issuer and their respective directors, officers and employees, the Canadian selling group and the Canadian Managers and other representatives) should not issue press releases or engage in conferences, speeches, magazine or newspaper interviews or like activities in Canada which relate to the offering or to the Issuer and which might be construed as encouraging the sale of the Issuer's shares in Canada.
- Since material published in Europe is frequently picked up by wire services or publications circulated in Canada, publicity activity in Europe, including press conferences relating to the offering, should avoid predictions, projections, forecasts or opinions with respect to value which in any way depart from the information appearing in the Offering Memorandum. In addition, members of the Canadian press should not be invited to any press conferences in Europe relating to the offering.

Distribution of Brokers'/Banks' Research Reports

At present, there are no express statutory restrictions on the use of research reports in connection with a private placement in Canada. The prospectus exemptions in certain provinces depend upon or require in effect that there be no advertising, marketing or media contact in connection with the Canadian private placement. The circulation of a research report by virtue of its timing and content could be considered to be an advertisement of specific securities and thereby jeopardise the prospectus exemptions.

The research report could also be considered to be 'a document purporting to describe the business and affairs of an issuer that has been prepared primarily for delivery to and review by prospective investors so as to assist those investors to make an investment decision in respect of the securities being sold' in the offering. If so, it must comply with the rules governing offering memoranda including the restrictions on the use of future oriented financial information such as projections and forecasts set forth in National Policy No. 48 of Canadian securities regulatory authorities. This policy also places restrictions on the distribution of forecasts and projections in any form during the course of a distribution of securities. Any adviser or dealer in Canada that recommends the purchase of securities must disclose any financial or other interest it may have in the securities.

Approved, independent broker research material prepared by brokers which are not prospective members of any syndicate or research that would be eligible for safe harbour treatment afforded by SEC Rule 139 is generally regarded as not constituting a document prepared primarily for the purpose of promoting a specific offering. However, an independent research report prepared well in advance of the proposed offering which is circulated along with an offering memorandum (draft, preliminary or final) could be considered to form part of the offering memorandum. If so it must comply with Canadian rules as to content of offering memoranda or else it may jeopardise the availability of prospectus exemptions. Because of concerns in a number of provinces that the circulation of reports in connection with a proposed distribution of securities could constitute 'trading' in such securities, reports may be distributed only to institutional investors and, in Ontario, only by Ontario registered dealers.

The most recently expressed position of the Canadian securities regulatory authorities in respect of the use of 'advertisement' in connection with the offering of securities in Canada is Draft NP 43, which as discussed, contains significant content requirements on Advertisements and places restrictions on the ability of issuers and dealers to disseminate any information that falls within the definition of 'advertisement' in connection with an offering of securities in Canada. The provisions of Draft NP 43 do not apply in relation to research reports distributed by a registrant in the ordinary course of its business and not produced for the purpose of facilitating a distribution of specific securities. Although it must be stressed that Draft NP 43 is not yet in force, it may be prudent to ensure that the exemption set out above is available or that the terms of NP 43 be complied with.

For these reasons and common law concerns relating to liability, the common practice on global equity offerings that include both the US and Canada is as follows:

- no prospective member of any syndicate should distribute any of its own research in Canada or to persons resident in Canada until completion of the offering unless such prospective member currently publishes research on the Issuer and the reports:
  - are distributed to Canadian institutional investors with reasonable regularity in the normal course of business;
  - include similar information on a substantial number of companies in the same industry or sub-industry as the Issuer or contain a comprehensive list of currently recommended securities;
  - do not give materially greater space or prominence in the research report to the information, opinion or recommendation with respect to the Issuer than is given to other securities or companies;
  - do not contain a recommendation or earnings forecast for the Issuer that is improved from the last recommendation or earnings forecast published by such broker or dealer; and
  - are not directed at particular customers.
- prior to distribution of any offering document (draft, preliminary or final) the approved, unconnected broker research reports or reports satisfying the criteria set forth above may be distributed by prospective members of any syndicate but only to institutional investors and, in Ontario, only by Ontario registered dealers. Such research should bear an appropriate legend prohibiting its distribution in Canada or to persons resident in Canada; and
- no research material should be distributed in Canada or to persons resident in Canada after distribution of any offering document (draft, preliminary or final) to avoid potential contravention of the rules governing the content of an offering memorandum and advertising of specific securities.

Civil and Criminal Liability for Misrepresentation

The potential liability of the Issuer, selling shareholder and syndicate members (to the extent they are involved in the Offering in Canada) for misrepresentation in connection with the Offering in Canada should be no greater under Canadian law than under US law. The verification and other procedures which will be implemented in the US to avoid liability for misrepresentation should have the same effect under Canadian law.

Under Canadian securities legislation, statutory liability is imposed on, among others, issuers and their directors, selling security holders and underwriters for misrepresentations contained in prospectuses used in connection with public offerings of securities. However, in a private placement, the participants involved are not subject to statutory liability in Canada and as discussed above contractual rights of action are not required in certain provinces. Canadian purchasers advancing claims against such persons on the basis of misrepresentation will therefore be required to establish liability at common law.

If Canadian purchasers contract with both the Issuer and selling shareholder, they would have a right of action against both at common law. If the Canadian purchasers contract with the selling shareholder alone, purchasers' claims against the Issuer and their directors or other officers will need to be based on tort rather than breach of contract. Under Canadian law, claims brought against the Issuer or their directors or other officers by Canadian purchasers could be based on the torts of deceit[54] or, possibly, negligent misrepresentation. Both categories of tort are subject to limitations and impose substantial evidentiary burdens on plaintiffs.

The verification and other procedures followed in connection with the Offering in Europe and the US should serve to limit exposure to actions for deceit; firstly, by rooting out factual errors in the information contained in the offering documents and, secondly, by providing a basis to rebut allegations that representations in the prospectus forming part of the Offering Memorandum were made recklessly or with indifference to their truth.

It might also be possible to bring a tort action against the Issuer and their directors or other officers on the basis of negligent misrepresentation.[55]

[54] s.131(11). To succeed in a claim of deceit, a plaintiff must establish that:

(a) the defendant made a false representation of fact;

(b) the representation was made with knowledge of its falsity or with reckless disregard as to whether it was true;

(c) the representation was made with the intent that it should be acted upon by the plaintiff or by a class of persons which included the plaintiff, in the manner which resulted in damage to the plaintiff;

(d) the plaintiff acted upon the representation; and

(e) the plaintiff suffered damages by so doing.

Although it is well established that liability for deceit can be imposed on a director personally responsible for its commission, there is some question under Canadian law as to whether a company can possess the requisite 'intent' to be found liable for deceit as well. While the law in this area is still developing in Canada, it appears that the Issuer could only be held liable if the false representation in the offering document used in Canada was made by those directors who, for purposes of making the false representation, constitute the 'core, mind and spirit' of the Issuer.

[55] Such an action will succeed if a plaintiff can establish that:

(a) the defendant owed him a duty of care;

(b) the defendant breached this duty of care by making a negligent misrepresentation;

(c) the plaintiff reasonably relied on such negligent misrepresentation; and

(d) the plaintiff suffered damages as a result.

Unlike statutory remedies which create a presumption of reliance on a misrepresentation, the plaintiff in a common law action must establish that he relied on the misrepresentation to his detriment; the mere fact that the Offering Memorandum might contain a misrepresentation is, of itself, insufficient. A further obstacle would be in establishing that a duty of care was owed by the Issuer, directors or officers to investors who purchased the Issuer's shares pursuant to the Offering in Canada. While there is no Canadian case law directly on point, a number of decisions have established the general proposition that persons involved in the preparation of offering documents will be under a duty of care if they are aware (as here) of the purpose to which such documents will be put and that reliance will be placed on them by what might be regarded as a readily ascertainable class of persons (i.e., prospective Canadian purchasers).[56]

Again, the verification and due diligence procedures followed in connection with the European and US offerings should serve to minimize potential liability for negligent misrepresentation on the basis that even if the Offering Memorandum contains a misrepresentation, it was not made negligently. Of course, this is very similar to the 'due diligence' defence which can normally be raised by directors, managers and others in respect of claims founded upon statutory civil liability.

With respect to the potential liability of directors or other officers, it is clear that if he or she has participated directly in the making of a false representation and the other elements of the tort are proven, he or she can be held liable for deceit. The situation is less clear where no personal fault can be affixed to a director or officer of a company which is found liable for deceit. The mere fact that a person is a director or other officer of company does not, of itself, render him or her liable for torts committed by the company during the course of his directorship or office.

[56] Whether a Canadian court would extend this duty of care beyond persons whose business involves the giving of advice based on special expertise (e.g., accountants and lawyers) to find that a 'special relationship' giving rise to a duty of care exists between the directors of a company and, by the application of agency principles, the company itself, on the one hand, and purchasers of that company's securities in circumstances analogous to the Offer in Canada, on the other, remains uncertain.

4

The Law Applicable to Securities Transactions: Choice of Law Issues

PROFESSOR HANS VAN HOUTTE

INTRODUCTION

The law applicable to securities transactions is difficult to analyse within the confines of a short study. Securities transactions are often complex and multifaceted. Moreover, the applicable law in securities transactions has not yet been explored extensively. Indeed, conflict of law writers, on the one hand, have treated securities transactions in a stepmotherly manner. Academics are probably less familiar with and excited by the technicalities of securities transactions. Practising lawyers, on the other hand, are often shy to engage in conflict of law-exercises and prefer to ignore issues of applicable law.

As a result, this Chapter has extremely limited ambitions. It surely does not pretend to provide some exhaustive analysis or even a list of the problems raised. It only reveals a few lines of thought which may be helpful to locate the legal rules applicable to some securities transactions, such as the issuing and acquisition of securities. Moreover, this is done from a West-European perspective, mainly relying on West-European conflict of law texts and theory.

However, which rules are applied to a securities transaction depends to a large extent on the court which decides the case. Consequently, this Chapter will not only deal with the applicable law, but also with court jurisdiction over security matters.

THE ISSUING OF SECURITIES

Shares

Applicable law

In conflict of laws, questions related to share capital and issuing or subscription of shares are governed by the *lex societatis*, i.e. the law which governs the legal status of the company.[1] It is the *lex societatis* which determines:

- whether the shares have to be registered shares or bearer shares;
- whether the share capital needs to be expressed in the national currency of the company;[2]
- whether existing shareholders have a preferential right when new shares are issued;[3]
- whether existing shares can be split;
- whether shares may be discounted at the time of issue;
- whether the subscribed shares have to be paid in full;
- how payment has to be made (payment in valuta or in natura, compensation, etc.);[4]
- whether share certificates may be issued.

The *lex societatis*, which governs the issue of shares, also governs the rights and duties vis-à-vis the company emanating from the shares (what is called in German the *Rechte aus dem Papier*). It determines, for instance:

- to what extent the original and later shareholders may be held liable for company debts;
- to what extent shareholders are entitled to receive dividends;[5]
- to vote at shareholders meetings;
- whether minority shareholders are entitled to specific protection.

In Western Europe, two different criteria are used to determine the *lex societatis*. The UK and the Netherlands for example, accept that their domestic law is applicable as lex societatis for companies which have been incorporated within their country (*incorporation theory*). France and Belgium, on the other hand, accept that French or Belgian law is applicable whenever the company has its 'actual seat' (*siège réel*) in France or

[1] For a curious example, see the Eurotunnel Prospectus 1994 which indicated that the shares of the French and English company were governed by respectively French and English law.

[2] See for example England Re Scandinavian Bank Group Plc, [1988] Ch. 87 where it was held that Section 2(5)(a) of the Companies Act 1985 does not require a company to have its share capital denominated only in sterling. 'Provided in the case of a public company, the statutory minimum is in sterling, a company may denominate its share capital in different currencies for different classes of shares' (L. Collins, Dicey and Morris on the Conflict of Laws (12th ed.), vol. 2, London, Sweet & Maxwell, 1993 at p. 1587).

[3] See e.g. the German Bundesgerichtshof, March 7, 1994, which facilitated the access of German stock corporations to foreign equity markets by easing the restrictions on the pre-emptive rights of existing shareholders to subscribe for newly-issued shares (International Financial Law Review, June 1994, p. 51).

[4] The issue whether payment in natura or through clearing is acceptable, is decided by the '*lex societatis*'. However, the question whether the assets have been transferred to the company, is governed by the '*lex rei sitae*' of these assets; the question whether the clearing occurs, by the law which governs the clearing contract.

[5] See e.g. Terca Brick Industries, Shares Prospectus, June 1994 where section 4.2.4. stated that Belgian law would time-bar payment of dividends after 5 years.

Belgium respectively ('*seat theory*'). The problems which arise when a company is incorporated in a country which accepts the incorporation theory and has its seat in a '*siège réel*'-country—or when it is incorporated in a '*siège réel*'-country and has seat in an 'incorporation'-country—may excite some academics but are true nightmares for practitioners.[6] Attempts to introduce uniform criteria to find the *lex societatis* through international treaties, have failed: the Hague Convention on the Recognition of Foreign Companies (1956) and the EEC Convention on the Mutual Recognition of Companies and Legal Persons (1968)[7] never came into force. As a result, legal practitioners therefore still have to navigate through the incorporation and seat theories.

Shares are issued to be purchased. It could therefore be tempting to consider the acquisition of newly issued shares as a sales contract for conflict of laws purposes. However, the subscription of newly-issued shares, which implies a contribution to the company's capital, seems so closely related to the operation of the company that it should be governed by the *lex societatis*.

The proprietary aspects of the acquisition of shares is governed by the law of the place where the security is located at the time of issue. The issue documentation and the law under which the security was created, determine where the security is located when it is subscribed by the new shareholder. For instance, registered shares are located in the company's seat where the register is held; bearer shares are located at the place where the bearer certificate, eg the share warrant, is. Share prospectuses often state that the shares will be 'at the disposal' of the purchaser. This implies that the shares will be delivered at the issuer's seat or at the place where the issuer's agent is established.

Jurisdiction

The Brussels and Lugano Conventions on Court Jurisdiction, which are applicable in many West-European countries, require proceedings concerning the validity of the constitution, the nullity or the dissolution of a company or concerning the decisions of their organs to be brought exclusively before the courts of the convention-state in which the company has its seat.[8] However, as the issuing of shares is not covered by that provision, there is no exclusive jurisdiction over that matter and the general convention-principles on jurisdiction apply.

[6] See e.g. G. Grasmann, System des internationalen Gesellschaftsrechts, NWB Berlin 1970; O. Sandrock, Sitztheorie, Ueberlagerungstheorie und der EWG-Vertrag, Recht der internationalen Wirtschaft, 1989, pp. 505–13.

[7] See B. Goldman, The Convention between the Member States of the European Economic Community on the mutual recognition of companies and legal persons, C.M.L.R., 1968, p. 104.

[8] Article 16 para. 2.

In general, a claim can be brought in the court of the country where the defendant is established. A company from a convention-state may thus be sued in the country where it has its seat, if that country is a 'seat theory'-country; in the country of its incorporation, if that country is an 'incorporation theory'-country.[9] When the shares are distributed through a third party, complications arise : did this third party operate as an independent operator or as an agent? If the former, he can be sued qualitate qua before his own court; if the latter, the issuing company itself has to be sued before the court of the country where the company's seat is established.

Claims can also be brought before another court depending on their subject matter. There are indications that the Court of Justice—for the purpose of the Jurisdiction Convention—would characterise the issuing of shares as a contractual matter.[10] For such matters, 'the court of the place of performance in question' also has jurisdiction.[11] Consequently, claims from the shareholder against the company concerning the delivery of the shares or concerning their non-conformity with what has been promised, can be brought before the court of the place where the shares have to be delivered; claims from the company against the shareholder for payment of the price can be brought before the court where this payment has to be made. However, with regard to the place where the shares have to be delivered and the place where payment has to be made, is it the seat of the issuing corporation or the place the shareholder obtains the shares? These issues are often specified in the issue documentation and, if not specified, by the law applicable to the transaction.

In order to avoid uncertainty regarding which court will assume jurisdiction over disputes concerning the issuing of shares, the issuing company may include a jurisdiction clause in its issuing documentation.[12] It also may have stated in its by-laws that all disputes between the company and its shareholders have to be submitted to a specified court, which, for instance, may be the court of the company's seat.[13] The shareholder may be deemed to have accepted the jurisdiction clause by accepting the offer from the issu-

[9] Articles 2 and 53.

[10] See Court of Justice, March 22, 1983, Peters v. Zuid Nederlandse Aannemers Vereniging, case 34/82, E.C.R. 1983, 987 where the Court characterised the claim for payment of membership dues by an association against its member as a contractual claim although the relations between an association and its members are not considered contractual in nature in many convention states. Similarly, the Court could characterise the subscription of shares as a contractual issue although it is not considered as such in many jurisdictions.

[11] Article 5 para. 1.

[12] See e.g. Eurodisney capital increase, June 1994:

'Toute contestation aux émissions visées dans les précédentes Sections du présent Chapitre II sera soumise aux tribunaux dans le ressort desquels est situé le siège social de la Socité lorsque la Société est défenderesse, ces tribunaux étant désignés en fonction de la nature des litiges, sauf disposition contraire du Nouveau Code de Procédure Civile.'

[13] See Court of Justice, March 10, 1992, Powell Duffryn Plc. v. Wolfgang Petereit, case C-214/89, E.C.R. 1992, 1745.

ing documentation or by buying the shares (at least when he could have known the terms of the issuing documentation or of the by-laws).

Finally, the Brussels and Lugano Conventions allow a 'consumer', i.e. 'a person who concludes a contract (for the supply of goods) for a purpose which can be regarded as being outside his trade or profession', to sue in his own court and to be sued there.[14] It has been stated that this provision grants jurisdiction to the court where a private person, who invests in futures and options, is domiciled provided that the investment firm is established within a convention-state.[15] It could be argued that this provision is also applicable to the acquisition of newly-issued shares.

The company may also include an arbitration clause in its issuing documentation or its by-laws. However, it has to be carefully checked whether this arbitration clause would be valid under the various legal systems.

Finally, and as a matter of curiosity, reference is made to the Swiss Private International Law Statute (1989) as this statute exceptionally contains several provisions on securities. Under its Article 151, when shares have been issued in Switzerland, claims concerning the issue can always be brought before the Swiss court of the place of issue, even when the parties have accepted a jurisdiction clause in favour of another jurisdiction. It seems to be accepted that this provision is however excluded by the Lugano convention, when applicable.[16]

Other Securities

Applicable law

Shares are closely interwoven with the legal operation of the company. The issue of shares is therefore governed by the *lex societatis*. Other securities, such as bonds, investment fund certificates, SICAVs, futures and options, do not have the same links with company law. As a general rule, they should be governed by contract law.[17]

However, the law of the issuer will determine whether the issuer was entitled to issue the securities. Moreover, their existence as a title and the rights to which they give rise are covered by the law of the place where they have been created. Finally, the law of the issuer will determine the extent to which these rights are still effective in the event that the issuer becomes insolvent.

[14] Articles 13 and 14.

[15] See Court of Justice, January 19, 1993, Shearson Lehman Hutton v. T.V.B., case C89/91 E.C.R. 1993, I, 139, concl. Adv. Gen.Darmon, nr. 76 and September 15, 1994, W. Brenner v. Dean Witten Reynolds, case-318/93, E.C.R. 1994, I, 4275.

[16] A. Heini e.a., IPRG Kommentar, Schulthess Zürich 1993, p. 1333.

[17] See A. Heini, e.a. op cit., p. 1362.

There are no clear rules to determine the law which governs the acquisition of newly issued securities. Even if the acquisition is governed by the law of the contract, is this the law of the issuer's country of residence,[18] of the place where the authorized dealer is established,[19] of the place where payments are made or of the currency of the paper? To avoid uncertainty the issue documentation sometimes contains a choice of law clause, which is generally the law of the issuer.[20] In certain situations, the issuer may even submit particular parts of the issue documentation to specific legal systems.[21] The legal opinion, requested for the issuing of the security, should examine to what extent this choice of law will be upheld.[22]

The proprietary rights to the issued securities are governed by the law of the place where these securities are located.

Jurisdiction

The issue documentation sometimes contains a choice of jurisdiction[23] or arbitration clause.[24] It should be ascertained whether, and if so, to what extent this clause will be upheld and to what extent the chosen jurisdiction will respect the choice of law of the parties.

[18] The Rome Convention on the law applicable to contractual obligations (1980) Art. 4, presumes that the contract is governed by the law of the party who delivers the 'characteristic performance'. When securities are issued, the 'characteristic performance' is made by the issuer. Whether the Rome convention is applicable to securities transactions will be discussed later. However, the 'characteristic performance' is also the general criterion used to determine the proper law in many conflict of laws systems.

[19] See e.g. decision of the Oberlandesgericht Dusseldorf, which decided that the authorized dealer is the person rendering the characteristic performance, reported in International Financial Law Review, December 1993, p. 46.

[20] See e.g. for the issuing of:

- SICAVs: BBL (L) Investment Prospectus, December 1993, section 23: 'La loi luxembourgeoise est applicable pour toute contestation'.
- Bonds: Compagnie Nationale á Portefeuille, Prospectus, March 1994: 'L'emprunt est soumis á la loi belge'
- Warrant calls and Warrant Puts: Kredietbank-Petercam-Derivatives S.A.: 'Les Warrants et le Warrant Global sont soumis á la législation belge et sont interprétés conformément á cette législation'.

[21] See for some examples of such 'split law transactions':F.G.B. Graaf, Euromarket Finance: Issues of Euromarket securities and syndicated Eurocurrency loans, Kluwer 1991, p. 115.

[22] A number of jurisdictions have mandatory rules on i.e. currency, compounding of interest and collective representation of bondholders. Moreover stock exchanges where securities are listed may impose restrictions on the choice of applicable law.

[23] See e.g. Audiofina Bond issue 1994:

'Tout différend entre les obligataires d'une part, et la Société d'autre part, auquel le présent emprunt pourrait donner lieu, sera soumis aux tribunaux luxembourgeois compétents'.

[24] See e.g. Lernout & Hauspie Speech Bond Issue 1994:

'Tout litige entre l'investisseur et la Société relatif à la validité, l'interprétation ou l'exécution de ce Statut sera réglé selon le réglement CEPINA par un collège composé de 3 arbitres désignés conformément à ce réglement. Le lieu d'arbitrage est Bruxelles et la langue utilisée lors de la procédure est le néerlandais.

La clause d'arbitrage mentionnée ci-dessus n'exclut pas que l'investisseur ou la Socité puisse intenter une action en référé auprés du Président du Tribunal de Commerce'.

Public Offering

Applicable law

In many legal systems securities regulations oblige companies to give adequate and factually correct information about the securities which are being offered for sale. These regulations are applicable to public offerings within their scope. Attempts by issuers to exclude such regulations as being inapplicable,[25] are ineffective. Statements by the issuer that regulations from a specific country are applicable to a given prospectus,[26] do not prevent regulations from other countries from applying as well.

Securities regulations of the country where 'direct selling efforts' were made, where the securities have been obtained, where the securities have been introduced on the stock exchange, or where the issuing company was located, may be applicable to transnational offerings.[27]

- It appears logical that companies, which issue securities, should observe the securities regulations of the country where they are established. This country will moreover generally constitute the main marketplace for such securities. However, should companies also observe the law of their seat, when all the shares are issued abroad?[28]
- When securities can be subscribed in different countries through issuing agents, it could be argued that the law of the country where the securities actually were subscribed, is applicable. However, even when

[25] See e.g. Prospectus relating to Mexican Investment Company Luxemburg:
'Most or all of the protection afforded by the United Kingdom regulatory structure will not apply. The rights of shareholders in the Fund may not be protected by the investors' compensation scheme established in the United Kingdom.'

[26] Take over bid by Royal Oak Mines Inc. of Lac Minerals Ltd., Prospectus July 1994, stating that Canadian law entitles shareholders to civil actions whenever there is misrepresentation.

[27] See e.g. concerning Euromarket securities: F.G.B. Graaf, Euromarket Finance: Issues of Euromarket securities and syndicated Eurocurrency loans, Kluwer 1991, p. 114:
'Regardless of where the issuer is domiciled, its liability for misleading offering material may be governed by the laws of a number of countries:
- the country where the offer is made; or
- the country where the issuer is domiciled; or
- the country where the securities are listed; or
- the country where the investor is located.

[28] 'I would even suggest that a company should not be allowed to organize an issue without respecting its own securities regulation. In other words, it seems to me difficult to justify allowing an American company to make an issue without respecting the SEC rules. Foreign investors should know that they have the same protection if they buy American securities, quite irrespective of the place of transaction' (A. Hirsch, Worldwide Legal Harmonization of Banking Law and Securities Regulations in Buxbaum e.a. e., European Business Law, Legal and Economic Analysis on Integration and Harmonization, p. 360).
See the decision of the House of Lords in Secretary of State for Trade v. Markus, [1976] A.C. 35, where the English Prevention of Fraud (Investments) Act 1958 was applied to a director of a Panamanian fund who sold shares from his London base to German investors.

securities are traded in a number of different places, it could make sense to submit their issue to the law of the country where the issuing company is established. Indeed, most professional investors do not instruct their broker to buy shares on a particular market, but under the best conditions. These shares could be bought in Brussels, London, New York or Tokyo, depending on where the best conditions will be offered at that particular time.

- The securities regulations of a country may finally also be applicable because of the mere fact that 'direct selling efforts' (distribution of prospectus, circular letters and unsolicited telephone calls) are made within that country.[29]
- Most often the country where the 'direct selling efforts' are made is the country where the investor is located and where he buys the securities. However, is the law of the country of the investor still applicable when he was solicited through foreign television and newspapers and when he subscribed to the shares outside his own country?[30] US courts, for example, have the tendency to apply US regulations to purchases made abroad, when substantial information was provided within the US territory.[31]

Referring once again to the Swiss Private International Law Statute, Article 156 provides that claims arising from public offerings of shares and other securities through prospectuses, circular letter or other means can—at the claimant's option—be brought either under the *lex societatis* or under the

[29] See e.g. Securities and Investments Board v. Pantell S.A. [1989] 2 All E.R. 673 where SIB started proceedings against a Swiss company which sent advertisements offering investments advice to the UK public from Switzerland: 'The question that arose was whether, by sending circular advertisements from outside the United Kingdom to persons within the United Kingdom, Pantell and its associates were or were not carrying on an investment business in the United Kingdom. In my judgment it is plainly arguable that they were' (p. 676).

See also Securities and Investment Board v. Vandersteen Associates N.V. [1991] BCLC 206, where SIB started proceedings against a Belgian company which solicited money for investment in options and futures by unsolicited telephone calls ('cold calling') and through advertisements in England and Wales.

[30] In *Bersch v. Drexel Firestone Inc.*, 519, F. 2d 974 (2d. Cir.), the prospectus stated that the shares of the Bahamian company were not being offered in the US. Nevertheless, US courts assumed jurisdiction to apply US Regulations as at least 22 US residents purchased shares.

In *Consolidated Gold Fields v. Minorco*, 871, F. 2d 252 (2d Cir. 1989) the offering documents were only sent by Minorco, a Luxemburg company, to British nominees of American shareholders. Nevertheless, the US courts applied US regulations as Minorco knew that the British nominees were required by law to forward the tender offer documents to the US shareholders.

In *Paulson Investment Co v. Norbay Securities Inc.*, 603F Supp. 615 (D. Ore 1984), the US court did not assume personal jurisdiction over a Canadian company (BMI), whose unregistered securities were bought by US investors in Canada: 'For the foreign acts with forum effects principle to apply in this case, the person sought to be charged must know, or have good reason to know, that his conduct will have effects in the state seeking to assert jurisdiction over him'.

[31] See *Leasco Data Processing Equipment Processing Corp. v. Maxwell*, 468F. 2d 1326 (2d. Cir. 1972) where misrepresentations by R. Maxwell to induce American investors to purchase securities of an English company in England, were made in the US.

law of the country where the securities were issued. As the place of issue is considered to be the place where the securities actually have been issued or where they have been introduced on the stock exchange, the fact that prospectuses have been distributed is not taken into consideration.[32] However, misrepresentation in prospectuses may give rise to a claim in tort governed by the law where the prospectus was distributed.[33]

From the above it follows that regulations from various countries with different requirements, may be applicable to a transnational offering. Issuers thus have to publish documents and follow procedures which comply with each of the regulations which may be applicable; or they have to adopt specific issuing procedures and documents for each separate market.

Issuers can try to simplify matters by restricting the offer to residents of a specific country and by stating that no offer is made to residents of other countries or by making the offer conditional on conformity with local regulations.[34] It is, however, doubtful whether such restrictions are effective. Transnational issuing would undoubtedly be facilitated if the various countries were to adopt uniform rules for the issuing of securities. Unfortunately, an attempt within the Uruguay Round negotiations to harmonize securities regulations failed. In the Annex on Financial Services to GATS, member states have reserved their national measures 'for prudential reasons, including for the protection of investors'. Member States of the European Union (EU) are somewhat obliged to recognize a prospectus which complies with the regulations of another EU member state, although national particularities may still be imposed.[35] Moreover, some countries have excluded from their securities regulation public offerings which only concern their territory to a limited extent, for example because primary issues were made outside the country or because the issue is mainly addressed to non-residents.[36]

Jurisdiction

Jurisdiction over public offerings is very important. When the regulations have not been respected, e.g. whenever there is misrepresentation or insufficient information, administrative authorities may block the issue or courts

[32] See A. Heini, op cit., p. 1361.

[33] See A. Heini, op cit., p. 1363.

[34] See e.g. the Take over Bid Prospectus by Albert Fisher Group Plc. concerning the Rahbeck Group, 1994.

[35] See Council Directive 80/390 of March 17, 1980, O.J. 1980 L 100/1 as amended by Council Directive 90/211 of April 23, 1990 (mutual recognition of public offer prospectuses) and as most recently amended by Directive 94/18 of the European Parliament of May 1994 (admission of securities to the official stock exchange listing). See also Rovinescu and Thieffry, supra, at pp. 46–7, 49–50.

[36] See e.g. for the US: SEC relaxes rules for non-US issuers, International Financial Law Review December 1993, p. 29; For Australia: Exemptions on offer for overseas securities in Australia, International Financial Law Review, September 1994, 33. For the position in the United Kingdom, see Rovinescu and Thieffry, supra, at p. 36. For a detailed analysis of some of the relaxations in the US and Canada, see Rovinescu and Thieffry, supra, at 51–68.

may grant an injunction against the company which is issuing its securities. As a general rule, administrative authorities or courts will have jurisdiction to do so when they deem their local regulations to be applicable to the public offering. In this respect applicable law and jurisdiction are intertwined.

Moreover, an investor who feels cheated may also file an action in court because of misrepresentation. At present, not much litigation is conducted because of misrepresentation in securities offerings within Western Europe. However, such litigation is quite frequent in North America where disgruntled investors do not hesitate to sue whenever the prospectus contained incorrect information. It may be expected that this trend will extend to Europe.

In some legal systems (e.g. France and Belgium) a claim between issuer and buyer because of misrepresentation will be considered as a contractual matter because of the contractual context. In other legal systems, such as English law, a claim based on misrepresentation would be considered as an action in tort.

When the action is based on breach of contract, the claim should be brought in the court of the defendant (issuing company and/or its issuing agent) or in the court of the place where the securities, which were bought because of misrepresentation or insufficient information, were issued.

When the action is based on a tort, the claim can be brought before different courts. The claimant can bring an action before the court of the place where the party who gave the incorrect or incomplete information has his domicile or residence; he also can bring the claim before the court of the 'place of tort' (locus delicti).[37] In a transnational issuing of shares, this 'place of tort' could be (i) the place were the information originated,[38] (ii) the place where it was received by the investor, (iii) the place where the investor decided to act on the basis of this information[39] or (iv) the place where the shares were issued. Under the Brussels and Lugano Conventions on Jurisdiction it is rather difficult to bring an action in tort in the place where the shareholder is located and suffered the financial loss because of the misrepresentation.[40] However in other countries the financial effects-test may provide a basis for jurisdiction in tort.[41]

[37] For instance, the Brussels Convention as well as the Lugano Convention on Court jurisdiction, Article 5 para. 3, provide that a court action can be brought in the court of the place where the harmful event occurred'.

[38] Psimenos v. E.F. Hutton, 722 F. 2d 1041 (2d Cir. 1983) (a flyer containing a tear-off post card to be sent to an American office for more information).

[39] See Multinational Gas and Petrochemical Co. v. Multinational Gas and Petrochemical Services [1983] Ch. 258 at p. 267.

[40] See e.g. Court of Justice, January 10, 1990, Dumez v. Hessische Landesbank, E.C.R. 1990 I 49, C. 220/88.

[41] See however, Psimenos v. E.F. Hutton, 722 F. 2d 1041 (2d Cir. 1983): 'Since we find that there is jurisdiction under the (conduct test), we do not need to reach the question whether the effects test provides an independent basis for jurisdiction'.

Transnational offering of securities is greatly burdened by the fact that courts from various countries may exercise jurisdiction over the issue and apply different standards thereon. It will be difficult to streamline the different countries in the exercise of court jurisdiction to sanction their securities regulations . The respective interests to have these regulations respected, are too important.[42] However, in the US, where the theory of 'forum non conveniens' is applicable, courts sometimes use this theory to refuse jurisdiction over securities suits with a substantial foreign element.[43]

TAKE OVER BID

Applicable Law

Securities laws and regulations impose many constraints on transnational takeover bids.[44] The *lex societatis* determines the conditions which the offeror will have to observe in carrying out the takeover bid (i.e prior authorisation from local authorities, notification of the company, treatment of minority shareholders).

Surprisingly, the documents for the public offer appear not to indicate the law which governs the acquisition of shares. The question which law is applicable, then remains open. Is it the law of the offeror, the law of the target company, or of the place the shareholders are established?

Moreover, specific regulations in the respective jurisdictions impose detailed conditions for takeover bids, e.g. as to the information to be given in the prospectus. These regulations may be applicable under different criteria: they may be applicable because the target company is located in the country;[45] because the public offer is made in that

[42] See G. Schuster, Extraterritoriality of securities laws: an economic analysis of jurisdictional conflicts, 26 Law & Policy in International Business (1994), 165.

[43] In Nathan Gordon Trust v. Northgate Exploration Ltd. (1993), the Southern District Court New York for instance dismissed a case where the stockholders had purchased securities on foreign stock exchanges and where the reports, which contained the alleged misrepresentations, had been prepared and disseminated in Canada (International Financial Law Review, August 1993). See also US rulings on forum non conveniens, International Financial Law Review, June 1994, 22.

[44] See e.g. Constraints on Cross Border Takeovers and Mergers, International Business Lawyer 1991, 58.

In M.C.G. Inc. v. Great Western Energy Corp., 896 F. 2d 170 (5th Cir. 1990) the Court dismissed a complaint from a US Corporation, which bought shares of a US Company on the London Stock Exchange for lack of subject matter jurisdiction.

[45] The English Code on Takeovers and Mergers seems only applicable when the target company is resident in the UK (see e.g. P. Lee in Les prises de participations: l'exemple des offres publiques d'achat, Lausanne, 1990, 656 and 660 ('We have learnt that it is crazy to bite off more than we chew').

country;[46] because most[47] or some[48] shareholders are established in that country;[49] because the stock is listed on the local stock exchange. Often these criteria will not be tested in depth because in the country where the offer is made, many shareholders are also established and the stock may be listed on the stock exchange.

Jurisdiction

Infringement of the regulations on takeover bids can be sanctioned by the authorities or courts of the countries, whose regulations are applicable. One of the parties concerned (i.e. the target company or shareholders) may, for example, seek an injunction to block the takeover bid. Moreover, an unsatisfied shareholder or even a third party may ask for other relief, such as compensation.

The same principles on jurisdiction as discussed with regard to the public offering of securities apply, depending upon whether the claim for compensation is brought in contract or tort.

[46] See Plessey Company Plc. v. General Electric Company, 628 F. Supp. 477 (D.Del. 1986) where the information of a takeover bid by a British bidder of a British target company was as much as possible withheld from the American press. In that case the takeover bid did not come within the scope of US legal and judicial jurisdiction because 'the only possible American consequence is aroused investor interest due to American newspaper accounts beyond the control of the offeror'.

[47] See A. Hirsch, art. cit., p. 361: 'For the 'takeover' of a company whose securities are traded in more than one country, it again seems irrational to apply different rules for the takeover of the same company, especially as the rules in different countries are not only different but also contradictory in principle, one should once again apply the regulations of the 'main market' of the target company.

[48] For example, the Belgian takeover-statute (Act of March 2, 1989) and the so-called the 'De Benedetti-decree' (Royal Decree, November 8, 1989) do not contain precise criteria for their territorial scope. It can be assumed that these statutory provisions are applicable as soon as shares of the target company are held by the Belgian public. It does not seem to be a requirement that the offer and/or the target company are established in Belgium (see S. Vandeginste, Het toepassingsgebied van de Belgische regeling inzake openbare overnameaanbiedingen vanuit grensoverschrijdend perspectief, Tijdschrift voor Rechtspersonen en Vennootschappen 1991, p. 400 at p. 401).

The anti-fraud provisions of the US securities laws were declared applicable to Luxembourg company, which had made an offer to take over an English company because 2.5% of the latter's shareholders, owning 5.3% million shares with a market value of about $120 million, were American residents (Consolidated Gold Fields v. Minorco, 871F. 2d. 252 (2d. Cir.). The same statute was declared applicable to a Bahamian company which had sold shares to at least 22 US residents (Bersch v. Drexel Firestone Inc., 519F, 2d. 974 (2d. Cir.)).

These provisions, however, were not deemed applicable to a purchase by a foreign investment trust, of which only 2% of the trust fundholders—about 300 investors—were US citizens or residents (IIT v. Vancap Ltd., 519F, 2d. 1001 (2d. Cir.)): 'It was unknown how Americans came to invest in the trust since the shares of the trust apparently were not intended to be offered to American residents or citizens' (p. 1017)).

US regulations likewise were declared inapplicable to a British bidder of a British target company when 98,4% of the relevant shares were held outside America (Plessey Company Plc. v. General Electric Company, 628F. Supp. 477 (D. Del. 1986)).

[49] In this respect it also could be relevant whether these shareholders are institutional or private investors and whether the shares are spread among the public at large in the country.

OTHER SALES OF SECURITIES

On Securities Exchanges

Applicable law

The purchase of securities on a stock exchange is in principle governed by the law of the state where this exchange is established. Indeed, it is there that offer and acceptance meet and that the transaction takes place. Moreover, in their rules, stock exchanges generally provide that transactions are governed by the law of the country where the exchange is located. The transfer of proprietary rights would also be governed by this law as the securities are deemed to be present at the exchange when offered for sale.

The purchase of securities at a stock exchange is not governed by the Vienna Convention on the International Sales of Goods (1980) for a dual reason: the Convention is neither applicable to the sale of 'shares and other securities' (Article 2, d), nor to sales 'by auction' where the seller does not know who the buyer will be.

Jurisdiction

The rules of the stock exchange generally provide for a choice of court or an arbitration clause to settle disputes related to transactions on the exchange. This clause will be binding in most cases.

However, transactions on an exchange are conducted through a broker, admitted at that exchange. Disputes do not so much concern the transaction at the stock exchange itself, but the way the broker has conducted his business. For example, the broker may be challenged because he did not respect the instructions of his customer or, when he has discretionary powers to invest, because he made erroneous decisions. Brokers very often include jurisdiction or arbitration clauses in their instruction forms. However, the validity of these clauses should be carefully examined. For instance, a few recent German court decisions have set aside arbitration clauses in a contract under which German private investors have given instructions to an English broker to invest on the international futures and options market. The respective contracts contained a choice of English law and provided for arbitration in London. German courts nevertheless assumed jurisdiction because they considered the German private investor protected by the German Börsengesetz, which in the courts' view entitled them to repayment of the amounts invested in the futures and lost afterwards.

Not on Securities Exchanges

Applicable law

Securities are often transferred outside any exchange. Share participations in companies move between investors. Companies generally are acquired through stock purchase from the previous owners. Conflict of law rules have to determine the law applicable to these acquisitions.

Within most countries of the European Union, the Rome Convention on the law applicable to contractual obligations (1980) determines the proper law.[50] Under this Convention, parties are entitled to chose the law which will govern the acquisition. Whenever the parties did not opt for a specific legal system, there is a general presumption that the contract is governed by the law of the seller. However, it may be that other elements point to another legal system, which then could be considered as the proper law. For instance, it may be argued that the location of the company whose shares are acquired is less relevant when only a few shares are bought, but that it becomes essential when all shares—or even a controlling participation—is obtained so that the real subject matter of the transaction became the acquisition of the company.

The transfer of proprietary rights is determined by the law of the place where the securities are located in law (*lex situs*).

Jurisdiction

The purchase contract very often contains a jurisdiction or arbitration clause. Particularly when shares are purchased to acquire a company, an arbitration clause is well advised. Indeed, disputes over the representations and warranties, which accompany the acquisition, are so technical and complex that they are better settled by arbitration than by state courts.

CONCLUSION

The law applicable to securities transactions is a complex matter, which requires careful analysis of the documents and a thorough investigation of the legal systems concerned. This Chapter gives only a general overview of some aspects of this question.

[50] It is true, the Rome Convention, Article 2 para. 2(c) explicitly excludes in an illustrative and non-exhaustive manner from its scope contracts concerning questions 'governed by the law of companies and other bodies corporate, such as the creation, legal capacity, internal organisation, winding up . . . and the personal legal liability of officers and members for the obligations of the company'. However, the acquisition of shares from a previous shareholder is not explicitly excluded; moreover it appears too removed from the illustrative examples to be covered by the exclusion.

5

Selected Issues in Securitisation

FIDELIS ODITAH

INTRODUCTION

In the last decade, securitisation has been one of the most significant innovations made by the financial markets. In the United Kingdom, the development of securitisation, in the sense in which that expression is hereafter used, has occurred since the mid 1980s.[1] As far as secondary securitisations in the modern form are concerned, the United States of America has led all the way; its market is the most matured. Although the United Kingdom has been the most developed of the European markets, secondary securitisation in Europe is still very much in its infancy. However, in the United Kingdom, the sale of receivables has existed in some form for a very long time indeed. What securitisation has done is to reinvent the wheel by 'wrapping' the sale of financial and trade receivables around marketable securities. Assignment, which provided the basic framework within which sale of receivables was consummated from the 17th century onward, still provides the basic structure for vesting the securitised assets in the special or multi purpose vehicle which modern secondary securitisations utilise.

The development of secondary securitisation in the United States is said to have its roots in the Depression of the 1930s. In order to help mortgage originators deal with the default risk of borrowers, the Federal Housing Administration ('FHA') was established in 1934 to provide government guaranteed mortgage insurance. In 1938, the Federal National Mortgage Association ('Fannie Mae') was created as the first government agency to provide a secondary market in government insured mortgages. In 1957, the Federal Home Loan Bank Board ('FHLBB') was established. Notwithstanding this early start, no active secondary market in the United States emerged until the 1970s, when the Federal Home Loan Mortgage Corporation ('Freddie Mac') was established in 1970, with power to

[1] It has been suggested that securitisation in the sense of asset-backed bonds have existed for over a century and that in the 1920s, private title and mortgage insurance companies in New York State sold 'guaranteed mortgage participation certificates' secured by single mortgage loans or pools of mortgages: see Shenker and Colletta, Asset Securitization: The Evolution, Current Issues and New Frontiers (1991) 69 Tex L R 1369 at 1380–2.

purchase both government insured mortgage loans and loans originated by private lenders.[2]

In the United Kingdom, the emergence of a secondary market in second-hand receivables is entirely attributable to the private sector. Government response has been aimed at containing the development from a regulatory point of view. No single factor can be said to account for secondary securitisation in the United Kingdom. What seems clear is that the origins of modern securitisations must can be traced to the desire of banks and non bank financial intermediaries to sell their loan assets. The forces which have driven and informed this desire are diverse, albeit closely-linked to the asset being sold. In relation to sovereign debt, for example, sales have been fuelled by the collapse in the credit rating of many sovereign borrowers especially in the less developed countries. Capital constraints may have contributed to the emergence of a secondary market in mortgages[3] and syndicated loans to corporates.

WHAT IS SECURITISATION?

Securitisation is a buzz word lacking any technical meaning. It is a market usage which can mean different things to different people. It is therefore important to identify at least some of the market usages in order to ensure that we are all using securitisation in a common and easily understandable sense. Three usages may be distinguished: first, securitisation is used to describe the transmutation of illiquid assets, e.g. mortgages, into tradeable securities. This involves the pooling, unbundling, repackaging and refinancing of existing income producing financial assets into securities that can be sold to investors in the capital markets. Mortgage securitisation is the best example of this. Secondly, securitisation is often used to describe any sale of financial assets, whether or not involving the creation of securities. The sale of participations in syndicated loans is perhaps the best example of this. Where participations are sold by assignment or sub-participation, no new marketable security is thereby created, but the transaction is often described as securitisation. Even where existing participations are novated by the filling and filing of the prescribed forms with the agent bank, the prescribed form itself is not a security, although often referred to as a transferable loan certificate.

Thirdly, securitisation is sometimes used to describe the *process* of issuing tradeable debts, whether or not the traded securities are backed by some

[2] For a good account of the historical development of the secondary market in mortgages in the United States, see Murray and Haddaway, Mortgage-Backed Securities: An Investigation of Legal and Financial Issues (1986) Jo of Corp Law 203 at 204–6; Shenker and Colletta, op cit, at 1383–8.

[3] For the background to the development of the United Kingdom mortgage-backed securities market, see Eilis Ferran, Mortgage Securitisation: Legal Aspects (Butterworths, 1992), 6–16.

underlying receivables. This emphasis on the *process* rather than on the form of asset being sold, has a close affinity to disintermediation. In this Chapter, the third meaning is referred to as primary securitisation; the first as secondary securitisation. The second meaning, like secondary securitisation, involves the sale of an income producing financial asset and raises similar issues, but differs structurally from secondary securitisation. Both differ from primary securitisation in the sense that primary securitisation does not involve the sale of second-hand financial assets, although securities issued in primary securitisation could be unbundled, repackaged and then sold as new asset-backed securities in a secondary securitisation. If we accept the second meaning of securitisation as involving true securitisation, two additional distinctions are possible: one is between domestic and international securitisation; the other is between securitisation of retail credit and securitisation of wholesale lending. The two distinctions overlap, but not completely. Securitisation of mortgages, credit card, auto and other consumer receivables would count as domestic and retail credit securitisation while securitisation of sovereign and international corporate debts would be international securitisation of wholesale credit. However, the overlap is incomplete because cross-border securitisation of mortgages and consumer debts is an international securitisation of retail credit.

Securitisation in all three senses raises a variety of issues. Some relate to the marketing of the securities and depend upon the type, place and manner of issue and marketing of the securities; some relate to the assignability of the underlying receivables and the requirements of different national laws as to the creation and perfection of the sale of receivables and the security interest, if any, which secures the marketable securities; some relate to credit, liquidity, reinvestment and insolvency risks; some concern the accounting treatment which the vendor or originator of the pool of receivables requires; tax considerations play a dominant role as do capital adequacy and other regulatory constraints.

Two areas of great difficulty are, first, the extent to which professional trustees used in securitisations can virtually abandon the discretion vested in them by acting on expert reports almost in a purely ministerial capacity; secondly, what is the liability of the rating agency? Most vehicles used in securitisations are thinly capitalised, established specifically for the purpose of acquiring the assets to be securitised, the acquisition of which is financed by the issue of loan notes. Most securitisations in the United Kingdom have been assigned a triple A rating, a rating which is often higher than that of the originator of the receivables. Rating is vital to the pricing of the notes and provides assurance to prospective purchasers of the notes who have neither the time nor the resources to evaluate the assets to be securitised.[3a] If the

[3a] Barratt, infra, at pp. 101–3, examines the types of ratings available as well as the criteria for assigning ratings to securities.

rating proves to be erroneous and the issue goes wrong, the question arises as to the liability, if any, of the rating agency. Rating agencies naturally take the view that they cannot be liable to purchasers of notes which they have rated, whether in contract or tort. As regards contract, rating agencies are on a firm ground as there would usually be no privity of contract between them and the purchasers; the possible claims in tort are more problematic, however. Two such claims are misrepresentation and negligence.

As regards misrepresentation, rating agencies insist that rating is really no more than an expression of an opinion rather than a statement of fact. However, given that they are experts holding themselves out as such, there would be little difficulty in concluding that their rating 'opinion' is indeed a representation of fact. Subject to questions of reliance (which would be easy to establish) and causation, they could arguably be liable to purchasers for misrepresentation. The usual disclaimer of liability would of course be subject to section 3 the Misrepresentation Act 1967 and would be enforceable, where English law applies, only if it passes the test of reasonableness.

The claim in negligence would of course be for pure economic loss. The courts in the United Kingdom have vacillated on the question of the circumstances in which it would be appropriate to impose such liability. Rating agencies may take comfort from the fact that given the sophistication of the participants in the market for securitised debts (usually institutional investors and sophisticated and wealthy private investors), the courts are unlikely to be eager to impose liability on grounds of negligence for errors in rating opinions.

I do not propose to discuss these issues in this Chapter. Instead I shall concentrate on some of the economic rationales which drive securitisation as well as the impact of securitisation on depository institutions and corporates which are not depository institutions.

SECURITISATION AND DISINTERMEDIATION

Historically depository institutions such as banks and building societies are and remain the primary sources of retail credit in the United Kingdom. However, commercial banks and building societies are not the ultimate providers of the retail credit which extend. Instead, they intermediate credit by mobilizing deposits and on-lending them to the ultimate borrowers on different maturities. In this role, commercial banks are but indirect sources of the credit which they provide and they do so by transforming short-term liabilities (deposits) into long-term assets (loans and other forms of credit). This is traditional or institution-based intermediation. In its simplest form, financial intermediation is simply broking: borrowers and lenders or vendors and purchasers are brought together for a fee. This fee, in the context of traditional intermediation, is usually in the form of a margin between the interest rate paid by the bank to depositors and the interest rate charged on bank lending. Traditional intermediation is nothing but 'spread' or 'margin' banking. It follows that disintermediation is the reversion to direct finance, in which the services of an intermediary are dispensed with and the ultimate borrowers and lenders deal with each other. The link with securitisation comes if this direct finance is conducted by means of marketable securities.[4]

Both primary and secondary securitisation involve disintermediation in this sense. In primary securitisation, where an issuer sells its own debt instruments to investors in the market, there is plainly disintermediation of banks in the sense that bank credit is by-passed in favour of direct finance from the market. In secondary securitisation, the disintermediation is only partial and incomplete because the existing structures do not involve any direct relationship between the ultimate lenders (noteholders) and the ultimate borrowers (mortgagors, credit cardholders and other consumer debtors). There is partial disintermediation of banks, building societies and other providers of consumer credit because their role is limited to origination of the receivables pool and its administration after securitisation.[5] By selling relatively young receivables for the outstanding principal amount of the pool of receivables, the originator ensures that the receivables are funded by holders of notes secured on the receivables pool.

Securitisation has threatened the role of depository institutions in their traditional financial intermediation. If large corporates continue to by-pass depository institutions in favour of capital market intermediated credit, securitisation, which enables this to happen by channelling debt finance directly between borrowers and lenders, would reduce the role of traditional intermediation in corporate finance and enable large corporates who have access to the capital markets to avoid the costs associated with traditional intermediation. At the same time, it has led merchant and investment banks into another form of financial intermediation, namely capital market-based intermediation. Instead of earning a margin or spread (interest income) through traditional lending and intermediation, the emphasis has shifted to non-interest income from services associated with arranging, placing of debt securities with investors, underwriting the issues and trading in the securities. Underwriting, broking and placing are all forms of market-based intermediation which are income producing for the depository institutions. As with traditional intermediation, lenders and borrowers are brought together

[4] Gardner & Revell, Securitisation: History, Forms and Risks (Institute of European Finance, 1988), 17.

[5] Compare Gardner & Revell, op cit, for the argument that secondary securitisation does not involve disintermediation because the second-hand financial assets generally remain in the hands of the banks or other financial institutions after their sale. Although this is perhaps true of the sale of syndicated loans by assignment or sub-participation, it is not generally true of the structures used for secondary securitisations in the United Kingdom.

through placing and underwriting. In underwriting, for example, the borrower is generally guaranteed a predetermined amount of funds at a known price on a fixed date or at a fixed period. Underwriting provides liquidity in the capital markets because the underwriter, for a fee or spread dependent upon uncertain market conditions, absorbs the uncertainty about the market demand for the borrower's debt securities. These off-balance sheet activities, which have become more common in the United Kingdom following the 'Big Bang', are now significant sources of funds for banks without tying up bank capital. Therefore, although primary securitisation has led to some loss of opportunity to lend to the blue chip corporates, depository institutions have responded and adapted to this challenge by assisting the corporates to raise funds from the capital markets in return for a fee. Securitisation, by disintermediating depository institutions from their traditional role of providers of intermediated credit, has, in relation to large corporates, partially crowded them out of the corporate financing sphere.

THE ECONOMIC RATIONALE FOR SECURITISATION

Financial innovation can be classified in different ways. One approach is to classify financial innovation in terms of the type of financial intermediation performed. On this approach, the following classification emerges: (a) risk transferring innovations (these transfer risk in existing positions); (b) liquidity enhancing innovations (these liquefy hitherto illiquid assets); (c) credit, debt or equity generating innovations (these give access to debt or equity markets).[6] Financial innovation can also be classified according to the effect which it has on the user of the innovation. On this analysis, the following distinctions emerge:[7] (a) those which provide access to financial sources which were previously unavailable ('the financial constraint effect'); (b) those which provide cheaper sources of finance ('cost of capital effect'); (c) those which allow the borrower a better financing of working capital or a better covering of the risks arising from its investment or financing decisions ('efficiency of capital and cost of capital effects').

Securitisation provides access to cheaper and alternative sources of debt finance for the person using it. This is true of primary and secondary securitisations. One explanation for the incidence of traditional intermediation is the presence of information assymetries between corporates and other borrowers, on one hand, and investors in the capital markets, on the other. These assymetries create market imperfections. Banks and building societies, by using their intrinsic credit analysis and risk monitoring skills, are

[6] Paul Fenney, infra, note 8, at 22–3.

[7] Vinals & Berges, Financial Innovation and Capital Formation in Arnold Heerje (ed), Innovation, Technology and Finance (Basil Blackwell, 1988), 169.

capable of bridging the capital market imperfections and thereby add to the overall efficiency of the financial system.[8] However, this is not costless. The most significant costs of traditional intermediation are the 'regulatory taxes' imposed on banks and building societies in their deposit-taking business. Two such 'regulatory taxes' are the capital constraints imposed to ensure the solvency of depository institutions and consequently the protection of depositors, and deposit insurance premium. Regulatory taxes increase the cost of funds (deposits) to depository institutions. Another source of costs is the relative illiquidity of the traditional assets of depository institutions compared with the assets of a merchant or investment bank. This illiquidity may mean that depository institutions are likely to require higher returns on their assets (loans) than investors in the capital markets. A third source of costs in traditional intermediation arises from bundling together the risks inherent in the credit process (extension, funding and servicing) by vertical integration of all aspects of the credit process. These costs associated with traditional intermediation increase the costs of borrowing from depository institutions as they are passed to borrowers in the form of higher rate of interest.

Both primary and secondary securitisations unbundle the risks inherent in the credit process. One aspect of this unbundling property is the breaking down and diffusion of credit risk in the capital market. In primary securitisation, the credit process is segregated into its discrete steps, credit risk can be insured; an active secondary market for debt securities ensures liquidity; the funding is separated from the trading and from the servicing. Each step in the credit process requires special skills. Unbundling enables institutions to concentrate on specific parts of the credit process and to build up competitive advantage through specialisation. This can reduce the costs of borrowing from the capital market and in part explains why market intermediated credit is cheaper than traditionally intermediated credit through depository institutions. Another aspect of the interest reduction is that many of the special purpose vehicles used in secondary securitisations are able to issue notes at rates of interest lower than the originator can borrow. Because the notes are triple A rated, the coupon attached reflects the high quality of the notes. The special purpose vehicle passes the proceeds of the notes to the originator as the purchase price of the receivables purchased from the originator. By pooling and repackaging existing receivables and selling them to a special purpose vehicle, an originator is able to enjoy a much lower rate of interest. Even when the considerable transaction cost involved in securitisation is taken into account, there is still a net saving in interest rate for the originator.

[8] Paul Fenney, The Economics of Securitisation (Chartered Institute of Bankers Occasional Paper Series, 1992), 21, 62.

Secondary securitisation leads to diversification and diffusion of the various risks inherent in the credit process. How does this work? Traditional intermediation is a closed market credit. Through securitisation, a closed market credit is transmuted into an open market credit—a security—and the product elements that make up the credit process are unbundled and repackaged as marketable securities. The credit risk is taken out (unbundled) from that of a closed market lending arrangement and diversified into two dimensions: time and between investor groups that buy the debt securities in the market.[9] By unbundling and dispersing the risks inherent in the credit process, secondary securitisation reduces the credit risk concentration in the closed market traditional intermediation. This insulates depository institutions from the impact of default in the assets sold by spreading this risk among purchasers of the asset-backed securities.

Secondary securitisation also reduces 'regulatory tax' and enables depository institutions to earn income through off balance sheet services without locking up their capital. Where a securitisation is accounted for as a true sale of the securitised assets from an originator to an issuer, for example, by derecognition or linked presentation under the Financial Reporting Standards 5 (FRS 5), Application Note D, it will generally result in the removal of the securitised assets and any associated liabilities from the originator's balance sheet; accelerate the recognition of profit or loss by the originator; and improve the return-on-assets and capital-to-assets calculations. Instead of receiving a series of small payments from individual debtors over a considerable period of time, an originator is able to receive the proceeds of sale of the securitised assets soon after the securitisation. This unlocks the capital with which the securitised assets were created and the capital so unlocked could be used to generate new financial assets which could again be securitised. In the case of depository institutions, if the regulatory criteria are met, they need not set aside any capital for the securitised receivables and this eases their capital constraints. Secondary securitisations therefore help to unlock assets, increase liquidity of assets, give an originator access to a wider and cheaper source of funding, help in balance sheet management, ease capital constraints and improve the return on capital.

[9] Gardner & Revell, op cit, 27, 63–6.

IMPACT OF SECURITISATION ON BANKS

As I have already pointed out, one effect of primary securitisation is the shift from traditional intermediation of credit through depository institutions to capital market intermediation. As banks lose lucrative lending opportunities, they have responded to the loss of interest income by assisting corporates to raise funds from the capital markets, by advising, arranging, underwriting, marketing and trading in corporate debt securities. These off balance sheet income sources have enabled banks to adjust to the challenges of securitisation as they move from 'spread' or 'margin' banking to 'conduit' or 'service' banking. Fundamentally banks have not actually been disintermediated; what change there has been has been in the shift in emphasis in the type of intermediation which they provide. Whereas traditional closed market credit intermediation tied up bank capital and subjected them to regulatory constraints, the new forms of intermediation enable banks to improve their return on capital without some of the 'regulatory taxes' inherent in deposit-taking business.

Secondary securitisations have also helped to diffuse and spread the risks inherent in traditional intermediation. The incidence of risk realisation, the ultimate burden of risk, is spread over many investors. In theory at least, this diffusion of risk increases the potential strength and at the same time reduces the fragility of the financial system, as risk bearing is not concentrated on a few institutions. However, not all the credits claimed for securitisation are real. First, leaving aside 'regulatory taxes', it is difficult to imagine the circumstances when market intermediated credit would be cheaper than retail deposits as alternative sources of finance. This perhaps explains why building societies and banks in the United Kingdom have not rushed into securitisation despite its obvious appeal.[10] Secondly, while secondary securitisation may reduce the risk of the originator of financial assets, it does not seem to reduce the overall risk of the banking system. There are at least two reasons for this: one is that many of the purchasers of the debt instruments issued in the process of securitisation are depository institutions. This is true of both primary and secondary securitisations. Another is that some of the instruments used by large corporates to ensure liquidity such as revolving underwriting facilities (RUFs) and multiple option facilities (MOFs) can expose depository institutions to liquidity risks if they are activated by a large number of borrowers at the same time. The commitment to lend inherent in an underwriting arrangement may involve a longer term credit risk than the receivables which depository institutions sell in secondary securitisation.

Thirdly, depository institutions may increase the concentration of their

[10] Eilis Ferran, op cit, 4.

credit risk in another sense and that is the adverse selection problem. As prime and blue chip corporates increase their reliance on the capital markets for most of their debt finance, depository institutions are left with lower rated medium and small sized businesses that have no access to the capital markets. Although depository institutions can charge such businesses a wider margin, they do so at the expense of the poor credit risk which they retain in their loan portfolios. Finally, securitisation can lead to systemic risks. As the Bank for International Settlements ('BIS') put it, 'the question whether new financial instruments (such as securitised instruments) contribute to an increase in systemic risk depends in part on whether the various risks inherent in them are appropriately priced. That is, whether they produce sufficient profit margins on average to cover the potential losses from market, credit or other risks, both in the short and in the long run'.[11] Insofar as systemic risks are perceived to arise from underpricing, this is likely to be a temporary phenomenon, explained by, first, the inevitable learning curve and, secondly, the young and growing nature of the market for securitised debt. In these formative years, competitive pressures are likely to cause underpricing because the drive to earn and retain a market share may lead market participants to underprice the risks associated with market intermediation in order not to price themselves out of what they consider to be a potentially lucrative market. In the medium to long term, however,it is unlikely that underpricing would persist as the learning process would have ended and most of the risks would have been identified, evaluated and appropriately priced.

IMPACT OF SECURITISATION ON CORPORATE FINANCE

What lessons can corporates learn from primary securitisation? If securitisation helps in managing, if not totally eliminating, the financial constraint effect and produces a reduction in the cost of debt finance, how does one explain the incidence of traditionally intermediated credit among blue chip corporates? If anything is clear it is that primary securitisation provides access to cheaper sources of debt finance and widens the financial alternatives available to corporate borrowers by widening the class of immediate lenders to the large corporates. In addition, securitisation enables such corporates to escape the control which depository institutions exercise indirectly over their investment or capital budgeting decisions by their power to determine which projects to fund and which ones to turn their backs on, even when corporate managers consider the rejected projects to have a positive net present value. It must be said, however, that the ability of deposi-

[11] The Bank for International Settlements (BIS), Recent Innovations in International Banking (1986), 199.

tory institutions to control the investment decisions of companies which have no access to the capital markets is likely to be inversely related to the economic strength of the particular company. The stronger the company, the more constrained is their control over its investment decisions likely to be.

Although depository institutions may lose some of their customers as a result, corporate users of securitisation must bear in mind that capital markets are transaction-based and that investors purchasing their debt securities may not be interested in relationship lending which is so often taken for granted in traditionally intermediated credit relations; secondly, the capital markets can be thoroughly irrational and may not in any event be as accommodating as depository institutions. Therefore the access to the cheaper debt finance which securitisation affords may be at a price. In practice, three factors militate against the perceived irrationaility which can sometimes characterise the capital markets. The first is the use of professional trustees for most debt issues; the second is the scope of discretion usually given to the trustee; finally, there is the fact that in noteholders' meetings democracy is the rule. While all three factors suggest that receivership is likely to be more constrained in market intermediated credit than in bilateral traditional intermediation, none is likely to prevent market irrationality from depressing the market price of a company's outstanding debt securities and by implication limiting its ability to raise additional debt finance by further issues of debt securities.

One question remains, however, and it is this. If securitisation reduces the financial constraint effect for corporates and provides cheaper debt finance, why is it that the patterns of corporate finance do not reflect these benefits? In other words, if it is financially inefficient for corporates to use traditional intermediation because of its greater cost why do large corporates with access to the capital markets still use traditionally intermediated credit? Young companies or older ones that have done poorly are said to be the only corporate users of traditionally intermediated credit while more successful ones use capital market intermediation. The argument is that successful companies have more 'reputational capital' at stake and therefore have more to lose by taking inefficient actions. For such companies it is inefficient to incur the costs associated with traditional intermediation. The younger companies, in comparison, have not had time to develop a track record and are consequently unknown or unfavoured by the capital markets while older companies which are known to the market are unfavoured and therefore have no reputation to lose. For these two categories of corporates, incurring the costs associated with traditional intermediation is efficient given the inaccessibility of the capital markets.[12] This may be true but

[12] See Paul Fenney, op cit, 64 where this argument is summarised.

it does not explain why the older more successful companies which have 'reputational capital' still use some traditional intermediation.

One explanation may be that for the large corporates traditional intermediation forms only a small part of their debt financing and even then they are able to borrow from depository institutions at rates which are only marginally higher than those prevailing in the capital markets. Why do they choose to pay this premium? Two explanations offer themselves. The first is that it is simply a relationship premium. A second is that it is an insurance premium to protect large corporates against the rainy day. Large corporates maintain credit relationships, mainly in the form of undrawn commitments, as an insurance against sudden and unanticipated liquidity requirements and also against possible loss of their 'reputational capital' due to deterioration in institutional or market conditions which might make their continued use of the capital market inefficient.[13]

CONCLUSION

As Paul Fenney observes,[14] if securitisation could be developed to a stage where all risks, maturities and values were catered for and traded on one world market, traditional intermediation would become superfluous. This is because depository institutions trade on market imperfections, information assymetries and on local knowledge. In a strongly efficient and complete market where the risks of all corporate borrowers can be correctly and efficiently identified, evaluated and priced, there would be no need for traditionally intermediated created. At the moment and probably for the foreseeable future, that state of affairs is an ideal to be aspired to rather than a realistic target capable of achievement.

[13] Op cit, 66. [14] Op cit, 27.

6

Financing Projects through the Capital Markets—a South East Asia Perspective

JEFFERY BARRATT

INTRODUCTION

Much excitement has been generated recently about the possibility of financing projects through the capital markets.

'Securitise your power station'
'144A your toll road'
'Finance your petrochemical plant through the capital markets'

But what does it all mean? Is this just 'hype' and bankers' jargon or can the massive funding requirements for the infrastructure projects required in the Peoples Republic of China (PRC) and Southeast Asia be met by some marvellous new financing technique?

The starting point we are told is that traditional funding methods cannot cope with the huge cost of meeting the infrastructure demands in the Asia Pacific region over the next period. A recent World Bank survey estimates the cost of new electric power projects alone in this region from 1995 to 1999 to be of the order of US$277 billion.[1]

Traditionally, projects have been funded by any one or a mix of funds provided by governments or supra-national bodies like the World Bank or the ADB, loans from Export Credit Agencies (ECAs), loans from commercial banks and equity financing.

The idea behind the move to 'securitisation' would be to open the capital debt markets for financing projects of this nature. Is this feasible? This Chapter examines some of the issues which need to be addressed in any proposed debt issue raised to finance projects. It also briefly examines how the capital markets are being used to raise equity for such projects.

[1] Moody's, The Outlook for Project Finance in the Asia-Pacific, March 1994 p. 1.

SECURITISATION—WHAT DOES IT MEAN?

Before considering the application of securitisation techniques to projects it is perhaps useful to examine what is meant by securitisation in the current context.[2]

It could be defined as: 'the refinancing (or, indeed, financing) of income generating assets in the form of tradeable debt instruments sold to the investing public which are secured on the assets refinanced and which are serviced from the cashflow which the assets yield.'

It could also be described as 'the transformation of an illiquid asset into a tradeable security with a secondary market.'

The definitions commonly used usually emphasise the 'refinancing' of an asset or a pool of assets. It is useful to extend the definition for present purposes to include bond or other securities issues used for the initial financing of an infrastructure project.

Securitisation, as it is most commonly known in the markets, first evolved as a means of enabling mortgage lenders in the United States to move large parts of their debt portfolio off balance sheet for the purpose of statutory accounting rules or for central bank capital adequacy rules which affected them.[3] This meant that those lenders could then make new loans without having to incur the cost of raising additional capital, while retaining an interest in the profits derived from the securitised assets.[4]

The structure of a securitisation commonly involves the following features:

(a) first, the pooling of assets that are to be securitised—for example residential mortgages, credit card loans or some other receivables owed by a large number of separate borrowers;
(b) secondly, a 'special purpose company' or trust which acquires and administers, or sub-contracts the administration of, the assets;
(c) thirdly, an issue of securities by the special purpose company, the return on which, either floating or fixed rate, depends on the ability of the company to generate income from the receivables, together with any supporting insurance proceeds, guarantees or financial facilities which may be available as credit enhancement; and

[2] Securitisation in its broader sense could include any form of financing involving the sale or trading of debt or income streams (or even equity) for example the trading of participations in the secondary debt market see. e.g. Selling Loan Assets, Butterworths JIB FL March 1993. See also Oditah, supra, at pp. 84–6.

[3] Numerous forms of assets or income streams have been securitised for example the GPA ALPS transaction involved aircraft leases—see also 'Securitisation New Look for the 1990s', 1993 1FLR pp. 9ff for a discussion of securitisation of service agreements.

[4] For a discussion of asset-backed securitisation in the United Kingdom, see Bank of England Quarterly Bulletin of May 1994.

(d) fourthly, the special purpose company obtains a rating for the securities it issues from a credit rating agency such as Standard & Poor's or Moody's, thus qualifying them for the investment purposes of insurance companies, pension funds and other institutional investors.

Assets have, to-date, usually been pooled for securitisation purposes. This can help to create a large asset value to make the process economically feasible in terms of transaction costs, and can also reduce risk through diversification. It also assists in enabling statistical analysis of the creditworthiness of the assets overall and hence a credit rating of the special purpose company's debt.

TYPES OF ISSUE—HOW CAN PROJECTS BE SECURITISED?

The starting point is perhaps to examine the possible ways in which capital market instruments may be issued. Broadly, there are three distinct possibilities:

(i) First, an issue by the company owning the project. Broadly, this would be a straight debt issue supported by the balance sheet of the owning company.
(ii) Secondly, an issue by a company whose sole asset was the relevant individual project. This would effectively be a debt issue with strictly limited recourse to the one particular project.
(iii) Thirdly, several projects could be 'pooled' into one company and the debt issued against the security of the combined projects.

The possibility described in (i) above is really no more nor less than a straight corporate debt issue; it is methods (ii) and (iii) which are of relevance for the purposes of this paper. Structure (iii) would be the project equivalent of a securitisation as described in the preceding section. However, very similar considerations will arise in both (ii) and (iii). The difference in (iii) being that if a number of projects are 'pooled' into one special purpose company, there is a diversification of risk. Thus if one project fails to perform or is nationalised or expropriated, there are still the remaining projects which can give investors their return.

FUNDING IN THE CAPITAL MARKETS

For the borrower and end-users of funds the main intention is likely to be to use the capital markets as an alternative to direct borrowing from banks as a means of obtaining long-term funds at lower cost or to raise finance off balance sheet.[5] A suitable credit rating (discussed below) for a new issue of debt instruments in the current financial environment in Asia must give rise to the possibility of reduced borrowing costs.

Access to one or other of the investor bases that make up the capital markets may be a more viable means of raising finance than seeking project lending from banks. The process of financing in the capital markets is different from borrowing from commercial banks. Bank financing tends towards a process of negotiation of the structure of the project from the point at which the banks become involved in the project, which means the period required to complete the financing may extend over many months. The marketing process in a capital markets issue is more centred on its pricing and investors will not be so directly concerned in the development and operation of the project. Therefore, structuring of the financing package has a more limited purpose, being to produce an investment which will sell at a certain price, and may be achieved more quickly and simply.

Although the market has yet to develop, banks could free up capital presently tied up in backing project debt by repackaging project loans as collateral for issues of securities (in the same way they have securitised their residential mortgage portfolios and other kinds of asset).

ADAPTING TECHNIQUES OF SECURITISATION

Issues arise in relation to financing of an infrastructure project through the capital markets which would not necessarily be the case if bank lending or other sources of funding were used or which require different approaches to the solutions applied in a bank lending.

Marketability Risk

The distinguishing feature of any 'project financing' is that, at least to some extent, lenders and providers of finance will share project risk with sponsors, contractors and others involved in the project. Because of the complex nature of most projects and the inter-relation of the various parties, risk allocation has assumed the dimensions of an art form. Assessing, analysing and allocating risk where part of the lending is provided through the medium of an issue to the public compounds the position still further.

For a project to be considered viable for securitisation the allocation of project risks will need to be considered carefully and everything done to

[5] There may well be other or different reasons e.g. in the recent Nigen refinancing in the UK the cost of borrowing increased but better terms in length of maturity and covenants were obtained—see also 'The Alchemy of Asset Securitisation' (1995) Stanford Journal of Law, Business and Finance.

ensure that the transaction is creditworthy enough to obtain a suitable rating or, at least, market support. The normal project risks will, of course, need to be analyzed, but some areas which will require different treatment as a result of the 'securitised' element of the financing could include the following:

Construction Risk—Financing During Construction

It may be necessary to finance projects through construction before refinancing on the capital markets because of the market's desire to avoid assuming construction risk and to invest in projects only at the stage when they can demonstrate solid cash-producing capabilities. An alternative would be to obtain a sponsor's guarantee pre-completion.[6]

Financing during the construction period of a turnkey project will inevitably require advances of funding on a large number of 'milestone' dates. Therefore, methods may need to be established to allow bonds to be issued on a number of dates throughout construction. The purchase of the relevant securities should on each of the issue dates be fully underwritten by subscribers with the cash resources available.[7] If other sources of funding are also being used, for example bank loans, it may be necessary to ensure that the utilisation of the loan facility and the bond facility remain in proportion throughout the construction period.

Operational Risk

The level of risk assumed by an operator under an operating and maintenance agreement is likely to be limited (and often much less than the level of risk assumed by the contractor under the construction contract). Lenders will look to the track record of the operator and may wish to have their own expert monitoring continuing performance. In certain types of project technology may be important. For example, in respect of a power project, combined cycle gas turbine technology provides proven and efficient technology which can be bought 'off-the-shelf' with low risk of cost overruns and delays.

Lending and security documents are likely to provide for operational responsibilities and the consequence of any failures to comply with such responsibilities. These could produce difficult areas for trustees monitoring compliance.

Currency Risk

Capital markets instruments will usually be denominated in some internationally traded currency, commonly US dollars. Unless the project income

[6] This is what happened in the Subic Bay Power offering, but completion was only a few months away when the issue was launched.

[7] There are examples in Malaysia where this role has been taken on by the Employees Provident Fund—thus combining 'state' funding with the possibility of future refinancing by the private sector.

is at least partially denominated in the same currency (which may be possible, for example, where the purchaser of the project's output has access to export revenues) there is clearly a risk of exchange rate movements reducing the income available to meet the US dollar debt obligations. In some jurisdictions, the availability of foreign currency itself may be uncertain. Governmental commitment may be needed to ensure the viability of a project in such circumstances.

Political Risk

International investors will carefully consider the political risks involved in a project. The most extreme form of political risk is that of expropriation. However, government influence over an infrastructure development is likely to be strong from the outset, since it will have granted the concession or licence to establish the project in the first place. Although the lenders' security over the project assets and contracts may give them the ability to step in and take control of the project in the event of a default, any radical measures such as replacement of the management of the project company may require governmental approval.

This risk could be limited by securitisation of a pool of projects in a number of different jurisdictions. In this respect, it is questionable whether diversification is really achieved where the assets are all based in the same industry and in one country. If, for example, a number of power projects in one country are 'pooled' for securitisation purposes, it is also conceivable that the power purchaser will, for each individual power station, be the same state entity. The much vaunted diversification achieved, for example by US mortgage-backed securities, will not be so easy to achieve in securitisation of infrastructure projects.

Lender Decision-taking

The use of securities to finance a project obviously gives rise to the possibility of the paper ending up in a multitude of hands. This can lead to difficult issues of lender decision-taking, particularly where there are other sources of equal ranking financing, for example, bank lending.

In the case of a project, probably the subject of long-term funding, there may be a number of decisions to be made by lenders. These can range from critical decisions on whether to enforce security in the event of non-payment, to minor issues, perhaps involving technical variations to project documents. Is it really practicable or reasonable to call for a vote by all bondholders on every issue which requires a decision by lenders? On the other hand, subject to the level of its financing involvement, why should a bondholder have less say on these decisions than a bank lender?

In traditional bank financing the covenants are often very tight so that the agent monitoring the project receives early warning of any adverse events and can work with the developer to resolve problems. It may be difficult for an issuer to obtain support in the same way from a disparate group of bondholders. Therefore, the covenants and events of default may be drafted to allow bondholders to participate in these decisions only when substantial issues arise threatening the ability of the project to meet its payment obligations or otherwise materially affecting the bondholders' interests. Certain discretions may be given to the trustee for the bondholders on more minor issues. On more important issues, the need for swift decision making is obviously important and even with tight time limits imposed for obtaining decisions from bondholders, it may take longer to resolve matters than with a bank syndicate, given the need for 14 or 21 days' notice of bondholders' meetings to be given. One possible solution is to subordinate bondholders to banks' decision-making authority, say during the construction period of the project, when the banks' experience of monitoring and ability to react to problems is most likely to come into play.

CREDIT RATINGS FOR DEBT ISSUES

A credible and marketable securitisation may require a rating by a rating agency. Generally, this will be by Standard & Poor's Corporation or Moody's Investors Services. It may be possible, if an issue is to be limited to a local market, for a national rating agency in the relevant country to provide the rating.[8]

The Ratings

A credit rating assesses the ability of an issuer to pay principal and interest on a debt in full and on time. Ratings for most categories of debt range from AAA to D.

AAA indicates that the capacity of the issuer to pay interest and repay principal is extremely strong. This is an assessment which the rating agency will only make if it is convinced that the integrity of the issuer and its cash flow is virtually assured, come what may. It therefore requires from the issuer and its financial advisers detailed cash-flow projections produced on a 'stressed' basis, i.e. on the basis of various near-disaster assumptions. This stressing enables the rating agencies to quantify the amount of capital and liquidity cover they will require to ensure that in the stressed situation the issuer will still be able to pay its way.[8a] It follows that whatever capital and other support the issuer may have must be 'copper-bottomed', not so much

[8] For example, the YTL Power bond issue was rated AA3 by the Rating Agency of Malaysia.

[8a] Oditah, supra, at pp. 85–6, argues that in certain circumstances a rating agency may be liable to investors on the basis of actionable misrepresentation or negligence.

in a liquidation of the issuer (since that is reckoned to be a remote eventuality) but in a liquidation of the provider of capital or other credit enhancement.

AA indicates a very strong capability to pay interest and repay principal and differs from the highest rated issues only to a small degree. As one goes down the scale one passes through various levels of creditworthiness. Debt rated BB and below is often regarded as having predominantly speculative characteristics and, finally, D indicates debt in default.

Criteria Applied in Fixing Ratings

What are the criteria applied by Standard & Poor's and Moody's for rating structured financing? Moody's will take into account the likely level of default and the level of subordination of the debt to be rated as well as the projected likelihood of default. The ranking of the capital markets issue against the rights of other creditors in the financing structure also needs to be considered.

Standard & Poor's rating process concentrates on three components of the financing:

(a) credit analysis, incorporating a review of the assets;
(b) payment analysis, analysing the application of the cash flow or market value derived from the assets; and
(c) legal analysis, relating to accessing and liquidating collateral for the benefit of the holders of the securities.

To quote from a Standard & Poor's publication: 'Unresolved concerns regarding any of these three components can prevent a transaction from being rated'.[9]

How are these criteria applied to projects? A Moody's publication states that 'As these projects are varied and complex transactions with unique characteristics, there are no simple formulae or standardised risk priorities that can be unilaterally applied.'[10] Thus each project is unique and must be analyzed on a case by case basis.

Against that background, it is likely that any rating of a project will be a time consuming and costly undertaking. Consider, for example, the credit analysis of a power station. A special purpose company is likely to be acting as issuer which probably has no real value other than its rights under the project documents and any shareholders' equity. The credit analysis of the transaction requires a review of the structure of the entire project, how project risks are allocated and the credit standing of the parties who are to provide financial support to the project or who otherwise have payment

[9] Standard & Poors 'International Criteria' 1993 p. 1.

[10] Moody's, Op Cit, at p. 8.

obligations in respect of the project. The creditworthiness of a power station project will depend on the availability of a reliable stream of income which will depend on the sale of power to suitable power purchasers.

Necessity

A rating may not be a pre-requisite for marketing an issue of bonds to finance a project.[11] But, a rating will broaden the potential investor base beyond the sophisticated few with the capability themselves to analyse the structure supporting an issue. It will also assist liquidity in the secondary market for the bonds, i.e. the investor's ability to sell. Although no Asian projects have yet been rated by international rating agencies, a recent report from Moody's reinforced the strong rating of six East Asian countries' sovereign credit strength, averaging in the medium investment-grade A rating level.[12] Hence, a project in one of those jurisdictions structured to deal adequately with project risks and which stands up to the analysis referred to above should be capable of gaining an investment-grade credit rating. There is also the possibility of one of the mono-line or other insurers giving their guarantee in support of a project to enhance credit rating. However, in certain countries particular problems clearly remain, such as the lack of developed legal systems and rules.

SECURITIES LAWS AND LISTING REQUIREMENTS

Most jurisdictions in which one would hope to raise finance from investors in securities carefully regulate the marketing and sale of securities.

Offerings of securities will necessarily involve consideration of prospectus laws and the liability (criminal as well as civil) that can attach to an issuer and its directors personally for misrepresentation, misleading information and non-disclosure. The marketing of asset-backed securities will require disclosure in relation to the quality of the underlying assets and the credit enhancement provided rather than the project company itself, which may have a limited financial history to disclose. It may well be necessary to describe project contracts in the prospectus or offering memorandum and a consideration of any applicable confidentiality clauses contained in those documents will be required to ensure their terms can be adequately described.

Application for a listing of the securities on a stock exchange (in the issuer's own jurisdiction where there is a domestic element to the offering or in one or more overseas jurisdictions where the target market is international,

[11] The Subic Power Issue was not rated.

[12] Moody's, Op Cit, p. 9.

or perhaps a combination of both) will often be desirable for marketing purposes. The Luxembourg Stock Exchange (which is often used for international placement) imposes the following general requirements regarding the information contained in the offering circular for an issue seeking a listing in Luxembourg:

'. . . information which, according to the particular nature of the issuer of the securities for the admission of which application has been made, is necessary to enable investors and their investment advisers to make a proper assessment of the assets and liabilities, financial position, profits and losses and prospects of the issuer, and of the rights attached to such security.'[13]

The listing rules of the London Stock Exchange contain specific requirements for new companies established to carry out major capital projects, and which therefore lack the three year trading record normally needed for a listing. In the United States, Rule 144A of the United States Securities Act of 1933, which provides a safe harbour from the registration requirements of the Securities Act for sales to 'qualified institutional buyers', has created significant opportunities for issuers which have not engaged previously in securities offerings in the United States due to the significant disclosure and other requirements of the securities laws applicable to public offerings.[13a]

THE ROLE OF EQUITY

The difficulties of raising equity capital for infrastructure projects through the securities market should not be underestimated, given the nature of the risks to which such projects are exposed, particularly the risks of major cost and time overruns during the construction period when they may not have access to sources of revenue other than the project. Nevertheless, various models may be pointed to as suggesting possible methods of sourcing equity.

Single Purpose Company

A current example from Asia demonstrates a structure which avoids investors taking construction risk. The privatisation of the Electricity Generating Company Limited (EGCO) by the Electricity Generating Authority of Thailand (EGAT) involves the sale of the Rayong combined cycle power plant for US$800 million. This facility is built and supported by a 20 year power purchase agreement with EGAT. EGCO has financed the purchase by selling 51 per cent. of its share capital to domestic and international investors.

[13] Handbook of the Luxembourg Stock Exchange Part II Article 8.

[13a] Rovinescu and Thieffry, supra, at pp. 51–7 examine in detail the applicability of the private placement exemption contained in Rule 144A of the United States Securities Act 1933.

Investment in Sponsor

Funds may be raised by the sponsor itself issuing shares to finance projects either on balance sheet or by means of onward investment in a special purpose company. The revenue and assets of existing businesses shield investors from the risks attached to the project, i.e. this is with recourse financing. To prevent dilution of existing shareholders, it might be appropriate to issue a deferred equity instrument such as a convertible bond. The right of conversion could be made exercisable at the time the project is due to start producing earnings.

As examples of the application of this method, one can point to recent Euroconvertible bond issues launched by Asian companies involved as sponsors in large infrastructure projects, many of which are still in the course of construction. The investors in the bonds may be attracted by the long-term earning potential of the project—a potential which they can tap by exercising the conversion rights attached to the bonds.[14]

Infrastructure Funds

Investment funds have been established to invest in projects in Asia;[15] a variant of this approach is Hopewell Holdings' transfer of an existing portfolio of equity interests in IPPs in China and the Philippines to a new investment company, which has 'securitised' the portfolio through an issue of shares to the public in Hong Kong and elsewhere. This approach does offer a diversification of risk across both different projects and different jurisdictions which echoes the advantages of 'pooling' assets which securitisation techniques traditionally involve.

[14] See for example, the Hutchison Delta Ports Convertible bond issue which was raised to finance Hutchison's port development activities in the PRC.

[15] The demands on sponsors for equity funding have led recently to the launch of funds such as the US$1.2 billion AIG Asian Infrastructure Fund and initial public offerings of shares by companies such as AES China Generating Co. Ltd. (a wholly-owned subsidiary of the AES corporation, one of the largest independent power producers in the United States) and Consolidated Electric Power Asia Limited, which raised HK$5.7 billion to acquire the equity interests of Gordon Wu's Hopewell group in various Independent Power Projects (IPPs) in China and the Philippines.

7

The Nature and Transfer of Rights in Dematerialised and Immobilised Securities

ROY GOODE

INTRODUCTION

Developments in the securities markets

The last thirty years have witnessed dramatic changes in the structure and organization of securities markets. Among the factors which have driven these developments are:

- a huge expansion in the amount of capital sought to be raised on the market
- a desire to promote cross-border investment and trading in securities
- the requirement for an efficient system of distribution among major investors
- the pressure to reduce delay, administrative burdens, risk and expense by curbing the volume and movement of paper (certificates and notes, transfer forms, and the like) and the number of transfers crossing the books of issuers
- the need to eliminate principal risk[1] by developing systems to ensure simultaneous delivery versus payment (DVP).

Among the steps which have been taken to meet these objectives are: the move from direct holdings of investments (that is, holdings direct from the issuer by entry on its registers or possession of bearer securities) to indirect holdings through one or more tiers of custodian; the development of dematerialised (uncertificated) securities in which transfers are effected purely by book-entry (a particular feature of government securities); the immobilisation of internationally traded securities by deposit with the international central securities depositories (ICSDs), Cedel Bank and Morgan Guaranty Brussels (MGB) as operators of Euroclear,[2] and by the issue of permanent global notes instead of individual definitive certificates; and the linkage of

[1] See n. 5, *infra*. [2] See infra, pp. 113–15.

securities transfer systems and funds transfer systems so as to ensure or facilitate DVP.

Risks

Over the past few years central and commercial banks, finance houses and other organizations have worked hard in collaboration to identify the major risks attendant on all this activity.[3] Specific types of risk include country risk, pipeline liquidity risk,[4] settlement risks of different kinds, such as principal risk[5] and replacement cost risk,[6] custody risk[7] and legal risk.[8] Overarching all of these is systemic risk, the risk that failure of a major player will have a domino effect on the market as a whole.

Though something will also be said about custody risk, which is of considerable importance to investors, this paper is primarily devoted to legal risk. Specifically it is concerned with the different types of risk[9] that arise where securities, instead of being recorded in the issuer's books as held in the name of the investor or a pledgee[10] of the investor, are held in the name of the custodian ('first-tier intermediary') with whom they have been deposited by the issuer[11] and credited in the custodian's books to the securities account of the investor or pledgee or of some depositor ('second-tier intermediary') which itself is acting as a custodian for the investor or pledgee.[12] To understand the nature of the problems it is necessary briefly

[3] See, for example, the Group of Thirty study, *Clearance and Settlement in the World's Securities Markets* (March 1989; the two reports by the Bank for International Settlements, *Delivery Versus Payment in Securities Settlement Systems* (September 1992) and *Cross-Border Securities Settlements* (March 1995); and the Euroclear discussion paper *Cross-Border Clearance, Settlement and Custody: Beyond the G30 Recommendations* (June 1993).

[4] The risk arising from delays through gaps between processing cycles of different ICSDs, CSDs and central bank payment systems.

[5] The risk that one party to a securities transaction may perform without reciprocal performance by the other.

[6] The risk of total non-performance of a transaction by one party, leading to a potential failure to realize an anticipated gain and a potential liability to others in a chain.

[7] The risk of loss through the negligence, fraud or insolvency of a custodian or sub-custodian.

[8] The absence of adequate legal rules in a given law jurisdiction to enable interests in securities to be efficiently and effectively acquired, enforced and transferred, and to be protected against the claims of third parties and given priority over other claimants on the insolvency of an issuer or intermediary, or to recognize and enforce such interests where created under the law of another jurisdiction.

[9] See infra, p. 117.

[10] The term 'pledge' is used in a non-technical sense to cover any form of security, possessory or non-possessory, and thus to include charges and mortgages.

[11] 'Deposited' is here used to cover not only the deposit of tangible securities but the holding of intangibles to the credit of a securities account.

[12] For brevity the term 'account-holder' is hereafter used to denote the party to the credit of whose account the security entitlement (see n. 18, *infra*) is held, whether that party holds for itself or for its own customers or by way of pledge. The customer of a second-tier intermediary may itself be an intermediary ('third-tier intermediary') holding for its own customer, and so on. As to the multi-tiered institutional structure of intermediaries see below.

to describe the different classes of security and the institutional structure of custodianship arrangements for securities issued, held and traded internationally.

THE CLASSIFICATION OF SECURITIES AND ITS SIGNIFICANCE

Classification of securities by type

Securities take a variety of forms. Classified by type they consist of debt (bonds and notes), equity (shares and stock), and a variety of hybrids such as debt convertible into equity, convertible warrants and depository receipts.[13]

Classification of securities by mode of transfer

More important for our purposes is the distinction between tangible securities, which are embodied in a negotiable certificate or note and transferable by its manual delivery, and intangible securities, which are not so embodied and are transferable only in the books of the issuer. In English law this classification corresponds exactly to the unregistered/registered classification. This is because a certificate issued in connection with registered securities is not the embodiment of title, merely evidence of title, so that the securities are not themselves transferable or negotiable by delivery of the certificate; such delivery is not effective to transfer legal title or to create a pledge and amounts at most to evidence of an intention to create a non-possessory mortgage or charge. So all registered securities, whether certificated or uncertificated, are considered intangibles in English law, and only unregistered securities represented by a negotiable certificate are tangible. By contrast under American law certificates to registered, as well as unregistered, securities are considered to represent the securities and to provide the holder with an alternative mode of transfer by indorsement and delivery which is effective as between the parties. Accordingly certificated securities are considered in the United States to be tangible, not intangible.

The diminishing importance of tangibility

The distinction between tangible and intangible securities has historically been of fundamental importance, affecting the mode of acquisition and

[13] Depository receipts are documents issued in one country entitling the holder to a given number and type of securities issued in another country. The holder is generally considered to have an equitable proprietary interest in the underlying security, not merely a personal right to delivery or transfer.

transfer of the security,[14] its pledgeability[15] and its legal location.[16] But tangible securities, though readily transferable, enjoy four major disadvantages. First, they entail the issue and physical movement of large quantities of paper, which in recent times grew to such dimensions that it threatened to swamp clearing and settlement systems. Secondly, the certificates and notes are expensive to produce, since they require security printing which incorporates numerous technical features designed to prevent forgery. Thirdly, they are risky, since title passes by manual delivery, so that if the certificates or notes are stolen the thief can pass an overriding title to a bona fide purchaser for value (holder in due course). Fourthly, their *situs*, and therefore the law governing their transfer, is susceptible to constant change, and where they are distributed over a number of jurisdictions a lender wishing to take security over the portfolio as a whole will have to comply with a diversity of national laws, each with its own distinctive perfection requirements and priority rules.

REDUCING PAPER AND ITS MOVEMENT

Two principal measures have been taken to deal with the problem of paper, dematerialisation and immobilisation.

Dematerialisation

The most complete method of eliminating paper is to dematerialise the security completely by having no instruments or certificates issued at all, even in relation to registered securities. The investor merely receives confirmation from the issuer's agent that securities of a stated type and amount have been issued to him. Except in jurisdictions where this method has been made compulsory by law, as in the case of France in relation to issues by public companies, dematerialisation has not in general found favour with investors except in the case of issues by government or other public bodies and has encountered significant legal obstacles in some jurisdictions. Dematerialisation does not by itself affect the direct relationship between investor and issuer.

Immobilisation: the breaking of the link between issuer and investor

An alternative measure, widely used in global trading, is to immobilise tangible securities by depositing them with a custodian on terms which prevent

[14] Delivery of the certificate in the one case, entry on the issuer's register in the other.

[15] In the common law sense of being able to be given in security by delivery of possession.

[16] Relevant in determining the law applicable to a transfer, the grant of a security interest and the priority of competing claims to the security, under conflict of laws rules.

a direct link between issuer and investor or which terminate a direct relationship previously existing and interpose the custodian as a principal, so that the custodian is substituted for the investor as the holder of record and the investor's entitlement is thereafter against the custodian, not the issuer.[17]

Immobilisation may be either compulsory and permanent, as where a new issue is by its terms represented by a single permanent global note lodged with an ICSD as custodian and not exchangeable for definitive certificates, or optional and revocable, as where certificated securities are deposited by the holder with a custodian on terms that they or their equivalent can be withdrawn at any time. In the former case the security is immobilised from the outset and typically remains so; in the latter, it is immobilised only from the time of its deposit by the investor, and any securities withdrawn thereupon become once again transferable *in specie* in the normal way.

A global note may be permanent, semi-permanent or temporary. A permanent global note is one which is deposited on the basis that the investor is not in the normal course of events entitled to have definitive certificates issued to him but merely to have a credit to his securities account with the custodian. It follows that the investor's relationship is solely with the custodian, and any transfers he makes will take place by book entry in the records of the custodian, not in the register of the issue. Further, except in extreme circumstances, such as where the issuer becomes insolvent or the permanent global note otherwise becomes void, the investor will never be able to take his security entitlement[18] in tangible form and will therefore never be able to put himself into a direct relationship with the issuer. A semi-permanent global note gives the investor the option of calling for definitive notes, in which case the global note is recorded as reduced *pro tanto*, but to the extent that this option is not exercised the security remains immobilised.[19] The temporary global note is one that is intended to be held for a limited period[20] and then to be exchanged for definitive notes.

Where securities are issued in certificated form at the outset or a temporary or semi-permanent global note is exchanged for definitive certificates, the investor may either choose to remain the holder of record or deposit the certificates with a custodian upon terms that he may at any time call for

[17] Such a custodian is to be distinguished from one who is a mere bailee, holding certificates to securities in physical safekeeping without replacing the investor on the issuer's register. See infra, p. 112.

[18] The term is taken from Article 8 of the Uniform Commercial Code, which refers to the bundle of rights held by an intermediary for its client as a 'financial asset' and its client's interests in those rights as a 'security entitlement' (section 8–102(a)(9),(19)). These labels are helpful in making it clear that what an account-holder has is not an interest in the underlying security but a sub-interest in the rights held by its intermediary.

[19] The international central securities depositories, Cedel Bank and Euroclear, have announced that they will not in future accept semi-permanent global notes.

[20] Designed to meet legal regulatory requirements.

their specific redelivery (if they are placed in a non-fungible account) or for other certificates of the same type and amount as those deposited (if they are placed in a fungible account). In either case the investor's holding is indirect so long as he maintains the deposit arrangements, but he can reacquire a direct relationship with the issuer by having certificates to bearer securities redelivered to him or certificated registered securities transferred back into his name.

The immobilisation of securities, whether it is permanent or temporary, has both legal and practical effects.

(1) Subject to the terms of the agreement and the applicable law, the investor typically gives up his ownership of the deposited security and becomes an account-holder, acquiring co-ownership of a pool of fungible securities of the same class, with a personal right to have securities of that class and to the value of his entitlement transferred or (if they are not permanently immobilised) to withdraw them in physical form.[21]
(2) So long as the securities are immobilised within the system it is the book-entry recording the investor's entitlement, not the certificates representing them, that constitute the source of his rights.
(3) As a corollary of the second point, transfers are effected through book-entries in the records of the custodian, not by physical delivery of the certificates or entries on the issuer's register.
(4) In determining the applicable law under conflict of laws rules the physical location of the certificates is irrelevant.

All this changes, of course, as regards securities temporarily immobilised if they or their equivalent are later withdrawn from the system, in which case the securities withdrawn revert to their former status.

INSTITUTIONAL STRUCTURES

The global custody network

The structure of relationships set up to accommodate cross-border trading in and custody of securities is complex and only a brief picture can be given here.[22] It is necessary to distinguish arrangements for physical custody of security certificates, in which the custodian is a mere bailee, from arrangements in which the custodian is a fiduciary holding securities or entitlements in its own name but on behalf of customers, recording their interests in its

[21] See further infra, p. 119.
[22] For further details see Fiona Christie and Herdeep Donsanjh, The Practical Elements of Settlement and Custody, infra, chapter 8.

books[23] and clearing and settling trades through its own or an external clearing system. As pointed out above, the ICSDs do not themselves hold physical custody of certificates or notes but control them through custody by their local depositories, who may in turn deposit them with the local CSD.

The present paper is concerned with physical custodians only to the extent of legal issues arising where paper they hold is lost or improperly disposed of. Our primary focus is on the fiduciary role of custodians and in particular the nature of the customer's security entitlement in relation to the custodian with which he has his account. Such an entitlement is typically reflected in a fungible account, in which the custodian is under no duty to deliver or redeliver the identical securities received from or for the customer but can deliver securities of the same issue, and the account is an omnibus account which does not identify certificate numbers or differentiate between one customer's holding and that of another. Though the custodian is accountable to its customer for securities received from or for the customer, it will not necessarily have physical custody of the certificates to the securities in question.

A global custodian[24] will normally hold securities it receives in an omnibus customer account and will deposit certificates to securities issued in or denominated in the currency of other countries with its appointed subcustodians located in those countries and having specialised storage facilities. The principal players (banks, brokers, etc.) in a particular country will be members of and maintain securities accounts with a central depository institution (CSD) and transfers among members will be effected by book entry through the books of the CSD, which will usually act also as the clearing house for clearance and settlement of trades.

Euroclear and Cedel Bank

Euroclear is a clearance and settlement system purchased from its creator, Morgan Guaranty, by an English company (itself controlled by some of the system participants), licensed to a Belgian co-operative owned by the English company and most of the participants and operated on its behalf by MGB.[25] The rights of depositors are governed by Belgian Royal Decree

[23] Article 8 of the Uniform Commercial Code makes this distinction clear by referring to fiduciary custodians as securities intermediaries, 'securities intermediary' being defined in s. 8–102(14) as (i) a clearing corporation or (ii) a person, including a bank or broker, that in the ordinary course of its business maintains securities accounts for others and is acting in that capacity.

[24] Which in the context of this paper denotes a bank or other organization offering custody services in relation to investments originating and traded or settled not just in its own country but in other major markets around the world.

[25] To make clear which system is under discussion future references are to Euroclear. However, it should be borne in mind that in relation to Euroclear account-holders MGB acts

No. 62 made in 1967 and amended in 1995. Cedel Bank is an independent clearance and settlement system, established by the market for the market, owned by market participants and incorporated in Luxembourg. The rights of depositors are governed by the laws and Grand-Ducal Decrees of Luxembourg, and in particular by a decree made in 1971 and amended in 1994.

The ICSDs were initially set up to provide a clearance and settlement system for dealings in Eurobonds but now accept a wide diversity of both Euro-instruments and domestic securities. The main functions of the ICSDs are to provide a clearance and settlement system for securities and cash, to collect payments of interest, dividends and redemptions, to facilitate lending and borrowing and repurchase arrangements between participants and to arrange for custody of securities. Neither of the ICSDs holds physical custody of securities deposited with it. Global notes are lodged with a common depository of the two ICSDs, definitive notes and other certificates by each ICSD with one of its specialised depositories, generally located in the country in whose currency the notes or certificates are denominated or in which the issuer is located, who may in turn deposit them with a local CSD.

Transfers between participants of a particular ICSD are effected by entry in the books of that ICSD; transfers between a participant of one ICSD and a participant of the other are effected over the 'bridge' linking the two systems. Securities are received into an ICSD system by deposit through the ICSD's local depository for the particular security. Transfers to counterparties outside the system are carried out, in the case of tangible securities, by mailing or other delivery to the participant's designated securities intermediary via the ICSD's depository link in the domestic market or, in the case of intangible securities, by transfers through that link. The ICSDs also receive deposits of certificated securities[26] and cash from depositors and arrange deliveries to buyers.

Chain of entitlements and the multi-tiering of intermediaries and security entitlements

The relationships between the various parties engaged in trade in an international issue can be viewed from opposite ends of the chain: from the issuer through the various tiers of intermediary to the ultimate investor and from the ultimate investor back through the different intermediaries to the issuer. This can best be illustrated by two examples, a new international

as principal, and their entitlements are against MGB, not against the English company or the Belgian co-operative.

[26] Neither Euroclear nor Cedel hold dematerialised securities directly from the issuer, though both have accounts with particular national clearing systems who themselves hold such securities.

issue in which the issuer deposits a permanent global note with the two ICSDs to be held in agreed proportions with a common depository, and a receipt into an ICSD or other depository of securities already in issue.

In the case of the new issue, participants pay for their participation through their account with their ICSD, which transfers funds to the lead manager for payment through the common depository against delivery of the global note. The ICSDs are the sole holders of record in the books of the issuer and in the ordinary way no investor will ever come into a direct relationship with the issuer or have a direct claim on the issuer. Since the global note which represents the underlying security is permanently immobilised, customers of the ICSD cannot normally acquire definitive notes or procure physical delivery; their interest takes the form of a securities entitlement against their ICSD, with associated rights to dividends, interest, redemption payments, etc. It is not an entitlement to a specific security from the issuer but a right to share *pro rata* in the pool of fungible rights in the issue held by the ICSD. But a customer, in addition to taking an allotment for itself, may also hold for clients of its own, typically in a fungible or omnibus account for clients collectively, without segregation as between one client and another. Alternatively the customer, having initially bought on its own account, may sell the whole or part of its interest to a client. In either event the customer of the ICSD holds for its clients, and each client's relationship will be only with that intermediary (i.e. with the customer of the ICSD), not with the first-tier intermediary (the ICSD) or with the issuer. Not uncommonly there are lower tiers of intermediary and client.

Looked at from the other end of the chain, an investor holds securities through an omnibus account with his bank, a global custodian, and his rights are against that bank, not against the issuer. The global custodian will in turn hold accounts with its sub-custodians in different countries, and they will be account-holders with their local CSDs. Some CSDs have a direct relationship with an ICSD. In other cases the ICSD's relationship with a local CSD will be indirect, i.e. through a local bank which is a member of the CSD. Each account-holder's relationship is solely with the intermediary with whom his account is maintained.

Let us suppose that an ICSD is holding a permanent global note issued by I and that A Bank is a customer of the ICSD and has acquired a five per cent participation in the issue represented by the global note, of which one per cent is acquired for itself and the rest for its customers, including B Broker, who has in turn placed an order on behalf of its client, C. The ICSD is the first-tier intermediary, standing between the issuer and the primary investor, and A Bank's rights in relation to the ICSD can conveniently be described as a first-tier entitlement. A Bank is the second-tier intermediary and B Broker's rights in relation to A Bank constitute a second-tier entitlement. B Broker is the third-tier intermediary and C holds a third-tier entitlement.

LEGAL ISSUES

A critical question, which we shall address shortly, is the nature of each entitlement, and whether either of the lower-tier entitlements is to be considered original or to be considered derived from, or carved out of, the entitlement immediately above it.[27] But first it is necessary to devote a few words to the concept of fungibility.

Fungibility

A securities account in the name of an investor may be fungible or non-fungible. Property is fungible when any unit of it is considered interchangeable with any other unit for the purpose of delivery or transfer obligations. Whether property is fungible depends not on its physical characteristics but on the nature of the obligation owed with respect to it. If the depositee is not obliged to return the deposited property *in specie* but has the right to deliver its equivalent in type and number or amount the asset is fungible. Such a right is typically conferred by contract but may also be given by national legislation, as in the case of the Decrees governing Cedel Bank and Euroclear. If the depositee has to return the very same item deposited with him it is non-fungible. Securities are usually fungible if forming part of the same issue or of another issue made on identical terms.

The division between fungible and non-fungible entitlements is not the same as that between purely contractual and proprietary rights. There are fungibles and fungibles. In terms of pure exchangeability the deposit of securities in a fungible securities account is conceptually indistinguishable from the deposit of money with a bank. In either case the depositee is free to use the specific items deposited (securities, notes and coin) as its own, its obligation being merely to redeliver an equivalent type (securities) or amount (money). But whereas the depositor of money has a purely contractual claim, there being no obligation on a bank to segregate deposited funds for customers either individually or collectively, the custodian of securities in a fungible account will typically[28] be required by the deposit agreement or by law to hold the pool of securities of that type for all interested depositors collectively, whether by way of trust (as in England) or under some other legal regime which confers on depositors co-ownership rights (as in Belgium and Luxembourg). The distinction is of great importance in the event of insolvency of the custodian, for the depositor of money will be a mere unsecured creditor (though in some legal systems having priority rights), whereas the depositor of securities will have co-ownership rights and

[27] See infra, p. 121. [28] But see infra, p. 119.

the securities will not form part of the custodian's assets available for distribution among its creditors.

Tangible securities may be fungible or non-fungible. The position of intangible securities[29] is less straightforward. Where they are unnumbered they are clearly fungible, there being nothing to distinguish one unit from another. The same applies where, though numbered, they have been made fungible by contract (e.g. by agreement to credit them to a fungible account) or statute. The situation regarding numbered intangible securities which have not been made fungible by contract or statute is not so clear. Being intangible they are not capable of physical segregation, so that in principle one unit is the equivalent of any other unit, and a person who agrees to transfer securities bearing numbers different from those he actually holds is considered to have agreed to make the transfer from units of the numbers he does hold. But though intangible securities cannot be physically identified, their numbering could facilitate a tracing claim. For example, if a custodian, D, holds shares numbered 1–50 for A and shares 51–100 for B and without authority purports to transfer shares 51–100, then though these have no physical manifestation we can say that the transfer shows an intention to dispose of B's holding rather than A's. In other words, as has been aptly pointed out, though intangibles may not be capable of identification in the physical sense they *are* capable of allocation.[30] Securities traded internationally are usually fungible; indeed, Euroclear, unlike Cedel Bank, does not open non-fungible accounts. Cedel Bank treats all securities as fungible unless otherwise instructed by the customer.

The position of the indirect holder

Even a direct holder of securities carries the risk of insolvency of the issuer[31] but at least he possesses or controls the securities and associated rights. An indirect holder carries a triple risk: the inability to enforce rights directly against the issuer where the custodian is the holder of record and is unable or unwilling to do so on his behalf; the insolvency of the custodian,[32] to the

[29] I.e. registered (and in the US, uncertificated) securities.

[30] See Joanna Benjamin, 'Custody—An English Law Analysis' [1994] IBFL 188, which contains a penetrating analysis of the problem. It should be noted that 'unnumbering' of securities is a precondition of London listing.

[31] This is, of course, reduced to the extent that the issue is secured.

[32] The insolvency of the *issuer* is of little moment for our purposes, for this affects first-tier and lower-tier intermediaries alike. The main concern of lower-tier holders will be to acquire direct rights against the issuer—particularly in relation to proof of debt and to voting at meetings of creditors, including creditors engaged in a work-out—without being dependent on their custodian's co-operation. As regards securities which are not permanently immobilised the account-holder can surmount this problem by requiring the delivery or transfer to him of securities equivalent to those he deposited, thus reacquiring a direct relationship against the issuer. In the case of securities permanently immobilised in the form of a global note the

extent of any deficiency in the pool of securities available to account-holders; and the loss of securities held by the custodian in circumstances where it is able to disclaim responsibility for the loss.[33]

As regards permanent global notes, the right of direct enforcement, so far as not given by the applicable law,[34] can be taken care of in various ways: by provisions in the trust deed (where there is one) executed by the issuer; by an irrevocable deed of covenant executed by the issuer at the time of issue of the global note by which, in the event of the permanent global note becoming void, account-holders acquire direct rights against the issuer;[35] and by provisions in the global note itself entitling the custodian to exchange it for definitive certificates in stated events, such as an event of default.[36] In the absence of such an event the account-holder relies on the contractual duties assumed by the custodian to perform services on his behalf, such as collecting and crediting dividends, interest and redemption moneys, exercising voting rights, and the like.

For protection against insolvency of the custodian the account-holder (investor or secured creditor) needs assurance that the law will recognize the priority of his entitlement over the claims of the custodian's general creditors. Specifically the investor or secured creditor needs to know that securities in the hands of the custodian for his account will not be available to the custodian's own creditors but will be held for him to the extent of his interest or, if securities or moneys have been lost, proportionate to his interest.

This raises a number of potentially difficult questions. First, what is the subject-matter of the account-holder's entitlement? In particular, is it a proprietary right which can be asserted against the custodian's trustee or liquidator or the purely personal right of an unsecured creditor? Secondly, where the account holder seeks to rely on the right as proprietary, and in particular where he claims the status of a pledgee or other secured creditor, has he taken all necessary steps to perfect his interest under the applicable law and preserve its priority against other claimants, including a trustee in bankruptcy or liquidator? Thirdly, what law is to be applied to determine the first two questions? Fourthly, what is the effect of mandatory perfection requirements under the law of another State having a claim to regulate perfection, for example, the State in which the grantor of a security interest is incorporated? Finally, where the custodian has itself deposited the securities

account-holder can enforce rights direct against the issuer only if he can invoke a deed poll or agreement of the issuer or rules of the applicable law giving direct rights. See *infra*, p. 125 et seq.

[33] As where the security has ben lost or stolen by a sub-custodian for whose acts the custodian has effectively exempted itself from liability by the terms of the custody agreement. In England, exemption clauses in standard-term custody agreements depend for their efficacy on satisfying the requirement of reasonableness under s. 3 of the Unfair Contract Terms Act 1977.

[34] That is, the *lex societatis* of the issuer. See infra, p. 124.

[35] This is enforceable in English law because the deed is a deed poll, that is, a deed not made between or confined to particular parties.

[36] However, only the custodian could enforce this provision.

with a sub-custodian who becomes insolvent or causes loss of the securities through negligence or fraud, does the loss fall on the custodian or the account-holder, and what law governs this question?

In analysing these questions it is helpful to take separately the position of first-tier entitlements and lower-tier entitlements.

Possible characterisations of the first-tier entitlements

Where securities are deposited in an account with a first-tier securities intermediary there are at least three different ways in which the applicable law[37] might characterize the account-holder's entitlement:

(1) *As a mere personal right to the transfer or (in the case of tangible securities, delivery) of securities of the same type and value*

This, of course, would be disastrous for the account-holder. Yet it is a risk in jurisdictions (particularly civil law jurisdictions) which have not modernized their law. For example, many civil law jurisdictions do not possess the trust institution, insist on specificity or segregation of assets as a condition of ownership or security and do not recognize co-ownership of, or security interest in, pools of fungible assets. In these countries account-holders and pledgees may be at risk in the absence of appropriate legislation.[38] Several civil law jurisdictions have in fact provided co-ownership rights by statute.[39]

(2) *As continuing ownership of the deposited securities*

Under English law this is the case where the securities are deposited in a non-fungible account, so that the intermediary is under a duty to return them *in specie* and is thus a mere bailee of the deposited notes or certificates. However, if the securities are intangible securities registered in the name of the intermediary legal title will be in the intermediary and the account-holder will be an indirect holder having merely equitable ownership, whilst if the securities are bearer securities the location of the legal title will depend on the intention of the parties. In practice, most accounts in relation to internationally-traded securities are fungible accounts, and this will be assumed in what follows.

(3) *As a combination of personal rights and co-ownership of a pool of fungible securities*

The theory here is that all deposited securities of a given issue are fungible, so that the depositor transfers ownership of the particular securities to the intermediary and acquires in their place a personal right to the delivery or transfer of their equivalent in class and value and co-ownership of the pool of fungible securities held at any given time by the intermediary as

[37] See infra, p. 123.
[38] See generally Philip R. Wood, *Comparative Law of Securities and Guarantees*, Chapter 6.
[39] See generally Wood, *op. cit.*

custodian. How that co-ownership is characterized in different legal systems (beneficial ownership under a trust, legal ownership, etc.) is generally of no great significance in itself;[40] what matters is that the rights are proprietary in character and that the securities pool is not available to general creditors of the custodian. This is the position under Belgian law in relation to Euroclear[41] and under Luxembourg law in relation to Cedel Bank[42] and is the principle established in the newly revised Article 8 of the Uniform Commercial Code.

English law has no difficulty with the co-ownership concept so long as it forms an express or implied term of the contract with the custodian[43] or alternatively is established by a trust in favour of the account-holder. There is no problem of lack of ascertainment of the subject-matter, and no need for physical segregation, since what the account-holder acquires by the agreement is not an interest in unidentified securities forming an unsegregated part of a bulk of securities but co-ownership of, or (in the case of security) a security interest in, the entire bulk.[44] The position is otherwise where the depositor makes an unconditional transfer of ownership to the custodian and stipulates merely for a right to delivery or transfer to him of their equivalent in type and amount at a later date without any express or implied agreement for, or trust, of a share in the pool of deposited securities. In such a case he is a mere unsecured creditor, in just the same way as the depositor of money with a bank. The right to call for delivery or transfer is a mere personal contractual right, not a proprietary right, for that is the bargain.[45] In the case of bearer securities an undertaking by the depositary to hold for the account-holder a given number and value forming part of the total holding would fail for lack of ascertainment of the subject-matter in much the same way as in the case of an agreement for sale of an undivided part of a bulk of goods.[46] This is not so in the case of registered securities, since these are incapable of physical segregation.[47]

Similar considerations apply to a security interest. Under English law this

[40] For a brief discussion of what would appear to be the characterization in English law, see infra, p. 125.

[41] Royal Decree No. 62 dated November 10 1967, as amended by Act dated April 7 1995.

[42] Grand-Ducal decree dated February 17 1971, as amended by decree dated June 8 1994.

[43] Such a term will be readily implied from market usage.

[44] However, rights in security which is permanently immobilised through the deposit of permanent global notes or certificates possess distinctive features which appear to have no complete equivalent in English law. See infra, p. 125.

[45] Indeed, the right could not be characterised as proprietary even in equity, for the subject-matter is an interest not in the entire pool but in an unascertained part of the pool, so that there is no identified asset to which an equitable interest could attach. The position of the prepaying buyer of part of a bulk of *goods* has now changed and he is recognized as a co-owner under ss. 20A and 20B of the Sale of Goods Act 1979.

[46] *Re Wait* [1927] 1 Ch. 606. But in the case of the prepaying buyer the position is now otherwise. See Sale of Goods Act 1979, ss. 20A, 20B.

[47] See supra, p. 109.

can be created by agreement or trust relating to a fund of intangibles and is effective against the trustee or liquidator of the party granting the security interest so long as any applicable perfection requirements have been fulfilled.[48]

The nature of lower-tier entitlements

Let us go back to our chain of I (issuer)–ICSD–A Bank–B Broker. The first question to consider is whether the first-tier entitlement, namely that held by A Bank in relation to the ICSD, is proprietary or purely contractual in character; the second, whether the lower-tier entitlement is original or derivative, that is to say, whether its content is determined independently of the nature and quantum of the interest held by the securities intermediary with which the account is held or is derived from and a sub-set of the intermediary's own rights against the higher-tier intermediary with which *its* account is held. There are several different possibilities, depending on the legal regime applicable.

Let us assume in the first place that A Bank's rights against the ICSD are purely personal (contractual). We know that this is not the case as regards Cedel Bank under Luxembourg law or Euroclear under Belgian law, but we might hypothesize another ICSD governed by a different law under which the rights might be purely contractual. In that case it is obvious that B Broker cannot have proprietary rights in any part of the pool of securities held by the ICSD. At best it is the beneficial owner (e.g. under a trust or similar device) of A Bank's contractual rights against the ICSD, which would protect it against the creditors of A Bank on A Bank's insolvency but not against creditors of the ICSD if it were to become insolvent. But in jurisdictions which do not possess the trust concept B Broker might be no more than an unsecured creditor of A Bank.[49]

Our alternative assumption is that A Bank is co-owner of the pool of securities held by the ICSD.[50] It does not follow that B Broker's rights against A Bank (on the assumption that A Bank purchased part of its participation for B Broker) are themselves proprietary in character. That depends on the terms of the agreement between B Broker and A Bank and on the law governing the proprietary effects (if any) of that agreement. It is

[48] In relation to a security interest given by a company, see infra, p. 128. A security interest given by an individual or partnership firm over intangibles is not in general registrable except where constituting a general assignment of book debts.

[49] It will, of course, be borne in mind that B Broker is not a money creditor; his only entitlement is to a co-ownership interest in whatever part of A Bank's participation is held for A Bank's customers, including B Broker. If that participation loses value, as where the issuer goes into liquidation with insufficient assets to meet the claims of unsecured creditors, B Broker will have no claim on A Bank beyond a proportionate share of any dividend A Bank might receive in the liquidation.

[50] For brevity, co-ownership is used to include security interests.

perfectly possible to envisage a legal scenario in which B Broker has a purely contractual right to the portion of the issue acquired by A Bank in accordance with B Broker's instructions. In market terms such a result would be highly undesirable, since it leaves B Broker to bear the risk of A Bank's insolvency.[51] The needs of the market require that B Broker's entitlement should be treated as proprietary in character. That could be done by giving him direct proprietary rights against the ICSD. But that solution would breach another market requirement, namely that each account-holder's relationship should be confined to the intermediary with which the account is held. The only way in which both market needs can be meet is by characterising B Broker's interest as a derivative interest of the same character as the interest from which it is derived. In other words, B Broker would be co-owner with other account-holders of A Bank of such part of A Bank's participation as can be shown to have been acquired on their behalf. So A Bank would have a five per cent co-ownership interest in the pool of securities held by the ICSD, and B Broker and other account-holders of A Bank would be co-owners of the 80 per cent of A Bank's participation acquired by A Bank on their behalf.[52] Moreover, if lower-tier interests are characterized as derivative then it follows that (a) their value cannot exceed a due proportion of the recoverable value of the issued securities;[53] (b) transfers of or security rights over higher-tier interests which are effective under the law applicable to them are binding on the holders of lower-tier interests;[54] and (c) no holder of an interest can have rights to securities greater than those possessed by the holder of the higher-tier interest from which the former interest is derived.

So far we have assumed that the custodian itself holds a security entitlement sufficient to cover the security entitlements it has agreed to give its own customers. To the extent of any shortfall the security entitlements of those customers abate proportionately, though their personal rights remain unaffected. If the custodian has purported to credit its customers with an entitlement from an interest it has not itself yet acquired, their rights will necessarily be purely personal until such acquisition.

[51] It is also theoretically possible that B Broker could be treated as beneficial owner of A Bank's contractual rights against the ICSD, as under the first hypothesis. But a legal system which is willing to treat B Broker as having a proprietary interest in A Bank's contractual entitlements is unlikely to find any great difficulty in going the whole hog and treating B Broker as having a derivative proprietary interest.

[52] See, for example, UCC s. 8–503.

[53] See n. 49, *supra*.

[54] So in principle if a custodian sells or pledges its securities entitlement the sale or pledge will override the sub-interests of its account-holders in that entitlement. See, for example, UCC s. 8–511, which, however, makes the priority of the purchaser or pledgee dependent on his acquiring control of the entitlement.

The applicable law

In order for the account-holder or secured creditor to form a view as to whether he is adequately protected by the legal regime governing his entitlements it is first necessary to determine what law applies. This is controlled by the conflict of laws rules of the forum. For dealings in movable property English courts, in common with those of many other jurisdictions, apply the *lex situs*. However, in an extremely interesting and well-reasoned judgment Mr. Justice Millett (as he then was) held that whether the securities are tangible (i.e. bearer securities) or intangible, the applicable law is the *lex loci actus*, the place where the transfer is effected.[55]

In the case of tangible securities it is important to bear in mind that what is relevant is not their tangible character as such but the manner in which a transfer of them is effected. While they are immobilised in the vaults of a custodian and transfers are effected by book entry, the location of the certificates is irrelevant, for the transfer has not been effected by physical delivery but by book entry, and whether one applies the *lex situs* or the *lex loci actus* the applicable law is that of the place where the entry is made.[56] This approach corresponds closely with the terms of the recently revised Belgian decree governing the Euroclear operations, which make it clear that the decree applies, and the interest in securities (as defined by Belgian law) held by Euroclear, is to be considered located in Belgium, even if the certificates representing the securities are physically held by sub-custodians outside Belgium.[57] But if the custodian or sub-custodian of securities that are tangible under the law of the issuer's incorporation were to transfer them by physical delivery outside the ICSD system, the effect of the transfer would be governed by the place of delivery, which is the same as the location of the certificates at the time of delivery. The legal regime for Cedel Bank contains corresponding legislation stating that the *lex situs* of securities deposited with Cedel Bank is Luxembourg law, irrespective whether such securities have been deposited in a location outside Luxembourg.[58]

It is also necessary to treat each level of interest separately. Each tier of intermediary holds a bundle of intangible rights for its own customer and each bundle of rights represents a distinct interest. This follows from the fact that the book-entry entitlement of any customer features only in the records of its own intermediary, not in the records of higher-tier or

[55] *Macmillan Inc. v. Bishopsgate Investment Trust plc* (*No. 3*) [1995] 3 All ER 747, pointing out that in the case of shares the *lex loci actus* and the *lex situs* would almost always be the same. But the Court of Appeal (Unreported, November 2, 1995) held that the applicable law was the *lex situs*, which was taken to be the law of the place of the issuer's incorporation.

[56] *Macmillan Inc. v. Bishopsgate Investment Trust plc* (*No. 3*), *supra*. However, the place of the record, though perfectly satisfactory in that case as the determinant of the applicable law, is not necessarily a satisfactory criterion. See *infra*, p. 124.

[57] Royal Decree No. 62, art. 10.

[58] Grand-Ducal decree of February 17 1971, art. 8(3).

lower-tier intermediaries. So first-tier interests would be governed (according to the theory adopted) by the *lex situs* of that interest or the law of the place of its transfer.

We have noted that in the *Macmillan* case the applicable law for book-entry transfers was held, at first instance to be the *lex loci actus* and, on appeal, the *lex situs*. The *lex loci actus* does, indeed, appear to have much to commend it, since it looks at the way in which the transfer is effected rather than the nature of the security transferred and can thus be applied whether the securities are tangible or intangible and, in the case of tangible securities, whether the transfer is effected by physical delivery or by book entry. It also avoids the need to ascribe an artificial *situs* to the intangible securities. However, it suffers the serious disadvantage that in the case of an intermediary with an international network of branches or offices connected by a computer network the place of record of an entitlement or transfer may be quite arbitrary so far as the account-holder is concerned, and, indeed, may change from time to time, with consequent uncertainty as to the applicable law governing any particular transaction. Further, the rights of different account-holders might be governed by different laws. There is therefore much to be said for discarding both the *lex situs* and the *lex loci actus* as the law applicable to book-entry transfers and substituting the law of the intermediary's place of incorporation, or alternatively the law of the place where it has its seat.[59]

It is a generally accepted principle of the conflict of laws that the nature of a security issued by a company, including the question whether it is to be characterized as tangible (and thus transferable by mere delivery) or intangible, is governed by the *lex societatis*.[60] So if share certificates relating to registered shares issued by a New York company are deposited with a bank in London by way of pledge, an English court, applying New York law to characterize the transferability of the shares, will recognize the effectiveness of the pledge even though under English law registered shares are incapable of pledge. Conversely, if certificates to registered shares or bonds issued in England are pledged with a bank in New York, one might expect New York courts to apply English law to determine the character of the shares or bonds and thus to conclude that they are incapable of pledge.[61]

[59] The latter has the advantage that it could be applied equally to unincorporated partnerships.

[60] See Hans van Houtte, 'The Law Applicable to Securities Transactions: Choice of Law Issues,' supra, pp. 69–70.

[61] The deposit of the certificates might, of course, show an intention to create some other form of security,. such as a mortgage or charge. That would be a dealing off the register not dependent on whether the security was tangible or intangible and its effect would, it is thought, be governed by New York law.

Characterization of the account-holder's rights under English law

It has previously been remarked that English law fully recognizes the ability of parties to provide, by contract or trust, for co-ownership rights in a pool of fungible intangibles. It is not without interest to consider how English law would characterize the account-holder's co-ownership rights. American writers have wisely cautioned against attempts to fit this new form of security entitlement into a Procrustean bed of existing property concepts. But analogies, even if inexact, can help us to get a better picture of the nature of the bundle of rights under discussion.

As we have seen, the effect of immobilising a security is, in the case of the permanent global note, to shut out any direct link between issuer and investor and, in the case of securities issued in the normal way and later deposited by the investor with a custodian,[62] to suspend that link until such time as the deposited securities or their equivalent, if tangible, are physically returned to the investor or, if intangible, are retransferred into his name in the issuer's books. Until then the custodian is the legal holder of the securities by virtue of its possession or entry on the issuer's register. Moreover, the account-holder does not have even an equitable interest *in specie* in the deposited securities. What he does have is a co-ownership interest (or if merely a secured creditor, a security interest) in the pool or fund of securities of the same issue held by the custodian. So in English law the custodian is a trustee of a trust fund of security entitlements represented by the pool of securities of a given issue in its hands at any one time, and the account-holders have beneficial interests in that trust fund, though not in any particular securities from time to time comprised in it. Hence we can say that their position is in most respects the same as that of beneficiaries under any ordinary trust which is not simply a bare trust of specific assets. The only significant distinction between the trust created by the immobilisation arrangements and the normal fully active trust is that the custodian does not necessarily have (and in the case of the ICSDs does not in fact have) discretionary management powers. As under an ordinary trust, the account-holders do not have direct rights against issuers of investments held by the custodian; their entitlements subsist purely against the custodian itself.

There is a unitized equivalent of this in the United Kingdom securities market in the shape of the unit trust. The investor is co-owner of units in a portfolio of investments held by the trustees but has no relationship with the issuers of the securities. The only differences are that the entitlements are unitized rather than being expressed as amounts or proportions of a total fund and the unit trust is actively managed on behalf of the trustees rather than being a pure custody arrangement.

62 The word 'deposit' is here used to cover not only the physical deposit of tangible securities but the transfer into the custodian's name of intangible securities.

Second-tier interests can be regarded as sub-trusts derived from the trust for first-tier account-holders. That is, the second-tier intermediary holds his trust interest on a sub-trust for his own customers to the extent of their entitlements. The layering of custodians and interests thus produces a hierarchy of trusts, each lower-tier beneficial interest being an interest in a sub-fund derived from the fund or sub-fund above it. It is thus possible, applying equitable tracing rules or (preferably) those laid down by legislation, for the collective proprietary interest of the lowest-tier account-holders to be traced up the chain, though only through his own custodian (and then only where the latter agrees or is bound by contract or the applicable law to enforce his own entitlement for the benefit of the account-holders collectively to the extent of their interests) or alternatively by direct action against the issuer or a higher-tier intermediary where this is given by deed poll, contract or the applicable law. Of course, such tracing rights do not relate to specific assets, only to the fund or sub-fund from which the account-holders' own interests are derived.

The nature of interests derived from an issue represented by a permanent global note requires special mention. These can be equated with the interests of beneficiaries under a trust of a pool of non-assignable debts.[63] What such beneficiaries acquire is not a right to the debts themselves but a right to the sums received by the assignor from the debtor.[64] So also with account-holders in relation to the fund of securities held for them by their custodian. They have no claims against the issuer or a higher-tier intermediary but are entitled to the fruits of the securities entitlement coming into the hands of their custodian, that is, interest, dividends and redemption moneys paid to the custodian by the issuer or by the custodian's own intermediary.

The importance of the co-ownership concept

It has been recognized for some time that to treat the account-holder as the continuing owner of rights in specific securities deposited rather than as co-owner of a pool of intangible fungibles would seriously undermine the flexibility and efficiency of the market. In the first place, each account holder's securities have to be dealt with on an individual basis. Secondly, where the deposited securities were tangibles they would be considered located where they were physically situated, and dealings in them across the books of the custodian would in principle be ineffective unless effected in conformity

[63] That is, debts which by the terms of the contract giving them birth cannot be assigned so as to bring the debtor into a relationship with the assignee or otherwise require the debtor to recognize the assignee's interest.

[64] See *Re Turcan* (1886) 40 ChD 5; R.M. Goode, 'Inalienable Rights?' (1979) 42 MLR 553 in an analysis broadly endorsed by Lord Browne-Wilkinson in *Linden Gardens Trust Ltd. v. Lenesta Sludge Disposals Ltd.* [1994] 1 AC 85.

with the *lex situs*, which itself would change with each movement of the paper from one country to another.

A modern law for dealing and settlement of international securities, and indeed of domestic securities held indirectly through an intermediary, requires:

(1) that the deposit of the securities converts the holder's rights from ownership of the deposited securities into co-ownership of (or in the case of a pledge) a security interest in the pool of securities of the same issue held by the custodian;
(2) that the co-ownership rights or security interests created and perfected in conformity with the *lex societatis* of the custodian maintaining the accounts should be respected in the event of the custodian's insolvency and should not form part of the custodian's assets available for its creditors.

These requirements are satisfied under Belgian law as regards deposits with Euroclear and under Luxembourg law as regards deposits with Cedel Bank. In each of the two jurisdictions the relevant law is expressed to apply even in relation to securities deposited with sub-custodians outside that jurisdiction. Both Belgian and Luxembourg law also provide for the creation of a book-entry pledge without the need to comply with the formalities prescribed by the general law governing pledges of securities. However, Belgian law and Luxembourg law are restricted in scope compared with the new Article 8 of the American Uniform Commercial Code. In particular:

(1) they do not provide for the acquisition of direct rights against the issuer[65] in the event of the issuer's insolvency or default or the failure of the ICSD—these have to be secured by other means noted earlier;
(2) they deal only with relations between the ICSD and its own account-holders, and between pledgor and pledgee as regards securities in a pledged account, not with the rights of customers of lower-tier intermediaries (other than banks and national CSDs in the two countries) or the effect on those rights of dealings by higher-tier intermediaries.

The new Article 8

The revised Article 8 is concerned with deposits of domestic rather than international securities but it has much to offer to other national legal systems, since it covers all tiers of intermediary and makes express provision for the intermediary to act in accordance with the account-holder's instructions in exercising the corporate and other rights following from the

[65] Indeed, they could not effectively provide for direct rights against an issuer outside Belgium or Luxembourg (as the case may be), for the availability of such rights is governed by the issuer's law and the terms of the issue.

security or alternatively to place the account-holder in a position to exercise the rights directly.[66] Article 8 and conforming amendments to Article 9 also contain detailed conflict of laws provisions[67] which broadly track those outlined above.

Overriding law of another jurisdiction

Conflict of laws rules routing the selection of the applicable law to the country of the intermediary's records do not guarantee recognition and enforceability of interests created and perfected in conformity with that country's laws, because transfers may still fall foul of additional perfection requirements imposed by the laws of another country. For example, where a security interest created by a company incorporated in England falls within one of the registrable categories listed in section 396 of the Companies Act 1985 then under section 395 it is void against a liquidator and creditors of the company if not so registered, and this is so even as regards security over assets situated outside the United Kingdom. Such a requirement is plainly mandatory, for by its terms it operates irrespective of the *situs* of the asset and is therefore not displaced by a foreign *lex situs*.

Fortunately co-ownership and security interests in deposited securities will not normally fall within any registrable category. The only possible candidates are charges over book debts and floating charges. It is considered that securities held by a company are not book debts of the company.[68] Pledges of securities deposited with an ICSD will not normally constitute floating charges, despite the fungible character of the account-holder's entitlement, except where the terms of the pledge agreement confer on the grantor continued power to deal with the interest in the securities free from the pledge. This could happen (particularly where the chargee is the clearer) but would not normally be the case, since the pledgee as account holder will control dealings. It is true that the terms of the pledge normally empower the pledgor to substitute other securities, but this right of substitution is controlled legally by contract and often practically by automated control systems to ensure that securities are not released from the pledge except on the provision of the substituted securities or the existence of adequate value in what remains. Nevertheless it is common to register under section 395 *ex*

[66] Section 8–506.

[67] Section 8–110 (transfers); 9–103(6) (pledges).

[68] Section 262(4) of the Australian Corporations Law covers this point expressly by providing that a charge on a book debt does not include a charge on a marketable security. Section 396 of the UK Companies Act 1985 should, it is thought, be construed to the same effect. It should be noted that although s.396(2) expressly exempts from registration security over a negotiable instrument created by a deposit of the instrument this exemption does not apply to non-possessory security of negotiable instruments (*Chase Manhatten Asia Ltd. v. Official Receiver and Liquidator of First Bangkok City Finance Ltd.* [1990] 1 WLR 1181). Accordingly as regards book debts any exemption must rest on the basis that a marketable security is not a book debt.

abundante cautela. But other countries may have mandatory requirements that would apply and would vitiate the pledge if not satisfied.

The justification for the English rule is that potential investors and creditors of a company registered in England should have the ability to get an overall picture of securities given by the company, whether over UK or foreign assets, by searching in one place, the file relating to the company maintained in the Companies Registry. But mandatory perfection requirements relating to securities held by an overseas custodian are inimical to the safe and efficient functioning of the market. A creditor lending on the security of a book-entry entitlement should be able to perfect his interest by complying with the *lex societatis* of the custodian without also having to perfect under some other law. Otherwise a creditor taking security over a portfolio of investments issued in a number of different countries would have to check and comply with the perfection requirements of each of them, which could be exceeedingly burdensome. It is not unreasonable to expect unsecured creditors to be bound by a security interest duly perfected under the custodian's *lex societatis*.

Loss of securities

Co-ownership of a pool of fungible securities protects account-holders only to the extent that the securities are still in the pool. If they have been wrongfully disposed of in conditions under which the transferees acquire an overriding title the proprietary interests of the account-holders disappear and they are left to their remedies against the custodian. These, however, will be valueless where the custodian is insolvent or has effectively excluded liability for the loss. It seems that in most cases custodianship agreements expressly exempt the custodian from liability for the acts or omissions of sub-custodians in the absence of wilful default or negligence on the part of the custodian itself.[69] Thus however strong the custodian, its customer faces a potential exposure through the negligent or fraudulent acts of a sub-custodian. One approach to this problem would be to outlaw exclusion of the custodian's liability. To this custodians would answer that no custodian could assume risks of such potential magnitude, and their central bank regulators would be concerned about the capital adequacy and systemic risk implications. If this be so, then the only solution is rigorous regulatory control to ensure as far as possible that organizations carrying out custodial functions are adequately capitalized and run with efficiency and integrity and that custodians exercise proper care and supervision in the selection and oversight of their sub-custodians.[70]

[69] See the BIS study, *supra*, n. 3, at p. 108.

[70] Pure custodianship is not at present regulated by the Financial Services Act but is likely to be brought within its purview in due course.

The custodian's duties in regard to third party claims

It may happen that a third party lays claim to a security entitlement credited to an account-holder. What is the custodian's position in this situation? Can it safely honour instructions from the account-holder to transfer the entitlement? The traditional common law approach to these questions is through the concept of notice. If the custodian has actual or constructive notice of the third party's rights it is bound to respect them and is liable as a constructive trustee if it fails to do so.

One of the great achievements of the draftsmen of Article 8 is to recognize that the adoption of such an approach in regard to book-entry transfers of securities would constitute a damaging interference with the operation of the market, for if the custodian, having received notice of the third party's claim, declines to implement the transfer instruction, the burden of the loss falls not on the custodian but the intended transferee whose transaction with the account-holder is not carried out. As Professor James Steven Rogers has perceptively observed:

> 'Legal rules that do not insulate intermediaries from adverse claims are rules that create systemic risk.'[71]

Hence the sensible, if counter-intuitive, rule that a securities intermediary who transfers a financial asset pursuant to an effective instruction is not liable to a person having an adverse claim, even if it was aware of that claim at the time of transfer, except if it ignores an injunction or acted in collusion with the wrongdoer or if it acted with notice of the adverse claim in a case where a security certificate had been stolen.[72]*

[71] 'Policy Perspectives on Revised UCC Article 8', to be published in the June 1996 issue of the UCLA Law Review. For a shorter but penetrating analysis see Randall Guynn, 'Modernizing Securities Ownership, Transfer and Pledging: A Discussion Paper on the Need for International Harmonization' (International Bar Association, Capital Markets Forum, to be published 1995). The seminal article provoking the debate which led to the revision of Article 8 of the UCC is Charles Mooney Jr., 'Beyond Negotiability: A New Model for Transfer and Pledge of Interests in Securities Controlled by Intermediaries' (1990) 12 Cardozo Law Rev. 305.

[72] UCC s. 8–115.

* I am indebted to a number of people for their help in the course of writing this paper, in particular Joanna Benjamin of Clifford Chance, Margaret Conklin of Euroclear, Fiona Christie of Cedel Bank, Randall Guynn and other members of Davis, Polk and Wardwell, Alan Keat of Travers Smith Braithwaite and Philip Wood of Allen and Overy. To all of them I express my deep appreciation. I have also derived great assistance from the writings of Professor James Steven Rogers and Randall Guynn (see in particular the citations in n. 68, *supra*), Joanna Benjamin and Philip Wood and the Prefatory Notes and Official Comments in the revised Article 8 of the UCC.

8

The Practical Elements of Settlement and Custody

FIONA CHRISTIE AND HERDEEP DOSANJH

INTRODUCTION

This Chapter reviews the practical elements of settlement and custody in preparation for the analysis of legal risks.[1] The settlement framework starts with the settlement and custody of what is defined as first tier custody of immobilised securities and is built from here to include tiers of intermediaries and their Customers. There is reference throughout to the International Central Securities Depositories (ICSDs). This refers to Cedel Bank and Morgan Guaranty Trust (MGT/Euroclear),[2] who clear approximately 70,000 internationally traded securities.

FIRST TIER CUSTODY

An initial example of first tier custody is the safe custody of definitive Eurobond securities.

First Tier Custody-Immobilised securities

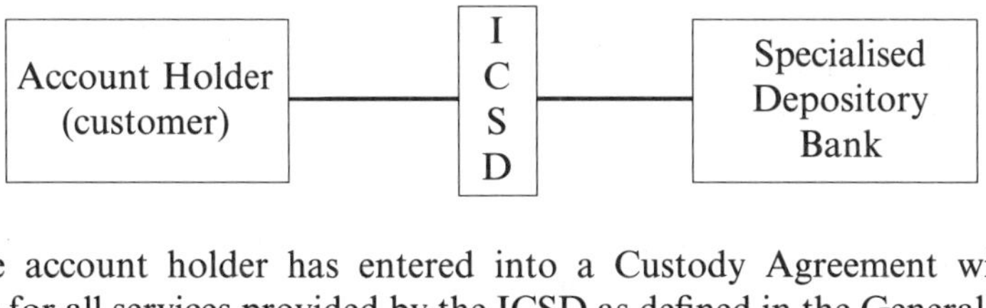

The account holder has entered into a Custody Agreement with the ICSD for all services provided by the ICSD as defined in the General Terms and Conditions and the Customer Handbook of Cedel Bank. These include cash management, securities lending and repos. The securities are definitive

[1] Roy Goode, supra, pp. 116–29, discusses the legal risks inherent in the custody and settlement of securities held through Cedel and MGT/Euroclear.

[2] For an analysis of Euroclear, see Roy Goode, supra, pp. 115–16.

printed bearer securities, held on behalf of the ICSD by an agent, the Specialised Depository Bank. The services of the Specialised Depository Bank are defined and agreed in a Depository Agreement, setting out the services provided to the ICSD. When a Customer delivers securities to the Specialised Depository Bank, the latter receives the securities and holds them on behalf of the ICSD, confirming receipt of the securities to the ICSD who in turn credits the account holder's securities account statement with a book entry credit of securities. These securities can be held in safe custody, held as collateral or traded free or against payment by book entry transfers between the accounts of Cedel Bank Customers or via the electronic bridge with MGT/Euroclear.

Against payment transactions from the seller must be matched by the purchaser and are backed by simultaneous transfers of cash into and out of the cash account linked to the account holder's securities account.

In this example, as these securities are in definitive printed bearer form, the ICSD Customer retains the right to request physical delivery of the securities. This transaction is the reverse of the initial delivery, the customer requests the ICSD to debit its account by book entry and make a physical delivery of the securities to the destination of its choice. As the pool of securities in the ICSDs is normally considered fungible, securities equalling the nominal value requested will be delivered, although these securities may not be the same definitive securities nor of the same denomination as those initially delivered. The ICSDs receive frequent requests from investors for delivery of definitive securities. These investors are affectionately called 'Belgian Dentists' and they are renowned for requesting definitive securities in small denominations to enable them to hold the securities under their mattresses and make physical coupon presentations for payment of gross interest!

There is also provision in Cedel Bank for the account holders to designate the securities as non-fungible; in this case the securities delivered by the account holder will be identified by their unique number, and the account holder would retain rights to these particular securities for safe custody, sales or transfers and physical delivery.

DEVELOPMENTS IN ISSUE STRUCTURES

Having described this first tier safe custody of definitive securities, it is now possible to see how developments in issue structures have impacted the custody and settlement for the ICSD account holders. Using the above example as a base, the first development to be considered is the form of the securities which may be held by the ICSD and reflected in the account holders statement.

With a view to reducing cost and risks inherent in the issuance of large volumes of security printed definitives, issues may be permanently represented by Global Notes, with a provision for definitive securities only in the case of default by the issuer or closure of the ICSDs. Global Notes had traditionally been produced to enable settlement of new issues. The Global Note is not security printed, but a legal document used to represent the issue during the forty day lock up period prior to certification of non US ownership. During the forty day lock up period, to comply with TEFRA D regulations, no sales may be made within the US or to US persons. On a practical level this also provides time for printing arrangements to be made and for definitives to be security printed. Interests in Global Notes can be held only by account holders of the ICSDs and the ICSDs in turn hold these Global Notes with a Common Depository, a bank appointed by both ICSDs as their joint agent to hold the Global Note in safe custody to their order.

There has been such a movement towards the issuance of Global Notes that (including temporary and permanent Global Notes) 60% of issues are now represented in global form. In the same manner as the Specialised Depository Bank has entered into a Depository Agreement with the ICSD, so the Common Depository has entered into a Depository Agreement with both ICSDs, agreeing the services to be provided.

In addition, and in recognition of the issuance of the Global Note, the issuer may enter into a Deed of Covenant, acknowledging that the account holders of the ICSDs have transfer and payment rights, evidenced by their participation in the Global Note as reflected in their account statement from the ICSD. As a Global Note cannot be delivered outside the ICSDs, participation in the issue must always be through the ICSDs' account holders.

SEMI-PERMANENT GLOBAL NOTES

In early 1995 this year the ICSDs rejected the semi-permanent Global Note structure. In this structure, provision was made for ICSD account holders with participation in a Global Note issue to request definitive securities for their individual participation. The aim of this structure was for issuers to meet the requirements of all note holders, both institutional investors and 'Belgian Dentists' and for the issue to be represented simultaneously by both global and definitive securities. Due to a requirement of the ICSDs that the security be in either definitive and deliverable form or global and non-deliverable form, these two forms of security had to be admitted for clearance and settlement under two separate security codes, making the issue, although technically fungible, operationally non-fungible. The market confusion caused by this resulted in the ICSDs' decision to refuse this structure for new issues closing on or after 1 March 1995. Whilst new issues are not accepted, existing structures remain with some investors' participation in the issue represented by Global Notes and others represented by definitive securities.

OTHER CSD LINKS—FIRST AND SECOND TIER CUSTODY

First and Second Tier Custody

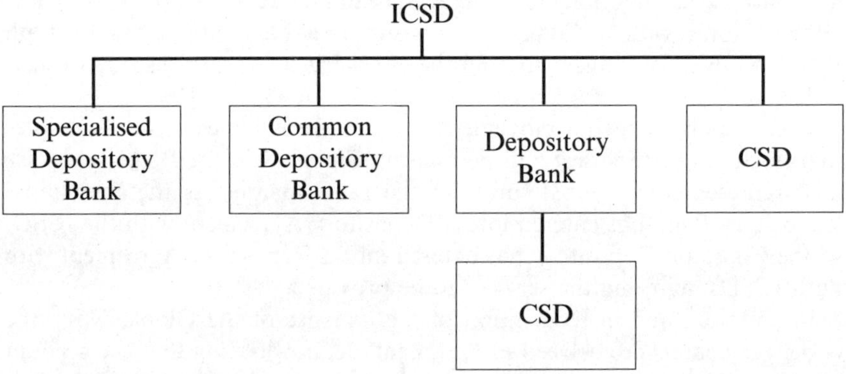

In addition to the form of these Euromarket securities held directly by the agents of the ICSDs, increasingly the ICSDs are forming links to other markets and other Central Securities Depositories (CSDs). The domestic market link is usually an indirect link to the CSD with a participant of the domestic market CSD acting as a depository bank for Cedel Bank. An example of this type of link is Cedel Bank's link to Necigef, the Dutch CSD, through ABN Amro Bank. Most of our links are indirect links, the only direct link being Cedel Bank's link with the AKV. The link with the market means account holders of Cedel Bank, rather than arrange domestic market settlement, can hold and trade securities within Cedel Bank. The first tier settlement system for the securities is the domestic market CSD, Cedel Bank is the second tier settlement system. Initially, either at the time of the new issue, or for initial deliveries over the link, the domestic market CSD will be aware of one transfer of securities to the account of Cedel Bank's representative. Once, however, there is a balance of securities in the accounts of the Cedel Bank account holders, transfers take place purely on Cedel Bank's books, between the Cedel Bank account holders and without impacting the records of the domestic CSD. This may result in easier or faster settlement in the second tier CSD than would be available in the first tier CSD or local market. Second tier settlement may be in a currency not eligible in the first tier CSD and outside the normal settlement processing of the local market. Should the domestic securities be in registered form, the first tier settlement CSD will show Cedel Bank's agent or nominee as the holder, and the records of Cedel Bank as the second tier settlement system will reflect the true positions of the note holders. The securities would therefore not be individually registered in the name of the beneficial owner.

FORM OF SECURITIES

As well as the ICSDs moving settlement from first tier to second tier, the securities from the domestic market are accepted in the form in which they are accepted for clearance by the prime settlement system. As well as securities in definitive or global form, securities may also be accepted in dematerialised, book entry form. In the Scandinavian market for example, the securities held by Swedish, Danish and Norwegian CSDs are about 95% dematerialised, with credits of securities made electronically reflecting confirmation of issuance. In these cases there is no physical evidence of the issue. It is interesting to note that preparations for CSDs in the emerging markets of Eastern Europe and Latin America have learnt from the experiences of other CSDs and are starting with dematerialised custody clearing and settlement.

CHAIN OF CUSTODIAN ARRANGEMENTS

The account holders of the ICSDs are financial institutions, who in turn may be global custodians or banks offering safe custody and clearing services for their clients. Cedel Bank also has accounts holders who are CSDs, who in turn have account holders and clients.

The end investor will pass instructions to his custodian who will arrange settlement and safe custody of the securities. The end investors' instructions will be communicated by the custodian, possibly through another intermediary CSD, to the ICSD. Each intermediary determines its own custody agreements, deadlines and settlement instruction formats, although ultimately all instructions to the ICSDs must meet the deadlines of the ICSD in the required format. When settlement occurs, the ICSD confirms settlement to the account holder, who in turn confirms settlement to its client(s), and reports holdings of securities.

Where the ICSD account holder is a global custodian, it is also possible for settlement of security trades to occur between customers of that global custodian. In these cases settlement will occur on the books of the global

Chain of Custodian Arrangements

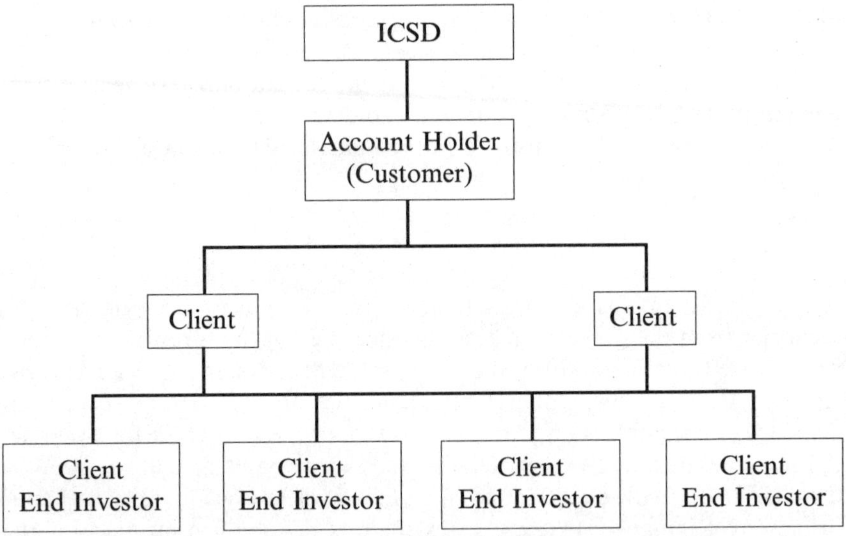

custodian, but there will be no reflection of the trades in the account of the ICSD account holder.

THE LUXEMBOURG LEGAL FRAMEWORK

Background

Cedel (the term originally stood for 'Centrale de Livraison de Valeurs Mobilières') was founded in Luxembourg on 28 September, 1970 to provide a neutral and independent clearing and settlement organisation to serve the international securities markets, primarily of Eurobonds at the time. Sixty-six institutions from eleven countries supplied the capital to establish Cedel, creating a co-operative to act as a general service provider for the international market. The independence and neutrality of Cedel is assured by both the restriction in its by-laws preventing any single shareholder from acquiring greater than five per cent of the total shares of Cedel, and by a policy of open membership to any institution which satisfies the requisite regulatory status and financial criteria.

On 1 January, 1995, Cedel changed its corporate structure, establishing a new parent company, Cedel International and five subsidiaries, including Cedel Bank which now contains the core lending, clearing and settlement business of the former 'Cedel' subsidiaries under the parent company, in line with international best practice.

Acquisition of banking status enables regulated banking customers to benefit from a Capital Adequacy Directive/Basle Accord capital weighting for cash deposits of twenty per cent and enables Cedel Bank to benefit from standardised accounting rules, a ‘passport’ for activities in the European Union and the ability to offer fiduciary services. Cedel Bank has been awarded the highest short term credit rating of A1+ from the International Bank Credit Agency (IBCA) and Standard and Poors. Cedel International is also regulated as a professional of the financial sector (the status of the former 'Cedel') in order that the Institut Monétaire Luxembourgeois may conduct comprehensive supervision of all Cedel Group activities.

Cedel Group Organisation Chart

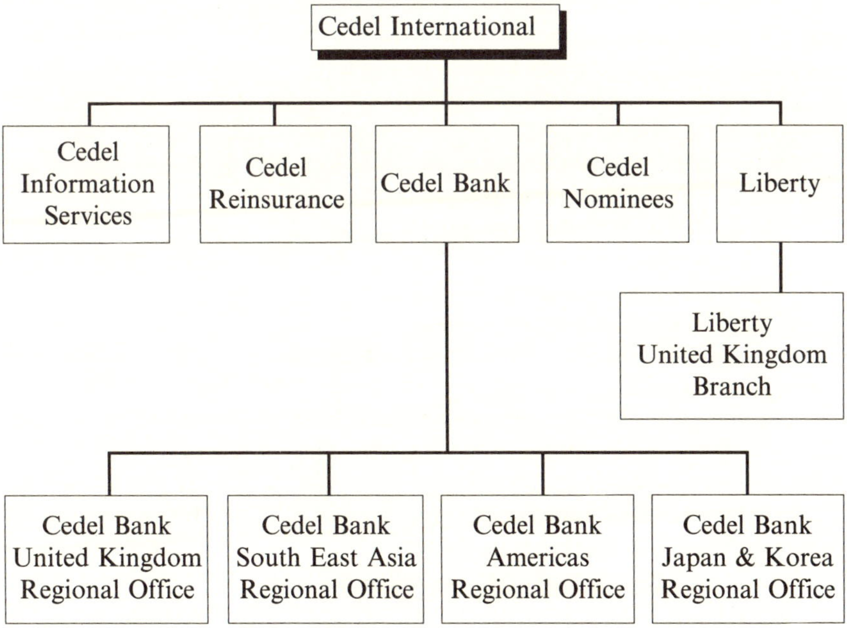

THE LUXEMBOURG LEGAL ENVIRONMENT

Luxembourg has continued to maintain an increasingly up to date legal framework to govern the custody, transfer and pledging of book entry securities. The obligations and interests of depositors of securities with Cedel Bank (‘Customers’) are governed by the laws of Luxembourg together with the General Terms and Conditions (and other Governing Documents) of Cedel Bank. Considering the relevant governing provisions of Luxembourg law in chronological order, it is possible to demonstrate the modernisation of Luxembourg law in conjunction with the increased sophistication of the financial world.

THE SECURITY INTEREST

The simplification of the creation of security interests was initiated in the Law of 1 June, 1929 which enables the validity of a pledge over registered or bearer securities without the necessity of any formal registration or notification to the debtor or to the company which is issuer of the securities. The same law also permits the substitution of collateral and envisages collateral being held in the possession of a third party, for example Cedel Bank. In addition to the creation and maintenance of the pledge under Luxembourg law, the realisation of the pledge is possible, by virtue of this law, by simple letter of notification from the creditor to the debtor. As a consequence of subsequent revisions to the Law of 1 June 1929, realisation of the pledge can be effected by appropriation by the creditor of the pledged assets at the market price rather than through sale of the collateral. Pending legislation also proposes to remove an existing mandatory notice period (eight days) required prior to realisation in certain cases.

THE CIRCULATION OF SECURITIES/FUNGIBILITY

The Grand-Ducal Decree of 17 February 1971 gave a statutory basis for securities accounts with banks and other authorised professional depositories. The concept of fungibility was also recognised and embodied in this Decree. Securities deposited in accounts without indication of their numbers are fungible. Cedel Bank, as depository, is not required to record the numbers of the securities which it safe keeps or transfers for individual accounts pursuant to this Decree. The Customer, in exercising his rights over such fungible securities is not required to establish the identities of the securities by means of any serial numbers. A Customer is free however to maintain a non-fungible account with Cedel Bank if so required, and a Customer may hold both fungible and non-fungible securities of a specific issue in addition to transferring securities between its fungible and non-fungible accounts. Unless otherwise instructed by the Customer however, Cedel Bank is permitted (pursuant to the General Terms and Conditions) to treat all securities received as fungible.

Article 7 of the Decree provides that at the time of deposit of a security in a current account of a depository such as Cedel Bank, it is the responsibility of the depository to verify that the security is not subject to any stop order/opposition[3] and in the case where a stop order/opposition is imposed subsequent to deposit, such stop order/opposition is without effect in Luxembourg. The provisions of this Decree are expressed to apply to foreign securities for which the legal regime is compatible with the regime of fungibility.

In addition, the Decree of 1971 also addresses the creation of a pledge over fungible securities enabling 'possession' of the pledged securities to be validly effected by the transfer of the pledged securities to a 'special' designated account. In the context of securities held with Cedel Bank, it is therefore possible to create a pledge in accordance with Luxembourg law by the notation of the pledged securities by book entry to a special account held to the order of either the pledgor or the pledgee.[4]

PROTECTION OF DEPOSITED ASSETS

To confirm the protection of assets deposited with authorised professional depositories, the Grand Ducal Decree of 17 February, 1971 expressly deals with the insolvency of such a custodian of securities. Article 9 provides that in the case of bankruptcy of a depository, the reclamation of securities is effected upon the totality of securities of the same nature deposited with the depository (or deposited to the depository's current account with other depositories). Should the total of securities available be insufficient to assure the full amount of restitution due, any insufficiency is borne by the depositors in proportion to their rights.

THE GENERAL TERMS AND CONDITIONS OF CEDEL BANK

Cedel Bank established revised terms and conditions governing the provision of services by Cedel Bank to its Customers in October, 1992. The General Terms and Conditions reflect the modernisation of Luxembourg law to define the framework for the custody, transfer and pledging of securities services provided by Cedel Bank. The Grand-Ducal Decree of 18 December, 1981 and the Grand-Ducal Decree of 8 June, 1994 have removed uncertainty as to the application of existing laws over many new types of financial instruments. They have substantially extended the existing definition of the categories of financial instruments for the purposes of the earlier laws to include registered or bearer securities, certificates of deposit, treasury notes, warrants and all other instruments representing property rights, credits or securities.

[3] General Terms and Conditions of Cedel Bank vary this by requiring a Customer warranty of good delivery.

[4] Further simplified by provisions for 'earmarking' of securities in Grand-Ducal Decree of 8 June 1994.

The General Terms and Conditions set out the rights of the Customers of Cedel Bank in accordance with Luxembourg law. In respect of non-fungible deposits (where securities are identified by means of a serial number), Customers of Cedel Bank have a right akin to a property right (which is similar to a *ius in rem*) in respect of the securities under Luxembourg law. In respect of fungible deposits, Customers do not have any right to specific securities but a credit to a Customer account creates an entitlement to require Cedel Bank to deliver an amount of equivalent securities to the Customer or to his designee upon demand.

THE RESPONSE TO THE GLOBAL MARKET

In recognition of the necessity of the legal environment of Luxembourg to reflect the increasingly diverse nature of the financial markets and cross-border transactions, the Grand-Ducal Decree of 8 June 1994 implemented three important improvements to earlier law. Firstly, as indicated earlier, the definition of securities was further extended to ensure that any securities and other financial instruments transferable on a fungible basis, including certificates of deposit, cash orders and any other securities representing rights of ownership, debts or stocks or shares whether materialised or dematerialised, transferable by book entry or physical delivery, in bearer or registered form, endorseable or non endorseable were encompassed by this and the earlier laws.

Secondly, the 1994 Decree affirms the 'earmarking' of securities in the system of the depository for the creation and perfection of pledges under Luxembourg law, and provides for the securities to be held in either the account of the pledgor or the pledgee with the depository. In addition, in the absence of notification from the pledgor regarding ownership of the pledged securities and rights of entitlement to create a pledge over such securities, the validity of the pledge is not affected by the fact that the pledgor has no, or insufficient, title to the pledged securities.

Thirdly, and significantly in the context of conflict of laws difficulties, the Decree states that the deposit of securities through book entry or by any other means by the depository, on his behalf with other depositories, either within Luxembourg or outside Luxembourg, does not alter the validity of the pledge created in accordance with the Grand-Ducal Decree of 8 June, 1994.

Similarly, the Law of 21 December, 1994 continues to respond to the needs of the global market to further address the issues of pledges and assignments of claims. The taking of cash accounts as collateral has been simplified and perfection of a security interest is permitted by an agreement and simple letter from the creditor to the debtor. On the same date, a separate law governing repurchase transactions was enacted. This Law explicitly recognises the effectiveness of absolute transfer of title pursuant to repurchase transactions. It also eliminates the uncertainty regarding the nature of the interest created in a repurchase transaction to remove the recharacterisation risk prevalent in some jurisdictions in respect of the treatment of a repurchase transaction in the event of insolvency of a counterparty.

LEGISLATIVE INITIATIVES FOR THE FUTURE

Two present initiatives are worthy of brief mention here. The Luxembourg Netting and Collateral Draft Bills are respectively intended to create the legal framework to permit netting of the widest range of financial obligations and to permit immediate foreclosure amongst financial professionals. The validity and enforceability of national and international netting agreements are clearly affirmed as a matter of Luxembourg law.

CONCLUSION

Legislators in Luxembourg have long recognised the necessity of adaptation and modernisation of national laws to keep pace with the increasing demands of the international securities markets. Cedel Bank operates its clearance and settlement system in a legal framework expressly designed to limit the risks to depositors using the system and specifically aimed to promote clarity and certainty. The integrity and success of this legal framework is supported by the twenty five year history and continued growth and evolution of the Cedel Group.

PART II

Market Regulation and Harmonization

9

Why Regulate Financial Services?

CHRIS FORD AND JOHN KAY

INTRODUCTION

One of the first things that strikes someone with a background in utilities regulation is the sheer extent of financial services regulation. Any one who wishes to offer investment advice must be authorised under the Financial Services Act 1986 (FSA); any one who takes deposits requires approval from the Bank of England—apart, of course, from building societies who are regulated by their own Commission; insurance companies are regulated both by the DTI and under the FSA. As a result, whereas the typical utility regulator deals with few firms—OFWAT regulates 31 and OFGAS and OFTEL are largely concerned with one alone—the Personal Investment Authority has some 5,000 members ranging from sole traders to some of Britain's largest companies.

There is an equally marked contrast in the regulators' attitudes towards the entry of new firms. In general, utilities regulators actively seek to promote increased competition. Regulation is intended to control the prices a dominant company charges—both to consumers and to other firms. This should allow such firms access to a network at reasonable cost. Whatever one's views about the success of the utility regulators, it is clearly a very different task from that adopted by financial services regulators.

Here the emphasis is less on promoting competition and restricting prices; more on controlling entry and behaviour. Firms must be 'fit and proper'; satisfy capital adequacy standards; and provide 'best advice'. Far from focusing attention on those firms that might be in a position to abuse market power, the costs of financial services regulation appear to fall disproportionately on smaller firms.

The objectives and origins of financial services regulation are not the same as those of utility regulators. We describe these differences further below. But the differences in regulatory approach and philosophy go far beyond those that these distinct objectives and origins would imply. The basic differences are that financial services regulation is principally aimed at *process*, and utility regulation at *outcome*. Utility regulators have a view of the structure of the industry they seek to bring about, and measure their effectiveness by reference to the range and quality of services available to customers and the prices they are charged. Financial services regulators would, in the main, be surprised by the suggestion that they should take a direct interest in these things. They are concerned to regulate the process by which services are delivered and, so long as that process is a proper one, what it is that is delivered is a matter for the market rather than the regulator.

This difference is the natural product of the difference between an economic and a legal approach to regulation. The design of utility regulation has mostly been shaped by economists; the design of financial services regulation by lawyers. These differences are self-reinforcing, since they are translated into the staff that each agency recruits. We shall be making the unashamedly self-interested claim that financial services regulation would benefit from the involvement of fewer lawyers and more economists. At the very least, we hope to show that an economist would ask questions about the nature and rationale of financial services regulation which would not naturally arise from a legal perspective.

Both the Gower Report and the resulting Financial Services Act 1986 start from the assumption that rules of conduct are required to deliver high standards of investor protection. Such a system has an inbuilt tendency towards the growth of regulation—a particular set of circumstances is not adequately dealt with in the existing rule book or that it is unfair to leave this product unregulated when a very similar product must comply with a detailed set of rules.

Although this concern about 'fairness' or 'consistency' is, in many ways, laudable, it often produces a far larger volume of regulation than was required to deal with the original problem. At its extreme, such an approach seeks to write a complete set of rules specifying what regulated firms should do in each situation. Such an approach fails for the same reason that central planners fail—information is costly. It is therefore always behind the game; attempting to plug the last loophole and repeatedly surprised by new developments.

The most recent of these new developments is the collapse of Barings. This is, of course, only the latest incident in a long line—in the last few years we have seen the problems of Orange County and Procter & Gamble in derivatives; Maxwell, home income plans and personal pensions in the retail markets. Although the details vary, there is a standard pattern—first the financial failure occurs and the papers speak of 'another scandal', then the responsible authorities set up a 'full enquiry' which duly prepares a detailed report with a series of recommendations. All concerned then promise to learn the lessons and try to make sure such an event 'cannot happen again'. Almost invariably, the solution involves more regulation.

In this Chapter, we want to suggest that the strategy of responding to each new regulatory failure by adding yet more rules is doomed to failure. Instead we need to take a more fundamental look at why financial services are regulated and what this regulation should try to achieve. It is only by becoming more realistic about what regulation can hope to achieve that we can break the present cycle of increasing cost and declining confidence in the regulatory system.

THE RATIONALE OF FINANCIAL SERVICES REGULATION

Systemic Collapse

The economist's traditional response to the question 'why regulate financial services?' is to talk about 'systemic effects' and 'asymmetric information'. It has long been recognised that retail deposit takers are uniquely vulnerable to contagious collapse because their liabilities are highly liquid—any of us can go to the nearest cash dispenser and reduce our balance without notice—whereas their assets are long term loans which can only be speedily liquidated for a fraction of their nominal value.

In the theoretical world of perfect information, this mis-match would give banks a strong incentive to behave prudently as strong banks would gain deposits whilst weak banks would quickly lose them. In practice such a system would be vulnerable to bank runs—if your bank is going to collapse, you want to make sure that this only happens after you have withdrawn your money. Because everyone wants to be at the front of the queue, the system is unstable—banks could collapse not because they are weak but because some depositors think that other depositors think that a collapse is possible.

To prevent this, governments protect depositors, either through explicit insurance schemes or by less formal support operations. Unfortunately, this solution removes the discipline imposed by the threat of bankruptcy. Once depositors know that the authorities will prop up their bank or that, in the event of a collapse, their deposit is safe, they are free to chase the highest interest rate without worrying about the bank's solvency. To pay interest rates that will attract deposits, banks are driven to undertake ever greater risks.

This means that the provision of deposit insurance must be accompanied by restrictions on the activities of the insured institutions. To see what happens if these restrictions are absent or inadequate one only need look at the expansion and collapse of the American Savings & Loans institutions.

However, we need to be careful not to draw too general a lesson. Systemic risk provides an argument for regulating certain types of financial service; not for regulating the industry as a whole. Indeed, the first question raised by the collapse of Barings is not 'why did the regulatory system fail to prevent the bank's capital being put at risk in this way?' but 'why was Barings being regulated at all?'

The answer clearly cannot be that the collapse of a relatively small merchant bank would have systemic implications for the UK banking system. Although a collapse would certainly have had some impact, the willingness of the Bank of England and the Government to allow the banking operations of Barings to go into liquidation if no bidder had come forward, suggests that they regarded the knock-on effects as manageable. Indeed, for several days it seemed possible that Barings' depositors would not be paid in full, and the systemic consequences described above did not take place.

The Scope of Banking Supervision

We believe that to explain why we have such an extensive system of prudential regulation, the chain of reasoning must run:

- retail deposit takers are prone to loss of confidence; therefore
- we need an insurance scheme; but
- this leaves banks free to take excessive risks; therefore
- we must control their lending; but
- these banks are also involved in capital markets; therefore
- capital adequacy requirements must cover all the bank's activities; but
- investment firms compete with banks in the capital markets; therefore
- it is only fair to also regulate these firms.

However, the apparent conclusion—that concern about systemic risk justifies regulating firms that have no retail deposits—is far from persuasive, and the style of argument potentially leads to the regulation of any activity which competes with any activity undertaken by a regulated firm. Whilst long-term loans can only be liquidated at a discount, if a firm's assets consist largely of marketable securities, their value will not be greatly affected by the firm going into liquidation. It should therefore be possible to avoid systemic risks by means of an orderly wind down. Provided investment firms are required to segregate investors' assets in special accounts that are protected against the claims of creditors in the case of insolvency, there appears to be little reason to impose capital adequacy requirements on investor protection grounds.

The belief that all banks and investment houses must be subject to a consistent set of capital adequacy requirements has spawned a vast industry debating what would be required to produce 'a level playing field'. However, the need for learned discussion of the appropriate split between the 'banking book' and the 'trading book' could be greatly curtailed if regulation was refocused on the original objective.

If the aim is to prevent systemic risk by regulating retail deposit takers and insuring their deposits, a regulatory system which focused on such risks would have a much greater prospect of success than one which seeks to control every activity undertaken by a retail deposit taker.

This could involve restricting deposit insurance to closely supervised 'narrow banks' Other institutions would only be allowed to own narrow banks if there were strong fire walls between the two. This would leave regulators free to concentrate on the narrow banks; an approach which is in some ways analogous to the focus of utilities regulation on natural monopolies with water or electricity companies being able to own non-regulated businesses operating in competitive markets provided these businesses are accounted for separately.

Fraud and Financial Market Regulation

Although the economist's immediate reaction to the question 'why regulate financial services?' may be to start talking about systemic risk, we are sure that a more typical response would be 'to stop crooks'. Even an economist can recognise that, for the criminal, the financial services industry offers special attractions. Investors are exchanging cash for a promised future return. Both the time lag (during which the investor need only be provided with a piece of paper indicating that the investment is growing safely) and the possibility of using funds provided by new investors to repay others give the unscrupulous more than adequate opportunity to depart with a large sum of money, leaving behind a crowd of dissatisfied clients.

The true deregulator would say that such scams will involve theft and breach of contract and can be left to the normal criminal and civil law. However, we do not normally rely solely on laws against theft; we also fit locks. In the same way, it makes sense for preventive action to seek to ensure that people who cannot meet certain basic standards of propriety are kept out of the financial services industry.

In doing this, the regulators have significant advantages over the judicial process. For one thing there are gains from specialisation. At least, in principle, regulators should have better sources of information and more experience than the police and so should be better at detecting many types of financial crime. Although there have been cases—BCCI and perhaps Barings—where the regulator's informational advantages might strike the outside observer as less than overwhelming.

In addition, the regulatory system can more easily use a different standard of proof. Whilst we are only prepared to jail people who are guilty beyond reasonable doubt, regulators might reasonably expect someone to answer any suggestions of criminal activity before being allowed to enter the financial services industry.

THE SCOPE OF FINANCIAL SERVICES REGULATION

Training and Competence

The present regulatory system goes much further than simply seeking to exclude the dishonest. Financial advisers are required to demonstrate that they are competent; or, more precisely, that they have completed the training and passed the examinations required by their regulator. In the case of independent financial advisers, the requirement is not only for 'competence' but for every client to receive 'best advice'.

At first glance this seems unremarkable—who could object to the idea that those who provide investment advice should have reached an approved level of competence and should provide the best possible advice?

However, such a requirement is not imposed on those who provide other retail services. Whilst travel agents are required to comply with various financial requirements, no one expects a regulator to ensure that the staff behind the counter have sufficient knowledge to advise on the holidays they sell. It is even harder to envisage a requirement to provide 'best advice' on a holiday—'are you sure you can afford to go away this year?'; 'wouldn't a British holiday provide a more economical means of meeting your needs?'.

Instead, it is for the firm to decide what level of training is required—balancing the cost of training against the risk of incompetent staff driving consumers away. The customer is left to decide whether the product on offer is suitable and good value.

Everyone would, of course, like to get expert advice on financial services, tailored to his or her individual circumstances if such a service were free. However, the requirement to offer 'best advice' really holds out a false prospectus. There are very few people with the expertise to assess someone's current financial position; survey the entire range of financial products and forecast which will be the best choice.

Let us take as an example the choice between a repayment and an endowment mortgage (only a part of the overall mortgage decision). This will require a forecast of the performance of equities over a 20-25 year time period, a view about interest rates over the same period, an assessment of the present tax implications and the likelihood of any change and an allowance for the client's attitude to risk. People who are capable of doing this are almost certainly able to find more lucrative employment than that provided by selling life assurance.

By promising something which cannot, in reality, be delivered, the regulatory system undermines the inevitable fundamental responsibility which consumers must take for their own decisions. As a result, when things go wrong, investors believe they are entitled to compensation, almost irrespective of the quality of the advice received.

The Costs of a Bespoke Service

It is not possible for the vast majority of investors to receive, or to pay for, the costs of providing 'best advice'. One indication of this is the limited demand and supply for fee-based independent financial advice. Attempting to meet the costs of extensive training and competence requirements through a system where advisers are paid on commission inevitably creates incentives to comply with the letter but not spirit of the regulations.

The alternative route is to accept that retail financial services should follow a similar path to other retail products. The vast majority of food products, clothes or electrical goods are no longer sold by specialists who have detailed knowledge of their product and provide something that precisely meets their customers' requests. Of course, it is still possible to go to an expert butcher or purchase a tailor-made suit; however, most people choose a supermarket or department store. The lower cost more than outweighs the limited range and absence of specialist advice.

Financial services are already heading in this direction. Major banks or building societies offer a limited range of products, which are designed at head office. This reduces the need for expertise at branch level; lower staff and training costs should make it possible to offer more competitive packages.

The standard response to this line of argument (particularly from those who are in the business of providing financial advice) is that it fails to understand the complexity of the products and the range of choice that must be considered. In fact, it is not at all obvious that the range of financial needs is greater than the range of, say, clothing needs. There are a relatively small number of basic products—life assurance, protection against sickness, savings including pensions—and a vast range of variations. The thousands of unit trusts are better regarded primarily as different patterns and colours than as different garments.

Of course, even in a world where most people buy packaged and ready-made goods, there is still a role for the specialist—providing a distinctive, expert service at a commensurately higher price. The problem arises if the regulatory system attempts to impose such standards and costs on all transactions.

Disclosure and Information Asymmetry

It is commonly argued that the best response to the problem posed by the asymmetry of information between buyers and sellers of financial services is a process of education and disclosure. Notice first that this is not how consumers normally buy complex products, such as cars or washing machines. They do not acquaint themselves in detail with the technical characteristics of the product. They assess some superficial characteristics of the product and rely on the reputation of the supplier as an assurance of quality, reliability and safety.

As we will go on to argue, firms that value their reputation will be careful to ensure that the information they do provide is accurate; those that do not will find themselves criticised in the press and facing large numbers of consumer complaints. However, information is a classic public good—regulators can therefore improve the quality of information available by requiring firms to correct misleading statements. Quite apart from the direct benefit of such corrections, the potential damage to a firm's reputation of being publicly reprimanded provides a further incentive.

When regulators turn to prescribing the format in which information should be disclosed to consumers, the argument becomes less clear cut. Although the desire to have comparable information about the cost of different life assurance policies is laudable, the new disclosure regime appears to give consumers more information than they either want or can understand. Such ill-targeted regulation is again an invitation to focus on the form of the rules rather than the substance. In practice what must often happen is that the salesman says 'I am sorry about all these numbers, I am required to give you the information but you really don't need to worry too much about it'.

Where disclosure has been successful is in enabling the press to use the information to construct league tables showing high cost and low cost providers. In addition, as Virgin's advertising campaigns demonstrate, firms can normally be expected to draw attention to their low cost products. Regulators should therefore focus on making reliable information available to anyone who wants it rather than forcing it on every investor. The objective is to provide information which contributes to the development of good and bad reputations, rather than to provide information to the customers themselves. This is how other markets deal with the information problems created by the complexity of modern products.

In addition to collecting and publicising information about costs, regulators should consider ways of improving consumers' knowledge of service quality. Information about the proportion of a firm's policy holders surrendering their long-term life assurance policies within a few years ('lapse rates') or about the number of complaints upheld by an ombudsman will give consumers a better sense of whether they should enter a long-term contract with that company.

HOW SHOULD WE REGULATE?

Rely on Reputation

This approach illustrates a more general point—that good regulation is designed to work with market forces. Most people will only make a handful of major financial services purchases in their lifetime. This means that there is little scope for learning from experience. As a result, a firm's reputation will play a large part in their decisions. In the long run, reputation can only be built by consistently delivering high quality. It is therefore a powerful form of investor protection.

Unfortunately, as the mis-selling of personal pensions has illustrated, the desire to maintain reputation was not sufficient to control sales forces motivated by commission. Recent sales figures show that the industry is now paying a high price for this loss of reputation.

Although, in the short term, this problem must be tackled and compensation provided for those who have been misled, it would be a mistake to use this as evidence that we need more rules or more intensive rules. Instead the system must recognise that, as it will never be possible to monitor more than a fraction of transactions, firms need to be given more incentives to police their own behaviour.

This requires firms with reputations which are sufficiently valuable that they are not willing to risk them for short-term gain. Although Marks & Spencers and Sainsbury's are subject to food safety regulations, the prime motivation for them to maintain high standards of hygiene is the impact any failure would have on their business, not the prospect of a fine in a magistrate's court.

Although the fines LAUTRO levied on a series of large life offices had a salutary effect in forcing their senior management to recognise that the problem was in the culture of the organisation and could not simply be blamed on a few rogue salesmen, such fines do not provide a long-term solution. A successful regulatory system must be based on more than simply keeping the threat of disciplinary action hanging over the largest companies in the industry.

Polarisation

This reference to Marks & Spencers and Sainsbury's raises the question of whether it is sensible to continue requiring all financial services firms which have own brand products to adopt the Marks & Spencers' approach and sell nothing but their own brand. Although the sharp division imposed by polarisation may have been helpful in the years immediately after the passage of the Financial Services Act 1986, it is not clear that the benefits still outweigh the costs imposed by reduced competition and restricted choice.

The present system means that firms are pushed towards providing a full product range (or, at least, towards rebadging products to give the appearance of a full range), even when they would be content to advise some clients to chose a product from another supplier. This disadvantages small firms, such as friendly societies who only offer a limited product range. It also makes innovation and entry more difficult by excluding the possibility—common in retailing—of persuading a chain to stock a new product on a trial basis.

Once one accepts that a bespoke service of genuinely independent financial advice is only going to be attractive to a relatively small proportion of the market, there is a strong case for allowing 'financial supermarkets' the option of selling both own brand and branded products.

Resist Calls for Further Extension of Regulation

We have already argued that banking regulation should be focused on a limited number of narrow banks. However, any one who suggests that the scope of financial services regulation should be narrowed quickly recognises that the prevailing current is flowing in the opposite direction. There have been calls for mortgages, permanent health insurance, and bank loans to be brought within the Financial Services Act 1986. Whilst I would not dispute the possibility of constructing an argument—of the type if you regulate X then why not Y and then why not Z—for each of these products, we need to recognise that this chain of reasoning will end up with virtually every transaction involving money (or money value) being subject to regulation.

The problem with such arguments, and with much of financial services regulation, is that they take no account of the costs of regulation. Although the Securities and Investments Board has recently sought to extend the use of cost benefit analysis, there are few aspects of the regulatory system that have been subject to a systematic appraisal of the costs and benefits. Too often the argument is simply that some rule is 'necessary on investor protection grounds'. The administrative cost of regulation receive much attention. The more important regulatory burden is the effect on innovative behaviour and on competitive response.

Whilst such an approach may produce a *process* which gives investors an admirable degree of protection, the danger is that the *outcome* is to exclude products which investors would wish to buy or to impose costs that discourage the purchase. In making this point, we recognise that a regulator is faced with a very real problem—there is little incentive to relax a rule if you know that as soon as something goes wrong in that area (whether or not it has anything to do with the rule change) everyone who has lost money will blame the regulator. However, this bias towards over-regulation makes it all the more important that advocates of additional rules are required to produce a quantified cost benefit analysis that can stand up to serious scrutiny.

OBJECTIVE

We have set out the case for a regulatory system which recognises that regulation is costly, focuses on a limited set of objectives, and seeks to work with market forces. Let us conclude by sketching the sort of financial services industry such an approach might produce. There would be a number of major retailers selling a range of standardised products (possibly made up of a mix of own brands and those of other companies) through their branch networks together with postal and telephone services. Most of the information provided at the branch would be in the form of brochures; only very limited advice would be available with more detailed questions being referred to central offices. There would also be a number of independent financial advisers providing a bespoke (fee-based) advice service, primarily for wealthier investors.

In such a system, the retailers primary asset would be their reputation. There would therefore be substantial common interest with the regulator who would be able to move away from a detailed, prescriptive approach to the conduct of business and focus on the problems of systemic risk and inadequate information.

10

Concepts of Regulation—The US Model

EDWARD F. GREENE, DANIEL A. BRAVERMAN AND JENNIFER M. SCHNECK[1]

INTRODUCTION

In most countries, the distribution of securities to the public is subject to significant regulation. The United States is no exception. The experience of the early part of this century, culminating in the market crash of 1929, illustrated the dangers in permitting virtually unsupervised sales of securities, often involving unsophisticated investors and unscrupulous or incompetent issuers and other market participants. The resulting lack of confidence in the integrity of the market meant that even legitimate transactions were tainted.

The market crash led to radical reform of the regulatory system. The distribution of securities, the activities of brokers and dealers, the operations of stock exchanges and numerous other activities related to the operation of the securities markets were made subject to detailed statutory provisions and regulations, and the ongoing oversight of a newly created administrative agency, the Securities and Exchange Commission (the 'SEC').

Since the enactment of the two principal statutes governing securities activities, the Securities Act of 1933 (the 'Securities Act') and the Securities Exchange Act of 1934 (the 'Exchange Act'), the US securities markets have undergone phenomenal growth. For example, the total amount of securities traded on the New York Stock Exchange (the NYSE) in 1937 was 409.5 million shares.[2] In 1994, that amount was 73,240 million shares.[3] In addition, there has been explosive growth in the types of securities traded, as well as the development of myriad new types of derivative instruments. There has also been a significant shift in who participates in the markets, with institutional investors now accounting for the bulk of investment.[4]

[1] Edward F. Greene and Daniel A. Braverman are partners, and Jennifer M. Schneck is an associate, at Cleary, Gottlieb, Steen & Hamilton. Edward F. Greene and Daniel A. Braverman are based in the firm's London office. Jennifer M. Schneck is based in the firm's New York Office

[2] New York Stock Exchange Fact Book 1965, p. 39.

[3] New York Stock Exchange Fact Book 1994, p. 94.

[4] Although truly comparative information is difficult to find, the NYSE has reported that in September 1952, 57.0% of the transactions conducted on the exchange were done by individuals while 24.6% were done by institutions (the remainder being done by NYSE

This shift has almost certainly been helped by the growth in mutual funds, through which retail participation in the securities markets can be transformed into institutional participation.

In addition to the growth in the US domestic market, there has also been an increase in cross-border transactions, both by US issuers and investors participating in markets outside the United States[5] and by foreign issuers and investors participating in the US domestic market. One consequence of the growth in international investment has been increasing conflict between the regulatory systems of various jurisdictions. Issuers and investors accustomed to the mechanisms of their home markets are faced with different and often inconsistent regimes when they venture into other markets.

The US market is the world's largest, accounting for nearly 40 per cent. of equity capital worldwide.[6] As a result, the US regulatory system exerts significant influence on the world's capital markets, both because it applies directly to a significant proportion of capital raising activities and because it is seen as a potential model for other regulators. However, because it is generally the most rigorous regulatory system of any major capital market, particularly in the area of accounting principles and disclosure standards, it is viewed as an impediment by many potential market participants.

This Chapter considers the system of securities regulation in the United States in light of the increasing globalization of the securities markets. It analyzes the mechanisms that are currently in place and some of their shortcomings. It proposes modifications to the current system to make it more responsive to the increasingly international marketplace. It also considers whether more fundamental changes to the regulatory system would better serve the regulatory goal of ensuring the smooth, efficient and fair operation of domestic and international securities markets. Pages 159–61 introduce three models of regulation: national treatment, reciprocity and deference, and discuss how the three can be applied exclusively or in an integrated fashion. At pages 161–9, the three models are illustrated by reference to the US system, which we know best. Although securities regulation in the United States comprises primarily the national treatment model, there has been a gradual loosening of standards so that in some instances reciprocity and deference have been applied. At pages 169–74, we consider some of the positive and negative effects of the US regulatory system, particularly as

members). In the fourth quarter of 1980, individuals accounted for only 25.7% of the transactions while institutions accounted for 47.4%. Business Research Division, N.Y. Stock Exchange, Public Transaction Study, Fourth Quarter 1980. It is likely that the differential has increased since 1980.

[5] As an example, in 1985 US investors acquired $24.8 billion of foreign equity securities and $85.2 billion of foreign debt securities. By 1990, those numbers had increased to $130.9 billion and $335.9 billion, respectively. See Securities Act Release No. 6902 (June 21, 1991), Section II, n.8 (hereinafter, 'MJDS Adopting Release').

[6] See SEC Annual Report (1994), p. 28.

they apply to cross-border transactions. We also propose ways the system can be changed to better serve the needs of today's market participants, including by moving toward common standards for regulation among various jurisdictions. At pages 174–5, we discuss the concept of regulatory competition, which occurs when applicable regulatory standards conflict. We conclude our discussion by considering the possibility and implications of a fundamental change to the US regulatory system, from registration of securities to registration of companies.

REGULATORY MODELS

In this Part we identify and describe three models that influence how jurisdictions formulate and apply their systems of securities regulation. The three models are: national treatment, reciprocity and deference. As we shall see, they are not mutually exclusive, but can each be applied to a greater or lesser extent.

National Treatment

The basis of the national treatment model is that all activities conducted within a jurisdiction, and all activities conducted outside that jurisdiction but which have a direct impact on the jurisdiction, are subject to regulation by the jurisdiction, whether or not they are also regulated elsewhere. Underlying this premise is the notion that residents of the jurisdiction are entitled to the protections afforded by its system of local regulation, and that anyone wanting the benefit of access to the jurisdiction's investors must abide by its rules.

Not surprisingly, the national treatment model is the basis for regulation in most jurisdictions. Such jurisdictions have their own sets of rules and regulations governing securities activities within their borders. In some cases, standards may be comparable between different jurisdictions, but compliance with any particular jurisdiction's specific regulatory system is a prerequisite to participating in that jurisdiction's securities market.

Under a strict national treatment model, the standards of the relevant jurisdiction are absolute and are applied equally to domestic and foreign participants, who must comply with those standards regardless of any external considerations. Such a system poses few difficulties when only purely domestic activities are involved. Market participants operating solely within the governing jurisdiction will be aware of the requirements and able to structure their operations accordingly. Such a system may also be workable when different jurisdictions adopt identical standards. In that case, activities that comply with the standards of one jurisdiction will also comply with those of the others.

Potential difficulties arise, however, where different jurisdictions impose different regulatory requirements. In such circumstances market participants may be forced to incur additional costs to comply with the different systems and compliance will almost certainly involve inefficiencies. In the most extreme cases, it will be impossible for the market participant to comply with conflicting requirements, foreclosing its participation in one of the markets.

Reciprocity

The realities of cross-border transactions mean that a jurisdiction that does not want to risk isolation is not likely to rely on a pure national treatment model of regulation. To a greater or lesser extent, it will accept standards applicable in other jurisdictions in lieu of its own. Reciprocity is the more restrictive model incorporating this acceptance of other standards. With reciprocity, jurisdictions agree that each will accept the standards applicable in the other as a substitute for the home country standard. The agreement can be between two jurisdictions or can cover a group of jurisdictions, with each agreeing to respect the standards of all the others.

Jurisdictions can agree to mutual recognition of each other's entire regulatory system, but in practice reciprocity is applied only in selected areas. Thus, for example, jurisdictions may agree to mutual recognition of each other's disclosure standards or capital adequacy standards without accepting other elements of each other's regulatory systems, such as regulation of financial intermediaries.

Deference

With reciprocity, a jurisdiction gives up some of its regulatory control, but only if its standards are accepted in return. There are times, however, when mutual recognition of standards is unnecessary or not feasible. In such circumstances, a jurisdiction may elect to defer to the standards of another jurisdiction. Deference involves either (i) acknowledging explicitly that the regulatory standards imposed by another jurisdiction provide sufficient protection so that they can be accepted in lieu of the home country standards or (ii) recognizing that for internal reasons, domestic regulation is not appropriate or possible. In this sense, the deference model is the opposite of the national treatment model. However, as with reciprocity, it is possible to apply the deference model to some elements of the regulatory system while simultaneously applying the national treatment model to others.

THE MODELS ILLUSTRATED—THE US SYSTEM

It ought to be readily apparent that no jurisdiction relies exclusively on any one of the models in its regulatory system. Rather, regulation is a combination of the three, with the mix varying from jurisdiction to jurisdiction and depending on the regulatory regime in place. The regulatory system in the United States probably comes closest to being one of strict national treatment in which the same rules are applied to domestic and foreign participants alike, but even the United States incorporates elements of reciprocity and deference.

National Treatment

As do most jurisdictions, the United States regulates a variety of securities activities conducted within its borders. Distributions of securities, the activities of broker-dealers and investment advisers, the operation of stock exchanges, the conduct of investment companies and a variety of other securities-related activities are subject to a comprehensive body of regulation. The US domestic regulatory standards apply to non-US market participants to the extent their activities directly affect the United States, which raises the possibility that the non-US market participants will be subject to inconsistent regulation. This problem is especially prevalent in the area of the disclosure required in connection with securities distributions,[6a] because the United States has a comprehensive set of requirements. The US accounting standards, in particular, cause difficulties for non-US issuers. The US requirements for financial intermediaries, such as broker dealers, impose significant US regulation on non-US market participants.

Disclosure

A fundamental tenet of the US regulatory system is that the market must be kept fully informed about issuers whose securities are offered and traded. There was a strong sense that a significant cause of the crash of 1929 was that investors were not adequately informed about the financial condition and business affairs of the companies whose securities they were buying.[7] As a result, investors, particularly retail investors, were making inappropriate investment decisions.

As part of the radical overhaul of US securities regulation in the wake of the market crash, a comprehensive disclosure system was implemented requiring any issuer wishing to sell securities to the public in the United States to register those securities with the SEC and to provide prospective

[6a] Some of these difficulties are discussed by Rovinescu and Thieffry, supra, at pp. 51–7.

[7] See H.R. Report No. 85, 73rd Long, 1st Session (1933) quoted in Edward N. Gadsby, Historical Development of the S.E.C.—The Government View, 28 Gev. Wash. L. Rev. 6,9 (1959).

investors with detailed information regarding its business and financial situation.[8] Moreover, an issuer that registers securities with the SEC, or whose securities are widely held in the United States, is obligated to provide ongoing disclosure.[9]

The rationale underlying the disclosure requirements is that retail investors need sufficient information on which to base their investment decisions. The view was taken that market forces alone were not enough to compel issuers to provide adequate information so the disclosure was made mandatory. The requirements are substantially the same for all issuers, to ensure that investors will be able to compare different companies.

The same considerations do not apply to certain institutional investors, who are deemed capable of looking after their own interests. It is thought they are better equipped both to know what information is important to their investment decisions and to obtain that information. Thus, offerings that are made only to sophisticated, institutional investors do not attract the same level of regulation.

In order fully to protect US retail investors, the disclosure requirements apply to all offerings that include such investors. Thus, a non-US issuer that wants to make a US public offering must provide disclosure that is, with limited exceptions, identical to that which a US issuer must provide. In addition, a non-US issuer that conducts a public offering, or lists its securities on a US stock exchange (or obtains a NASDAQ quotation), becomes subject to the ongoing periodic disclosure requirements of the Exchange Act.

For non-US issuers, the US disclosure requirements are generally viewed as being rigorous and difficult to comply with.[10] Particularly onerous are the requirements for the presentation of financial statements. Financial information must be either prepared in accordance with US generally accepted accounting principles (GAAP) or reconciled to US GAAP. Moreover, the financial statements must be audited in accordance with US generally accepted auditing standards. Preparing such information is a time-consuming and costly process and there are no exceptions to the requirement.

As cross-border activity has increased, the SEC has acknowledged that some concessions must be made to the difficulties faced by non-US issuers wanting to have access to the US markets, particularly as it wants to encourage such activity. Nonetheless, despite some movement towards

[8] See Securities Act §5; Forms S-1, S-2, S-3, F-1, F-2 and F-3 under the Securities Act. The specific disclosure requirements applicable to various offerings have been modified over time, but the underlying principle remains in place.

[9] See Exchange Act, §§12, 15; Forms 10-K, 10-Q, 20-F, 6-K and 8-K under the Exchange Act.

[10] See, e.g., Securities Act Release No. 6896 (Jun. 5, 1991), Section I; Securities Act Release No. 6866 (June 6, 1990), Section II.

acceptance of other regulatory standards,[11] the US disclosure requirements remain a prime illustration of national treatment.

In contrast to public distributions, there are no restrictions on investors purchasing securities of foreign companies in secondary market trading, and no obligation generally on foreign issuers to comply with US disclosure standards, irrespective of the number of US holders of their securities. The dollar amount of trading in the secondary market in the United States in both US and non-US securities far exceeds the amount of money raised in the primary market. While US companies are required to register classes of equity securities when their asset and shareholder bases exceed specified limits in order to provide periodic information to the secondary market, the same rule is not applied to foreign issuers; complete deference is afforded to local market requirements provided foreign issuers do not make a voluntary entry into the United States[12] by way of a public offering or authorization of their securities to trade in the United States on a stock exchange or to be quoted in the NASDAQ System.[13]

Broker-dealer Regulation

Brokers and dealers play a significant role in the smooth operation of the securities markets. They act as agents in the purchase and sale of securities by retail and institutional investors and conduct significant proprietary trading. Brokers and dealers played a major role in the 1929 stock market crash. Brokers had extended a large amount of credit to investors for the purchase of securities and many were undercapitalized. When stock prices started to fall, investors were unable to repay the loans and were forced to sell their securities at a loss, forcing prices down even further. A combination of incompetence, malfeasance, bad luck and bad judgment meant that the entire system was overextended and could not withstand the shock of falling stock prices.

Because of the importance of broker-dealers to the market, regulation of their activities was another major element of the regulatory reform after the crash. Key areas where more rigorous standards were introduced included capital adequacy requirements,[14] limits on the amount of credit that can be extended for the purchase of securities[15] and supervisory and recordkeeping requirements.[16] To ensure that US investors benefit from these protections, it is a requirement of the US regulatory system that only broker-dealers that are registered with the SEC, and are therefore subject to the regulations, can

[11] See pp. 164–9, infra.

[12] See Edward F. Greene, Daniel A. Braverman and Sebastian R. Sperber, Hegemony or Deference: US Disclosure Requirements in the International Capital Markets, 50 The Business Lawyer 413 (1995) for a full discussion of this dichotomy.

[13] Rule 12g3-2b.

[14] See Rule 15c3-1 under the Exchange Act.

[15] See Exchange Act §7.

[16] See, e.g., Exchange Act §§15(f), 17(a); Rules 17a-3 and 17a-5 under the Exchange Act.

deal with US investors.[17] Whereas distinctions were made in the Securities Act based on whether distributions were made to the public or only to sophisticated institutions, no such distinctions were initially made under the Exchange Act; broker dealer registration is required in order to do business with any customer in the United States.

A major consequence of the broker-dealer registration requirements is that non-US broker-dealers are precluded from interacting with US investors, even when the securities in question are those of a non-US issuer and investors are initiating contacts in the context of secondary market trading. The prohibition has proved burdensome as the securities markets have become increasingly global and US investors have become more interested in participating in markets outside the United States. In order not to lose out on this US demand, most major non-US broker-dealers have been forced to establish US affiliates which are registered with the SEC, thereby accepting the US national treatment standard with respect to their US operations.

Reciprocity

By and large, reciprocity is not a significant element of the US regulatory system. Indeed, a major complaint about the US system is the rigidity with which the SEC applies US standards, refusing to accept a non-US issuer's compliance with its home country standards as sufficient protection for US investors, at least in the context of public offerings. One significant exception to this policy has been the multijurisdictional disclosure system (the MJDS) between the SEC and provincial securities regulators in Canada.[18]

The MJDS

The MJDS permits certain US and Canadian issuers to conduct a variety of US/Canadian cross-border securities offerings and tender offers in both

[17] Exchange Act §15. Broker-dealers and others who provide investment advice to US investors must also be registered under the Investment Advisers Act of 1940 (the 'Advisers Act'). In one of the strictest applications of national treatment, the SEC for many years took the view that the provisions of the Advisers Act applied to all activities of registered advisers, anywhere in the world, regardless of whether those provisions were stricter than, or even conflicted with, local regulation. It was not until 1992 that the SEC announced it would consider applying a narrower, more territorial approach to the reach of the Advisers Act. See Division of Investment Management, SEC, Protecting Investors: A Half Century of Investment Company Regulations (May 1992), cited in Edward F. Greene, Alan L. Beller, George F. Cohen, Manley O. Hudson, Jr. and Edward J. Rosen, US Regulation of the International Securities Markets (Prentice Hall Legal & Business, 2d ed. 1993) (hereinafter, 'ISM Book') §10.02[1]. Even so, the SEC has indicated that it retains a strong interest in ensuring that the non-US activities of registered advisers or their affiliates do not have an adverse affect on the US markets. See Unibanco (avail. Jul. 28, 1992); Mercury Asset Management (avail. Apr. 16, 1993).

[18] See generally, MJDS Adopting Release; ISM Book, Ch. 5.

countries on the basis of their home country disclosure and other home country regulatory standards. It also permits such issuers to satisfy both countries' ongoing reporting requirements by meeting their home country obligations, as well as providing reciprocal recognition of the regulation of trust indentures and trustees.[19]

Under the MJDS, many Canadian issuers that have complied with the Canadian ongoing reporting requirements for a minimum of three years can register securities with the SEC merely by filing a Canadian prospectus, along with a US 'wraparound' containing a US-style cover page, certain standard-form legends and other technical disclosure. In addition, the issuer must file certain exhibits but as they consist only of the documents made publicly available in Canada in connection with the offering, as well as any documents incorporated by reference in the Canadian prospectus and the consents of any experts named in the filing; no additional disclosure is necessary.

Canadian issuers may rely on the MJDS to conduct an offering in the United States even if there is no simultaneous Canadian offering. The issuer must still prepare a disclosure document complying with Canadian standards and must designate one of the Canadian provinces as the reviewing jurisdiction which will approve the document, but the SEC will not normally subject the filing to any additional regulatory review.

In adopting the MJDS, the SEC acknowledged the significant growth in cross-border transactions involving both purchases of non-US securities by US investors and offerings outside the United States by US issuers.[20] The SEC also noted that non-US issuers were reluctant to extend various offers, including rights offers, exchange offers and tender offers, to US shareholders because of the necessity of complying with more than one regulatory system.[21] A primary reason for this reluctance on the part of non-US issuers is that the US standards applicable to such offers are generally more rigorous than the standards applicable elsewhere and complying with them adds significant time and expense to the process of completing the offering.[22] In light of these statements it is somewhat surprising that, for many offerings, the MJDS does not provide complete reciprocity; the SEC retained perhaps the most onerous of the US regulatory requirements, namely that an issuer's financial statements must be prepared in accordance with, or be reconciled to, US GAAP.[23] Notwithstanding that requirement, the MJDS has proved reasonably successful with over $9 billion of offerings done by Canadian issuers under the system by the end of 1992.[24]

[19] See MJDS Adopting Release, Section IIIA.

[20] See MJDS Adopting Release, Section II.

[21] Id.

[22] See id.

[23] See Securities Act Release No. 33–7004 (June 28, 1993) (hereinafter, 'MJDS Amending Release'); MJDS Adopting Release, Section IIIB.

[24] See ISM Book, §8.14.

Other Initiatives for Reciprocity

The MJDS with Canada was intended to be the first of a series of reciprocal arrangements with other jurisdictions.[25] Canada was chosen as the first jurisdiction for reciprocal recognition of regulation because of the 'significant presence of Canadian companies in the US trading markets'[26] and because there was already substantial similarity between the US and Canadian regulatory systems.[27]

To date, however, no additional agreements have been finalized. Notwithstanding the willingness of the SEC to pursue further initiatives, the MJDS is unlikely to prove a good model. It is a very complex system that was greatly facilitated by the existing similarities between the US and Canadian systems and the willingness of the Canadian regulators to adopt a number of new regulatory provisions comparable to those of the US when the MJDS was being negotiated, factors which may not be present in other jurisdictions.[28]

The current focus in discussions among securities regulators appears to have shifted away from bilateral agreements and towards harmonization—that is, agreeing regulatory standards among a large group of jurisdictions that would be accepted in all such jurisdictions. For example, efforts being conducted under the auspices of the International Organization of Securities Commissions (IOSCO) are aimed at agreeing common standards across a wide range of jurisdictions and a wide variety of regulatory topics, including disclosure, regulation of secondary markets and regulation of financial intermediaries.[29] In addition, the International Accounting Standards Committee is engaged in an ongoing effort to develop accounting standards that will be used in all the major markets.[30]

A fundamental question underlying any initiatives to develop global regulatory standards is whether the SEC will be willing to accept the standards of other jurisdictions in lieu of those currently applicable in the United States. Although the agency has taken some steps in this directions—witness the MJDS—it remains reluctant to relinquish its primary regulatory authority in what it perceives as key areas, such as financial statement disclosure.[31] As long as the SEC insists on the primacy of the US accounting

[25] See MJDS Adopting Release, Section I.

[26] Id., Section II.

[27] See ISM Book, §8.01, n. 2.

[28] See id.

[29] See International Organization of Securities Commissions, Annual Report 1994.

[30] See International Accounting Standards Committee, International Accounting Standards 1995, p. 7 et seq.

[31] For example, the MJDS as originally adopted provided that US GAAP reconciliation would not be necessary for offerings conducted after July 1, 1993. See MJDS Adopting Release, Section IIIA. In 1993, however, the SEC amended the MJDS to retain the reconciliation requirement, citing its belief that differences between US and Canadian accounting standards are significant enough to 'warrant retention of the currently existing reconciliation requirements . . .' MJDS Amending Release, Section I.

requirements, the MJDS model is not likely to be extended. The trend is more likely to be in the direction of harmonization of disclosure requirements and accounting standards through IOSCO.

Deference

As with reciprocity, the SEC's general unwillingness to accept the regulatory standards of other jurisdictions has meant that deference does not play a significant part in the US regulatory system. As discussed, this intransigence has proved particularly problematic in the context of financial statement disclosure since, in order to distribute securities widely in the United States, non-US issuers are required to present their financial information either in accordance with, or reconciled to, US GAAP. By contrast, most other jurisdictions defer to the US standards and do not require US issuers to conform to local accounting rules in order to market their securities.

Notwithstanding its general reluctance to accept regulatory standards of other jurisdictions, there are some areas where the SEC has adopted deference. By and large, these efforts have been limited and apply only to transactions involving only institutional investors or in situations in which the authority to impose domestic regulation is unclear. A useful example of the former is broker-dealer registration, of the latter, the fact that non-US companies are exempt from the periodic reporting requirements imposed on US companies solely by reason of their asset size and shareholder base exceeding specified amounts.

Broker-dealer Registration

As discussed above, a basic requirement under the US regulatory system is that in order to effect transactions with US investors, including offering and selling securities to those investors, a broker-dealer must be registered with the SEC.[32] The result of this requirement is that unregistered non-US broker-dealers are precluded from having any interaction with US investors.

Perhaps in recognition that the general requirement unduly inhibits the access of US investors to non-US markets, the SEC has implemented a limited exception to the registration requirement for non-US broker-dealers. Rule 15a-6 under the Exchange Act allows non-US broker-dealers to engage in certain types of business with US investors. For example, non-US broker-dealers can, without significant restrictions, offer and sell securities to US registered broker-dealers, as well as to various supranational organizations such as the World Bank and the African Development Bank.[33] Non-US broker-dealers can also offer and sell securities to a limited class of sophisticated investors, including banks, insurance companies, pension

[32] See pp. 164–5. [33] Rule 15a-6(a)(4) under the Exchange Act.

plans, trusts and charitable organizations, as long as the resulting transactions are effected by a US registered broker-dealer who also supervises any telephone conversations or meetings between the non-US broker-dealer and the US investor.[34]

The principle embodied in Rule 15a-6 is deference to the regulatory standards applicable to broker-dealers in other jurisdictions with respect to transactions involving investors which are thought to be sophisticated and therefore able to understand the risk of dealing with broker dealers not regulated by the SEC[35]. As long as the requirements of the rule are met, a non-US broker-dealer can conduct business with US investors on the basis of compliance only with the broker-dealer regulation applicable in its home jurisdiction. However, the restricted class of US investors with whom non-US broker-dealers can deal in reliance on the Rule means that, ultimately, the deference embodied therein is limited.

Other Examples of Deference

There are a number of other examples of deference in the US regulatory system. For instance, in the area of market regulation, where US regulation generally applies to activities of participants in a distribution anywhere in the world if the distribution includes the United States, offerings conducted by large issuers organized in Germany, France or the United Kingdom are now exempted from the operation of the market regulation rules for the portion of such offerings conducted outside the United States.[36] Another example is in the area of proxy rules, where non-US issuers are exempted from compliance with the US rules, even though they may have US shareholders.[37] Even in the area of financial disclosure, where the SEC has proved quite reluctant to make concessions, there are some examples of deference. Thus, non-US issuers that are subject to the periodic reporting requirements of the Exchange Act need not provide quarterly financial information if it is not required in the home jurisdiction.

There are two other areas where at first glance the United States appears to have adopted deference. Section 7(d) of the Investment Company Act of 1940 provides that the SEC can authorize non-US investment companies to conduct public offerings of securities without complying with the full panoply of regulations applicable to US investment companies. Similarly,

[34] Rule 15a-6(a)(3) under the Exchange Act. This subparagraph of the Rule does not permit non-US broker-dealers to market securities to US corporations that do not fit into one of the other specified categories.

[35] Interestingly, Rule 15a-6 does not require non-US broker-dealers to be subject to any sort of regulation in their home jurisdiction. It is sufficient that they are broker-dealers organized outside the United States.

[36] Deutsche Bank AG available October 6, 1993; Distributions of Certain French Securities (available June 7, 1994); The London Stock Exchange (available January 10, 1995)

[37] See Rule 3a12-3 under the Exchange Act.

section 310(a)(1) of the Trust Indenture Act of 1939 permits non-US entities subject only to regulation in their home countries to act as trustees for US public debt offerings. A closer examination of the two provisions, however, reveals that only entities whose home country regulation the SEC finds to be substantially equivalent to that of the United States can benefit. Not surprisingly, with very limited exceptions,[38] the SEC has not found such equivalence.

Other jurisdictions have taken a different approach to deference. Rather than relying entirely on the standards of another jurisdiction or using nominal deference simply to mask national treatment, this middle route involves two or more jurisdictions agreeing minimum standards for regulation that will be acceptable in each. A regulated entity that complies with its home country's standards is then permitted to conduct business in the other jurisdictions. This approach has been followed in the European Union where, for example, minimum standards have been established for listing securities on stock exchanges and for the continuing obligations imposed on issuers of listed securities that are applicable in all member states.[39]

The SEC has indicated that it will consider deferring to other standards in appropriate circumstances.[40] Indeed, it has greatly facilitated access by non-US issuers to the institutional market in the United States through the adoption of Rule 144A under the Securities Act. However, it remains unwilling to make cross-border investment easier for retail investors. For example, the NYSE has suggested that it might be appropriate for certain non-US issuers to be listed on the basis of their home country financial disclosure, without US GAAP reconciliation, but the SEC has resisted such efforts. Unless it becomes more willing to cede its primary regulatory authority, there is little likelihood of significant change.

ISSUES UNDER THE US SYSTEM

Impact of Strong Reliance on National Treatment

The United States is the world's largest securities market.[41] It is also one of the most highly regulated markets, and as such, influences the regulatory regimes of other jurisdictions. Many elements of the US system have provided models followed by other regulators. For example, the US has

[38] Certain non-US investment companies have been permitted to register under Section 7(d). See generally, Tamar Frankel, The Regulation of Money Managers, Vol. III, ch. XXIV, §4 (1980 and 1994 Supp.).

[39] See Council Directive of 5 March 1979, O.J. Eur. Comm. (No. L. 66) 21 (1979), discussed by Rovinescu and Thieffry, supra, pp. 49–50.

[40] See, e.g., Securities Act Release 6866 (June 6, 1990) (hereinafter, 'Multinational Tender Offer Release').

[41] In 1993, for example, US equity market capitalization represented over 36% of the world total. SEC Annual Report 1994, p. 28.

developed a comprehensive approach to ensuring the integrity of the securities markets. The US rules governing insider trading, market manipulation and reporting of transactions have served as the bases for comparable regulation in a number of other jurisdictions. Similarly, the concept of a statutory body charged with regulating securities activities has been adopted in several other countries. Furthermore, the US approach of making distributions of securities the focal point of regulation has been widely followed.

The US regulatory system generally works well in facilitating the smooth and efficient operation of the US domestic market and in providing protection to US investors. However, the continued adherence to a predominantly national treatment model focused on the distribution of securities in the face of the continuing globalization of the world's securities markets imposes increased costs and inefficiencies on non-US entities wishing to access the US market and hinders participation by US investors in other markets.

Increased Costs

The most significant additional costs are imposed on issuers wanting to sell their securities in the US public market. To do so, they must prepare a prospectus satisfying the rigorous US disclosure requirements, and must present their financial statements in accordance with, or reconciled to, US GAAP. The prospectus generally must undergo a review by the SEC, which can be time-consuming. Moreover, by undertaking a public offering in the United States, or by obtaining a US stock exchange listing, a non-US issuer becomes subject to the periodic reporting requirements of the Exchange Act, which obligate the issuer to, among other things, file an annual report with the SEC, which includes US GAAP or US GAAP-reconciled financial statements, as well as to the provisions of the US Foreign Corrupt Practices Act.[42] These ongoing requirements are generally much more onerous than those imposed by the issuer's home jurisdiction. Even in those instances where they are not, the simple fact that the issuer must comply with two sets of requirements means its costs are increased.

Nor is it only issuers who face increased costs in accessing the US market. As discussed above,[43] broker-dealers wishing to deal with US investors must be registered with the SEC. A non-US broker-dealer must therefore incur the costs (both financial and otherwise) of SEC registration either directly or by setting up a separate US affiliate in order to have full access

[42] In general, the Foreign Corrupt Practices Act (the FCPA) prohibits certain persons from making or promising to make payments or gifts to foreign officials, political parties or candidates for political office if the purpose is to induce the recipient to violate his or her lawful duties or use his or her influence to affect a governmental action so as to assist the giver in obtaining business from or directing business to any person. The FCPA also imposes certain requirements with respect to accounting practices and controls.

[43] See pp. 163–4 supra.

to US investors. Even if the non-US broker-dealer is willing to limit its contacts with the United States and rely on Rule 15a-6, it will incur some additional costs.

Increased Inefficiencies

The need to comply with the US regulatory requirements also results in increased inefficiencies for non-US market participants accessing the US capital markets. Perhaps the most significant inefficiency is the additional time a transaction takes. Generally, preparing a prospectus to US standards takes longer than preparing a prospectus for the issuer's home market, in part because of the SEC review process but mostly because of the additional information that must be included. Furthermore, in some instances, the US requirements conflict with those of the home jurisdiction.[44] In such cases, an issuer may be forced to conduct a separate offering in the United States or attempt to conclude a compromise with the regulators in one or both of the jurisdictions.

In extreme cases, the conflicts are irreconcilable, with the result that the US regulatory requirements effectively preclude access by non-US issuers entirely. A clear example of this result arises as a consequence of the US regulation of investment companies. An investment company must be registered with the SEC in order to conduct a public offering in the United States. However, as discussed above,[45] in order for a non-US investment company to be allowed to register, it must be subject to a regulatory system comparable to that of the United States. Since virtually no other country's regulation of investment companies is as rigorous, almost no non-US investment companies are registered or have conducted public offerings in the United States, despite the fact that investment in mutual funds has grown dramatically around the world and such funds are the subject of substantial regulation in most developed markets.

These increased costs and inefficiencies mean that non-US issuers are often reluctant to come to the US market. When they do include US investors in their securities offerings, it is often on a limited basis, since the regulatory requirements for offerings only to institutional investors are less burdensome. The ironic result, therefore, is that the very rules designed to protect US retail investors result in their being excluded from many offerings. In order to obtain the securities of many non-US issuers retail investors may be forced to participate in the local secondary market, where most non-US issuers are subject only to their home country regulatory

[44] For example, the rules governing tender offers in the United States conflict in certain key respects with the UK Takeover Panel requirements. Compare, e.g., Exchange Act §14(d)(5) and Rule 14d-7 under the Exchange Act (withdrawal rights available throughout a tender offer) with The City Code on Takeovers and Mergers, Rule 34 (no withdrawals permitted until 21 days after first closing date).

[45] See pp. 168–9 supra.

requirements and protection for investors is generally limited to the investment adviser's obligation to recommend only suitable investments. Moreover, execution costs and settlement risks are higher than if trading could be done in the United States.

Prospects for Change

The US regulatory system currently focuses on distributions of securities. The perceived need to protect US retail investors means that the emphasis is on national treatment, and there is a great reluctance to concede that other regulatory systems might provide adequate protection for US investors. Since the system was first implemented, however, there has been a significant shift in the nature of the securities markets. The dollar amount of secondary market trading now far exceeds the dollar amount raised in initial offerings on an annual basis and institutional investors make up a much larger proportion of market participants than do retail investors. The SEC has recognized that, in order to facilitate the smooth operation of the increasingly global capital markets, it needs to make changes in the US system.[46] Those changes are likely to be made, though, within the current regulatory framework, which was not designed with the goal of facilitating secondary market trading. While increasing the amount of deference or reciprocity applied under the existing regulatory system will ease the difficulties faced by non-US issuers, it may also be important to consider changing the underlying scope of regulation.

Increased Reciprocity/Deference

The amount of reciprocity or deference applied clearly will depend on the activity to be regulated locally. With respect to financial statement presentation, a major stumbling block for non-US issuers, there are strong arguments that strict adherence to the US GAAP standard is unnecessary, particularly for offerings with substantial institutional investors involvement. The participation by US institutions in Rule 144A offerings and other private placements by non-US issuers, where no US GAAP presentation or reconciliation is required, indicates that such investors are willing to make investment decisions without US GAAP information. Similarly, the significant US secondary market trading in the securities of non-US issuers indicates that investors, including retail investors, do not see the absence of US GAAP financial information as a deterrent.

The willingness of US investors to purchase securities of non-US issuers in private offerings and in the secondary market, where US GAAP presentation is not available, implies that the SEC could move toward deference

[46] See Securities Act Release No. 6896 (June 5, 1991); Multinational Tender Offer Release.

in the context of accounting standards. In particular, if it deferred to standards which were the equivalent of International Accounting Standards, other jurisdictions might move their standards to International Accounting Standards, and adoption of such standards would greatly facilitate the conduct of cross-border offerings.

One area where it might not be appropriate to defer to standards of other jurisdictions is the regulation of financial intermediaries, such as broker-dealers. Because the failure of a US broker-dealer could have a significant ripple effect through the entire US financial system, there is more justification for requiring entities that want to participate in the US capital markets to comply with whatever minimum standards are deemed necessary to safeguard that system. Currently, Rule 15a-6 does not require that a foreign broker-dealer be subject to any minimum standards.

Rethinking the Regulatory Approach

The United States, like most other jurisdictions, requires that a prospectus be delivered in public distributions of securities. However, one area that is ripe for change is the prospectus disclosure requirements. In order to ensure compliance with the US disclosure requirements, the document is often lengthy and complicated, with detailed information about the issuer, its business and its financial situation and a full set of the issuer's financial statements. Anecdotal evidence suggests, however, that very few potential investors actually read all or even most of the prospectus. At most, they appear to focus on the summary information generally presented at the beginning of the prospectus. If that is in fact the case, and if the distribution of securities is the primary focal point for regulation, investors might be better served if they were provided instead with a short-form prospectus that provides only key information in a more 'user-friendly' format. The issuer could still be obligated to produce a full prospectus for SEC review, which would be available to any investor requesting it (or which could be provided as a matter of course to institutional investors), but it would not have to incur the expense of producing full prospectuses for all retail investors.[47] A system like this is used in the United Kingdom where a 'mini-prospectus', containing extracts from the full prospectus, is provided to retail investors. Indeed, the SEC recently approved the use of a short-form 'profile prospectus' by mutual funds on a one-year experimental basis.[48] Any concern that investors would be disadvantaged by receiving less information could be ameliorated by retaining or even expanding the obligation imposed on broker-dealers to recommend only suitable investments to their

[47] This approach is already used to a certain extent in the shelf registration process, where an issuer's ability to incorporate significant amounts of the mandated disclosure by reference means there is flexibility as to how much information to include in the prospectus.

[48] Investment Company Institute (available August 4, 1995).

clients. The short-form prospectus approach would be more efficient for issuers and would provide investors with a manageable amount of information that is more likely to prove useful in making an investment decision.

A more radical change, but one that would facilitate the secondary market trading that now forms such a significant part of securities activities, would be to shift the regulatory emphasis away from a national treatment model focusing on distributions to requiring continuous disclosure to the trading market by all companies whose securities are actively traded globally. Such a change could involve new approaches to the need for, and the content and form of, prospectuses as outlined above as well as some increased forms of deference, particularly with respect to jurisdictions in which efficient markets are thought to operate.[49]

REGULATORY COMPETITION[49a]

The approach of the United States discussed above is premised on the concept of regulatory convergence, i.e., that because deference or reciprocity will be implemented on a restricted basis by the SEC, there will ultimately be a convergence of conflicting regulatory standards around those in effect in the United States. This stance is due in part to the perception that where there is competition between regulatory systems, each jurisdiction has an incentive to ensure that its system is the most attractive to market participants, and hence to make its standards less onerous. The result, it is posited, will be an inevitable lowering of regulatory standards at the expense of investors.

In reality, there are some natural limitations on how much standards can deteriorate. For example, some or all market participants will generally demand a minimum level of regulation in order to guarantee some order in the markets. In addition, not all jurisdictions will be willing or able to compete and strong markets, like the United States, are in a position to resist any pressure to lower their levels of regulation. Nonetheless, the theory holds that regulatory competition will result in lowered standards.

The existence of differences in regulatory standards among various jurisdictions means that some jurisdictions are likely to be more attractive to market participants than others. However, examples of jurisdictions tailoring their standards in an overt effort to entice market participants are comparatively rare.[50] Indeed, far from constituting a 'race to the bottom' of

[49] For a fuller discussion of the proposal to expand the use of deference, see Edward F. Greene, Daniel A. Braverman and Sebastian R. Sperber, Hegemony or Deference: US Disclosure Requirements in the International Capital Markets, 50 The Business Lawyer 413 (1995).

[49a] Kitch, infra, pp. 233 ff discusses the benefits, problems and limitations of competition between different securities markets.

[50] The clearest examples are the various offshore banking centers, such as the Channel Islands, the Cayman Islands and Bermuda.

constantly lowered standards, the competition among the world's major financial centers—London, New York, Tokyo and Frankfurt—has seen more of a convergence of standards. Although the various centers compete aggressively for business, their regulatory regimes have become increasingly similar. For example, the United Kingdom and Japan have adopted laws against insider trading not unlike those in the United States, and the UK Financial Services Act 1986 includes market manipulation regulation akin to that in the United States. Each market has its own comparative advantages, but by and large regulatory laxity is not a major feature.

REGULATORY TIMING

Regulatory systems cannot be static. As markets develop and grow, the applicable regulation must be adapted accordingly. In virtually all existing securities regulation regimes, it is distributions of new securities that attract regulation, notwithstanding that the amount of secondary market trading far exceeds annually the amount of money raised in primary offerings. Recently, however, the wisdom of focusing on distributions has come under scrutiny, as some regulators and market participants have questioned whether there might not be a better approach.

Regulation of Securities Distributions

Regulation of securities distributions usually means that there is uncertainty as to the timing of access to the capital markets, either because of regulatory review or inability to comply with current disclosure requirements. The United States began to address the consequences of that uncertainty by developing the concept of shelf registration. With shelf registration, companies register in advance securities of any kind they reasonably expect to sell during the next two years. Because the shelf registration statement has been reviewed and declared effective by the SEC in advance, offerings take place without any regulatory intervention. Takedowns occur by means of prospectus supplements to the core prospectus in the shelf registration statement and are delivered to investors with the confirmations. Moreover, the core prospectus and prospectus supplements build on prior disclosures to the market. Rather than repeating them to satisfy the mandatory prospectus disclosure requirements, the disclosures are incorporated by reference, thereby reducing the size of the prospectus while satisfying the mandatory requirements. Investors can, however, request the historical information that is incorporated by reference.

Shelf registration is possible because (i) the Exchange Act requires periodic reporting to the secondary market, (ii) the contents of that reporting are equivalent to the disclosure made in a prospectus during a distribution of securities and (iii) the theory of efficient markets suggests that for certain companies information previously disclosed is incorporated into the price at which securities trade in the secondary market and need not be reiterated during subsequent distributions. Thus, if distributions of securities are regulated and if there are mandatory disclosure requirements for prospectuses, these mandatory requirements can be satisfied by companies with a wide following in the market simply by incorporating the prior disclosure made in the periodic reports into the prospectus. The prospectus delivered will set out information about the offering, the securities and any new information necessary to make the incorporated disclosures not misleading. They will be short, easy to prepare and allow instant access to the market.

But even with the extraordinarily efficient shelf registration system, the focus is still on the distribution side, which is episodic—that is, disclosure about an issuer is only updated if there is a distribution. Thus, in the United States, there is currently discussion of a company registration proposal under which companies of a certain size would register, and provide continuous detailed disclosure to the market irrespective of the amount of securities sold in any one period. These companies would be able to offer securities at any time without any regulatory intervention. There would be no prospectus requirements; the market would dictate what information was delivered to investors, and that information would be subject to the same liability standard as disclosure provided pursuant to the continuous disclosure requirements. The focus of the agency would shift such that its review function would be substantially allocated to initial public offerings by companies before they became eligible for the company registration system and the continuous disclosure made to the market by companies in the system.

There are some significant concerns that need to be resolved if a company registration system is to be substituted for a system in which the focus is on distribution of securities. Prospectuses used in distributions are often reviewed by regulators and are typically subjected to a stricter standard of liability than disclosure to the market generally. That is certainly true in the United States, where companies have absolute liability for misstatements and omissions in a prospectus, but are liable only for fraud in connection with such misstatements or omissions in their periodic reports or press releases to the market. Thus, the quality of the disclosure is thought to be higher in distributions, even though the disclosure requirements are the same for prospectuses and periodic reports under the Exchange Act.

It may also be the case that the quality of disclosure is higher because of the role of gatekeepers. Regulation of distributions of securities often imposes liabilities on gatekeepers, i.e. experts such as accountants, underwriters and directors. They are expected to vet any disclosure made to the public when money is being raised, and in the United States are held liable for any misstatement or omission in the prospectus unless they exercised reasonable care. Should there be a gatekeeper function when the focus is not on the distribution of securities but on continuous disclosure to the markets? If so, should the gatekeepers be the same? Is it realistic to expect that underwriters can have any control of the disclosure process? Will the elimination of gatekeepers reduce the quality of disclosure to the secondary market? If so, what other techniques could be used to substitute for the gatekeeper function?

A change to company registration would bring the US regulatory system more in line with the current state of the market, at least insofar as the market has become predominantly one of secondary trading. The change would not, however, alleviate the difficulties faced by non-US market participants under the current system, because it does not inherently require a departure from the national treatment model. To address this issue, the SEC would need to be prepared to concede that the standards applicable in some other jurisdictions provide sufficient protection to allow issuers from those jurisdictions to participate in the US markets, under a company registration scheme, without becoming subject (or perhaps not fully subject) to the US requirements.

Although the concept of company registration would need significant further refinement before being a realistic alternative, it does have several inherent attractions. It would streamline the process of capital formation. Issuers would no longer be subject to a time-consuming process of preparing a detailed prospectus each time they wanted to offer securities. Instead, they would be able to take advantage of market opportunities on an expedited basis. Company registration would also keep the entire market informed. There is already tacit acknowledgment that information is important to the secondary trading. Company registration would ensure that the secondary market was kept fully informed.

THE FUTURE

If we are right and the focus of regulation may be shifting from distributions to secondary market trading, how should we regulate that trading in the context of cross-border transactions? More and more the markets are moving to dealer markets with screen based quotation and trading systems. What if the proprietors of a regulated screen based trading system, such as NASDAQ or SEAQ, wanted to install terminals with all brokers-dealers and institutional investors around the world interested in investing in that market? This surely would be a likely development if regulatory hurdles could be overcome, and would bring certain efficiencies to cross-border trading. But how should a regulator respond to such an initiative? For example, if such a proprietor wanted to install such screens in the United States, should the SEC follow national treatment as the model? If so, it would require the operator of such a system to register with the SEC as an exchange or a broker-dealer or a clearing agency, perhaps all three. Moreover, such a model would force dealers to distinguish between securities in the process of distribution and outstanding securities to ensure compliance with the Securities Act, and publish trade information on a timely basis. If the SEC decides that national treatment is appropriate, the system is not likely to be installed.

If, however, one considered alternative approaches, one could permit such an installation without necessarily complete deference to local regulatory oversight of the operator. Rather, one would consider certain factors in deciding how to proceed. For example, if such a system gave US investors direct access to the securities of non-US issuers, are there any minimum disclosure or market capitalization requirements for those companies whose securities are quoted in the system? Does the system only make available indicative quotes, with no capability of executing a trade? If trading can occur, are the trades reported on a real time basis, as is the case in the United States? Does the system include securities in the process of distribution? Does the local market bar insider trading? What degree of regulatory oversight exists with respect to such a system? Are information sharing arrangements among regulators in place? These are important issues to be considered, but they can be addressed in our view without automatically imposing a national treatment model, for if a regulator regulates such a system under that model, it may never become operational unless harmonization occurs. It would be short-sighted to take such an approach. Other regulatory initiatives will be necessary, involving agreeing minimum standards internationally and cooperation among regulators to permit distributions and trading systems to operate globally and efficiently. Regulators including the SEC must become more international in their outlook.

11

Approaches to Market Regulation—The United Kingdom

MICHAEL J. PERRY

INTRODUCTION

Until comparatively recently, an examination of approaches to market regulation in the United Kingdom would have primarily focused on the London Stock Exchange (LSE) as the predominant market. The LSE continues to have a pre-eminent role in the equity market place, both as a dominant force in the cash market trades of UK equities and as the leading international exchange for the trading of foreign shares. However, the market place has moved beyond the traditional concept of the central market in an organisation sense and UK investors (both institutional and retail) have a wider range of options to consider with regard to the market in which they may deal.

Firstly, the recognised exchanges in the UK look set to increase. At present there are exchanges for commodities (London Commodities Exchange LCE), metals (London Metals Exchange LME) and oil (International Petroleum Exchange IPE), the London International Financial Futures Exchange (LIFFE) is the exchange for futures and options, OMLX is the exchange for Scandinavian securities derivatives and Trade-Point has just been recognised by the Securities and Investment Board (SIB) as an exchange which will provide for its customers an order driven dealing service in securities. The likelihood is that the number of recognised exchanges will increase since, as will be discussed later on, the UK regulators, whilst not promoting competition, nevertheless wish to ensure that investors have the freedom to choose.

Secondly, over the counter (OTC) markets have developed strongly which primarily cater for institutional/professional customers who require a customised product (whether for hedging or otherwise) which is not available on an exchange. OTC derivatives are a well known example of instruments that are dealt in off-exchange.

ISDA (The International Securities Dealers Association, formerly AIBD) in accordance with the dealing and settlement rules of which the Euromarkets are conducted in London, is a hybrid market; it is not recognised (since its headquarters are in Switzerland) but has been 'designated' by the UK Treasury since it is such an important market and its rules satisfy SIB's requirements. The Eurobond market and the development of the Euro-equity market are the main reasons why London is the preeminent European/global financial centre.

The international nature of the London markets is illustrated by the fact that in 1994, nearly half of the LSE turnover of £1,275 billion was accounted for by foreign companies and the turnover in non-UK companies was £606 billion, twice that for 1990. The primary and secondary turnover in the Euromarkets in 1994 was US$440 billion equivalent and $28.963 trillion equivalent respectively. This latter statistic does not break down the turnover by location, but London must have the predominant share.

Thirdly, investors have greater and easier access to overseas markets which will be further enhanced with the implementation of the Investment Services Directive (ISD) in January 1996.

The recent SIB report on 'Regulation of the United Kingdom Equity Markets' (the UK Equity Markets Regulation Report) sums up the position thus: 'Today's equity market is more sophisticated and diverse than ever before. For any equity risk there are now many different ways of dealing—not only through the traditional cash markets, but through ADRs, warrants, convertible bonds, single equity and index futures and options and through contracts for differences. Moreover, investors can often choose where they deal and whether they deal on-exchange or over the counter'.

Consequently, in considering market regulation, it is necessary to look at the regulation of the intermediaries and professional participants in the markets as well as the exchanges themselves.

The regulators are faced with the responsibility of adapting the regulatory system to the realities of an increasingly liberalised and global market place and with striking the right balance—underpinning confidence in the markets while, at the same time, recognising that thriving markets depend on innovation and risk taking. As is stated in the UK Equity Markets Regulation Report 'Our [SIB's] approach must be firmly rooted in a practical understanding of how markets work and what market participants want'.

In this Chapter we will be looking at how the attitude to market regulation is influenced by the overriding principles of disclosure (openness, transparency) and fairness, the distinction between the wholesale and retail markets, pressures for change in the markets, the consultation process and the need of the regulators to respond to diversity and to ensure a proper coordination across a broader market place both domestically and internationally.

UK REGULATORY SYSTEM

A brief review of the system is necessary in order to understand the attitudes which underlie market regulation.

London has always been regarded as one of the major financial centres of the world, it offers a very diverse range of financial services across a broad range of financial markets on a global basis. This reputation and expertise has built up over many years. As a result the approach taken to regulation of the financial markets has evolved in line with the developments within the market place.

Prior to 'Big Bang' there were strict demarcation lines between the various functions within the City. Brokers, jobbers and bankers operated as separate entities. However, after the abolition of minimum commissions and the lifting of the restriction on corporate ownership of member firms these functions were joined within large financial conglomerates which offered a wide range of financial services to both wholesale and retail customers. As such the physical barriers which had existed between firms were removed almost overnight. The legal and regulatory system which existed at that time was not sufficiently developed to regulate effectively in the new market conditions. The deregulation also heralded a dramatic change in the pace of change in the operation of the City.

In January 1984 The Gower Report, commissioned by the Department of Trade and Industry, produced a full report into the question of investor protection. Whilst the proposals contained within the report were not directly applied, many of them were implemented by the Financial Services Act 1986 (FSA).

Regulation of the financial services industry became statute backed with the FSA. The FSA stated that any investment business conducted had to be authorised and that the supervision of this investment business was to be placed in the hands of SIB.

The system has been dubbed 'self-regulating' (which would be more appropriate to the Lloyds insurance market which was not covered by the FSA). However, that description is not strictly correct since the FSA gave statutory backing to SIB and set out its powers. SIB was originally established in June 1985 but actually assumed its regulatory tasks in May 1987. Under the Act, SIB has the power to delegate its regulatory responsibility to a number of authorised agencies, namely the Self Regulatory Organisations (SROs). As such a 'two tier' system of regulation has been created. SIB was intended to be an organisation which was in principle responsible for setting standards, developing an all-encompassing rulebook for the financial services industry whilst still concerning itself with public policy issues. The SROs, which now include the Securities and Futures

Authority (SFA), the Investment Management Regulatory Organisation (IMRO) and the Personal Investment Authority (PIA) (which is in the course of replacing FIMBRA and LAUTRO as the SRO for retail packaged products) were intended to act as the front-line regulators for their particular area of the financial services industry. SIB maintains, in practice, strict control over the SROs and has extensive powers to withdraw their recognition should it believe that the interests of the public and the industry are not being served. The SROs act not only to regulate their specific area of the financial services industry, but also to address the concerns of the participants of their particular sector based upon the specific knowledge they have developed into the workings of the industry. The rulebooks drafted and implemented by the SROs are based upon the rules contained in the SIB Rulebook.

A firm must be authorised by an SRO in order to conduct investment business on its own behalf and also on behalf of its customers. For example, a firm would need to be authorised by an SRO to conduct investment business as defined by the FSA and will also be a member of one or more recognised exchanges to enable it to transact the business on such exchanges. The regulations imposed by the SRO govern the authorisation of the firm, reporting and capital adequacy requirements and conduct of business rules in the execution of customer business. The key test for authorisation by an SRO is the 'fit and proper test' which is determined by reference to financial integrity, competence, good reputation and character and efficiency and honesty. Firms who are members of exchanges must also comply with the rulebooks of those exchanges of which they are members. These rules concern dealing practices and are designed to maintain market integrity.

Not only must firms be authorised but also, in the case of the SFA and more recently IMRO, individuals employed by those firms to conduct investment business must be registered to conduct investment business either on behalf of their employer or customers.

THE CHANGING ROLE OF THE SIB

In analysing the regulators' approach to market regulation, it is instructive to look at how the role of SIB has developed since it was first established pursuant to the FSA.

Whilst it may appear rather journalistic to describe SIB's role by reference to the three chairmen who have been in office, nevertheless, each chairman set his own agenda and therefore particular aspects of SIB's role were given greater prominence. A convenient summary of the transition could be characterised as a movement from 'Detailed Rules' to 'Core Principles' to

'Setting Standards and Supervision'. However, it would be fair to point out that these changes have arisen as part of the evolution of SIB and in response to market developments and not merely because of a change of chairman.

Sir Kenneth Birrell

As was acknowledged in the paper written by Andrew Large entitled 'Financial Services Regulation: Making the Two Tier System Work' ('the Large Report'), the setting up of the system in 1985 required an enormous effort on recognition, authorisation of firms and the establishment of the infrastructure for on-going monitoring and enforcement. The political imperative was to get a regulatory system in place as soon as possible including the creation of a rulebook covering the whole of the investment business. This rulebook provided a benchmark of 'equivalence' for the recognition of the SROs who had to have their own rulebook.

As Andrew Large stated:

> 'The equivalence process was a bruising experience for SIB and the recognised bodies. The industry wanted clarity and the lawyers sought detailed prescriptive rules. The rulebooks were drafted hastily and under considerable legal influence. The SROs themselves tended to favour a detailed approach to rule making because of the narrow view taken by SIB of the 'equivalence' standard.'

Sir David Walker

In 1989 a new Companies Act modified the FSA to create a new framework for rules. This was in the context of a climate that favoured more flexibility and less prescriptive rules.

Under the so-called 'New Settlement' announced by Sir David Walker, SIB laid down in April 1990 ten Principles intended as a universal statement of general standards expected of all authorised firms requiring high standards of integrity and fair dealing, acting with due skill, care and diligence, observing high standards of market practice, knowing their clients and giving sufficient information to them to make investment decisions and avoiding conflicts of interest, wherever possible.

These Principles (together with 40 designated rules made by SIB) form the basis of the rulebooks. They relate not just to conduct of business rules but also to capital adequacy, protection of client assets (money and securities) and the maintenance of proper internal controls and procedures (very relevant in the current debate on derivatives and Barings).

The test to be applied by SIB to the rulebooks of SROs became 'adequacy' rather than equivalence with the intention of providing greater flexibility. Furthermore, the regulators were required to consider the costs of compliance in deciding how the investor protection objective should be achieved.

The industry generally welcomed the changes but, with further rule writing involved and SIB's staff carefully vetting 'adequacy', some questioned whether this aspect of the New Settlement was real.

A Central Monitoring Unit was constituted in 1988 to supervise recognised bodies but, with little resource, did not become an effective tool.

In retrospect, the New Settlement did lead to a greater distinction between inter-professional dealing and personal investors in the retail sector who require greater protection (which distinction is discussed below), but the lighter touch in rule making was less than was hoped for.

Andrew Large

By the time Andrew Large became Chairman in 1992, the regulatory system of financial services was perceived as failing to detect major fraud even though some of the cases are outside the system and some arose before FSA became effective. Things came to a head with the Maxwell scandal and the Home Income Plan frauds. It was felt that there were a multiplicity of parties involved and that there was no effective supervision or enforcement.

The Large Report was occasioned by the Maxwell case which had potential severe repercussions for a large number of pensioners. The Large Report identified a need for a change of style, approach and outlook of relationships and regulatory method. As the title of the paper implies, the objective was to make the two tier system work. The recommendations were that:

(i) the objectives of SIB and the recognised bodies must be made explicit and public based on the priority of investor protection;
(ii) SIB must set standards which are to be benchmarks and provide a basis for measurements of performance and accountability;
(iii) the supervision of the recognised bodies must be strengthened. Performance targets should be set and maintained by SIB;
(iv) SIB should give strong enforcement leadership to the regulating community;
(v) a businesslike approach must be applied by regulators to cost evaluation and control.

The securities industry has generally welcomed the approach taken in the Large Report although it was recognised that better enforcement might require some legislative changes which appeared to have been beyond the brief of the Large Report.

One matter I would like to discuss further is the move from detailed rules to Principles which was generally welcomed. The ability to be flexible and responsive in a changing environment is important. It is difficult to foresee every situation which might arise in respect of which prescriptive rules may not be appropriate. However, a firm needs to know where it stands and whilst it is healthy that it must look to the spirit of the rules rather than the detail, the Principles are not always easy to apply in new situations since best market practice (for example) may simply not exist. Seeking the views of the regulators may not always result in a clear or quick answer. The notice issued by SIB following the controversy caused by the use of derivative instruments in the Trafalgar/Northern Electric bid illustrates the point. The Notice reminded authorised persons that when dealing in securities to hedge exposure in contracts for differences where one or both parties are in possession of unpublished price sensitive information, they could be in breach of SIB Principles even if their conduct may not infringe any law or rule. Whilst the Notice was clearly intended as a warning, it did little to help the practitioners because it was too general in its terms. The SIB is setting up a body, the Market Conduct Regulatory Group, mainly formed by members of the different regulatory bodies to give guidance on what is best practice and further advice is expected on the matter previously referred to. Only experience will show whether this body will provide quick, definitive and practical advice.

SIB's Principles have been incorporated by the SROs into their rulebooks and both authorised firms and registered individuals are bound by them. A somewhat disturbing feature, from the practitioners' viewpoint, is that the individual SROs are seizing upon the breaches of Principles on which to base disciplinary charges rather than specifying breaches of specific rules. Whilst this might appear admirable in concept, there is concern that the use of the Principles in the disciplinary process should only be in egregious cases or where there is a clear gap in regulation. As the Principles are widely drafted and seek perfection (rather like the Ten Commandments), in theory it would be possible for a regulator wishing to show its enforcement muscle to discipline a firm for being rather less than perfect, but some way short of being in breach of a rule that would have any impact on investor protection. As LIBA (the trade association for London Investment Banks) has pointed out, in expressing concern at this development, the SFA combines the roles of investigator, prosecutor and judge but the SFA, whilst appreciating practitioner concerns, believe their approach is justified by the seriousness of the cases concerned, speed and avoidance of legal nit-picking.

WHOLESALE AND RETAIL MARKETS—THE DISTINCTION

A distinction is made within the regulatory system in the United Kingdom between wholesale and retail business. The distinction is based on the type of customer. Essentially, a 'retail' customer will include individuals, small companies and trusts with other customers being regarded as 'wholesale'. The classification is based upon the financial standing and/or sophistication of the customer. The regulatory structure (both in the FSA and in the rulebooks of the SROs) recognises the need to provide the retail customer with greater protection.

Events of recent years (eg mis-selling of pensions, Home Income Plans) have demonstrated that some financially inexperienced retail investors have been sold products by persons with a strong material interest which were not suitable. Consequently they have suffered substantial losses. It is therefore essential that regulation within this area must be detailed and prescriptive and coupled with effective monitoring of the practices employed by participants advising retail investors.

For wholesale business, flexibility in the approach to market regulation is essential to preserve London's leading position as a financial centre. Financially sophisticated customers require speed and economy in all their dealings and are in a position to make an informed decision upon a particular transaction or portfolio strategy. They are also accustomed to take professional advice where necessary. It is clearly a situation where 'caveat emptor' should apply. United Kingdom regulation allows intermediary firms to classify financially sophisticated private investors as experts. Consequently, they receive less protection under FSA than private investors but in return have a greater degree of flexibility and more opportunities to participate in the wide range of financial products available. For example, IMRO does not allow its members to market OTC derivatives to retail customers nor to deal in such instruments for such customers.

In the US no distinction is made between the duties owed to retail and wholesale customers and there are indications that as a result, the efficiency of the wholesale market is unduly burdened by the needs of the retail market.

The extent of regulation may also be influenced by whether the market being dealt on is wholesale or retail. Prime examples of wholesale markets are the Euromarkets, the OTC derivatives business and the foreign exchange markets. Such markets are characterised by sophisticated financial products, high volume and value trading and participation by seasoned market players, namely financial institutions. The retail market may be characterised essentially by the use of packaged products and the participation of the smaller, less sophisticated investor. However, certain markets operate, to a greater or lesser extent, on both levels; for example LSE and LIFFE which although dominated by large financial institutions, encourage active market participation by the small investor. Accordingly, their rules for investor protection are stronger and surveillance for the exchanges themselves is more active.

DISCLOSURE AND FAIRNESS

In order that participants may use markets with confidence there must be fairness and transparency.

Disclosure has been the underlying principle of Anglo-American securities laws. Disclosure is also a regulatory tool for regulators and they have fleshed out what this concept means in relation to particular markets, products, and different kinds of investor.

In the primary markets, disclosure is a matter of the laws relating to public offerings and prospectuses. Full transparency comprises three elements: an efficient price formation which has integrity, pre- and post-trade publicity and disclosure of material interests in share holdings.

Fair disclosure means avoiding excessive disparity of information or factors likely to have an impact on prices.

However there is controversy as to how transparent all markets need to be. The LSE provides a good degree of transparency but some participants have objected to the late publication of certain large trades and the exemption given to market makers not to disclose holdings above 3%. These aspects were examined in the UK Equity Markets Regulation Report in relation to the findings of the Director General of Fair Trading and are still under consideration (The LSE has, in fact, taken action quickly and will now publish market makers' holdings of 3% or more in the FTSE 100 companies, 5% or more in the FTSE 100-250 companies and 10% or more in the remainder of the FTSE companies).

With regard to wholesale markets (such as Euromarkets) and particularly OTC markets transparency is not such a crucial element because either the participants should have a good knowledge of or access to competing quotes in the markets or the product is so customised that disclosure is relevant only to the investor of the key elements involved but not to the market in general. SIB recognises the valuable role OTC markets play in innovative market trading and acknowledges the practical difficulties involved in bringing OTC trading in general within transparency standards required of on-exchange trading. SIB may nevertheless seek disclosure of some standardised OTC contracts for differences.

A further complication with regard to exchanges is the fragmentation of the market place. Should a person dealing on the LSE have access to the best price in the same stock on Tradepoint Financial Networks plc? SIB would like to see, in the interest of competing trading systems, a consolidated tape of all price information on a particular stock from all the markets on which it is dealt. However, it shares the concerns about the costs of such an exercise and believes that initiatives by private commercial suppliers would be the most efficient way of meeting the need rather than through direct regulatory action. Ruben Lee, Director of the Oxford Finance Group, would go further and argue that the whole question of the appropriate level of transparency should be left to market participants and that mandated transparency by the regulators is not necessary to stimulate competition between exchanges.

There are, however, ways other than transparency of markets of protecting the investor.

We have already seen that SIB and the SROs place an obligation on investment firms to provide retail investors with sufficient information, to provide best execution (as regards price) and to act with integrity. There are also safeguards in the criminal law, the FSA and the rules of SROs and Exchanges against market abuse (insider trading, market manipulation, etc).

The regulators can also insist on reporting of trades even if they are not published. Such reporting would enable the monitoring of transactions which would assist in detecting and deterring market malpractice and reinforcing systemic safety and to ensure that OTC contracts are not being used deliberately to avoid disclosure requirements.

In the International Organisation of Securities Commissions (IOSCO) paper issued by the technical committee on Transparency on Secondary Markets it was observed that 'the effective monitoring and detection of insider trading, manipulation and best execution are in principle substitutes for real time reporting of secondary market information in the function of achieving fairness.' This, however, begs the question of how effective such monitoring is.

SIB have promised a new review of the best execution rule in the light of market diversity. They have also issued two consultative papers for the purpose of setting standards. The first is on the Overall Standard of Equities Market Integrity and covers such topics as: market counterparty, market transparency, fair treatment of market users, reliable price formation, a market which is not misled, manipulated or abused and cost-effectiveness.

The second relates to Standards of Market Integrity with relation to Market Maker Privileges and Obligations. This paper looks at the privileges, the abuse of privileges, market maker obligations and monitoring and enforcement.

It can be seen that the debate about transparency will be ongoing and regulators will regularly review the subject as markets evolve and change.

PRACTITIONER INPUT

The regulatory system has been characterised as statute-based with significant practitioner input although the 'self regulatory' label is being downplayed as being synonymous with a club-like atmosphere where strict enforcement may be perceived as lax or being identified with the Lloyds insurance market problems. The practitioners' input is, however, vital to having sensible regulation and markets which provide the opportunity for investors to exercise choice.

A significant element of practitioner involvement is also essential if regulation is to be effective. Practitioner participation has many benefits; not least of which are that it:

(i) harnesses the expertise of the regulated;
(ii) can monitor innovation in the markets;
(iii) can ensure swift regulatory response;
(iv) promotes cooperation by regulated firms and a common interest in effective regulation.

It is recognised, though, that while effective practitioner input is crucial, it needs to be balanced by an impartial and competent regulator in order that 'regulatory capture', by business or other interests, does not take place and that the interests of investors are adequately represented.

There are three particular areas in which practitioner input can be seen.

Personnel

People with significant industry experience are sometimes recruited to the regulatory bodies themselves (eg Andrew Large) or are appointed to Committees (eg on Conduct of Business, Membership, Enforcement, Capital Finance etc).

With regard to recruitment to the regulators, it is felt that the regulators are not in general attracting experienced practitioners partly because there is no predictable career progression or the rewards are insufficient. Moreover, working for a regulator (unless in a very senior position) does not carry the prestige which a term of employment with the SEC, for example, affords.

These problems may arise because the establishment of the regulatory system is so recent, but until there is greater public perception that the regulators are doing a good job or are seen to be more successful, working for a regulator may still not be seen as a positive career move for experienced practitioners.

However, the appointment of practitioners to the Boards of SROs and/or onto Committees appears to have worked reasonably well. There is a greater need for the public interest to be represented, but practitioners have played a very active part in the development of policy of the SROs.

Under the FSA, SIB must include 'persons with experience of investment business of a kind relevant to the functions of SIB and other persons, including regular users on their own account or on behalf of others of services provided by persons carrying on investment business . . .'. Furthermore, the composition of the Board '. . . must be such as to secure a proper balance between the interests of persons carrying on investment business and the interests of the public'.

The current Board has thirteen members of whom three are executive and six of the ten non-executive members are or were active in the financial services industry.

The matter of public interest directors is important to the perception of the role of the SIB and its independence and, following the Large Report, action was taken to underline the independence of the Board.

Andrew Large also recommended the use of advisory groups so that, in setting standards effectively, SIB could obtain close knowledge of the requirements of the main users of the financial services system.

The Board of SFA, as at 31 August 1994, comprised twenty four persons of whom seven were 'independent' of the securities industry and the Chief Executive was recruited from the Bank of England. Members of the Board are elected by the members, apart from the independent members, the Chairman and Chief Executive.

The members of the other Committees are mainly drawn from the Board but, there are a significant number of coopted members (who do not have voting rights) on the Conduct of Business, Capital and Membership Committees, where specialist input from the various sectors of the industry is important.

With regard to IMRO, over half of its Board is now made up of non-practitioners.

Consultation

A key feature of the regulatory process is consultation by SIB and the recognised bodies.

In the SIB report on the UK Equity Markets already referred to, SIB stated that it had undertaken an extensive process of consultation with UK and overseas investors, with market participants and with the relevant regulatory authorities. The consultations were said to have been of great value. Indeed, this particular report was preceded by the Agnew Report and other consultation papers issued by the London Stock Exchange and others.

If anything, the practitioners are currently suffering from too much consultation (or perhaps, more accurately, from too much rule making) from all the regulatory bodies who are taking advantage of the changes being required by the ISD and the Capital Adequacy Directive to rewrite substantial parts of their rules on transaction reporting, client money, disciplinary process etc.

The SFA has responded to concerns expressed by the industry on the cost and necessity for implementing new transaction reporting requirements by being more flexible on the timetable for implementation and providing a full explanation of why the rules are needed and how the information will be used. This is a good illustration of the consultation process working and not being a mere public relations exercise.

The diversity of the London markets, the fast pace of change and the many interests (domestic and international) represented in London and the importance to the UK of London as a financial centre make consultation a vital element in regulatory attitudes.

CATALYSTS FOR CHANGE

In the UK Equity Markets Regulation Report it is observed that securities markets world-wide are undergoing a period of unprecedented change. The liberalisation of capital flows; changes in the institutional framework in many countries; the increasing internationalisation of investment; the innovative powers of modern technology and market participants; and competitive pressures are among the factors driving the process of change.

Three particular pressures for change are examined below: innovation, EU regulation and political pressures in the light of scandals

Innovation

Thriving markets depend on innovation and risk taking and the UK regulators have publicly stated their approach must be firmly rooted on a practical understanding of how markets work and develop.

Both in the equity and debt markets there has been significant growth in the number of instruments through which they can acquire a proprietorial interest and/or (in the case of equities) an economic interest.

In equities we have seen the growth in convertibles and warrants, depository receipts, index futures and options, traditional and traded single company options and OTC equity derivatives. The growth of index derivatives has been particularly strong, providing investors with a new and liquid medium through which they can rapidly alter their economic exposure to markets or individual securities in size. LIFFE has recently announced a further innovation for the UK markets: the introduction of cash settled futures contracts on individual shares with associated options for physical delivery.

Developments in information technology have increased the opportunities for new screen-based order-driven markets to compete. Tradepoint has been recently recognised as an investment exchange to provide such a market.

The debt markets, particularly the Eurobond sector, have seen much innovation with structured notes, both listed and unlisted, meeting the needs of the investor and the issuer. Currency, interest rates and debt ratings all provide opportunities for arbitrage and hedging and, indeed, speculation.

EU Regulation

A number of EU Directives which have been implemented or are in the course of implementation have affected UK regulation. The principal Directives have related to Insider Dealing, Disclosure of Interests, Prospectus Requirements, Investment Services and Capital Adequacy Directives.

In January 1996, for example, if an EU market wishes to place screens in other member states, EU investment firms will be able to take advantage of their new right to access each others' regulated markets without the need to establish operations or seek authorisation in each member state. This is an example of technology enabling users to access markets anywhere in the world.

However, one aspect of the Investment Services Directive (ISD) (which provides a passport for any EU firm to carry on business in another member state) which could be of concern, if regulators do not coordinate effectively, is that the authorisation of firms (which in the UK is based on fitness and propriety) is a matter for the home state and the UK's strict disciplinary regime over both firms and registered persons may be weakened with respect to inwardly passported firms and their employees.

Political Pressures

There is nothing like a scandal involving the financial markets for stirring up a debate in the newspapers and in Parliament on the state of regulation and demands for changes whether structurally or in attitude.

The Large Report was commissioned in the wake of the Maxwell catastrophe. The terms of reference given by the Chancellor of the Exchequer to Andrew Large required him to 'take full account of SIB's assessment of its own monitoring of IMRO in the Maxwell affair and any consequent action taken by SIB and IMRO to improve their performance, as well as the general need to strengthen the implementation in practice of regulatory standards'.

As we have seen, the Large Report brought about some major changes in the supervisory approach of SIB and a very thorough reorganisation of IMRO (whose Chairman resigned) in the light of its perceived failures to spot or prevent Maxwell's mischief.

FIMBRA, the SRO which was formed to authorise independent financial brokers and advisers specialising in insurance related and packaged investment products, suffered a number of cases where investors lost their money through theft (Barlow Clowes) or fraud (the Home Income Plans). This SRO is being replaced by PIA (Personal Investment Authority) since it had largely lost the confidence of its members (and investors) and its financial viability was threatened by the number of compensation claims.

However, in many of the other cases which have caused critical public reaction, it was the perceived failure of the criminal justice system to achieve the convictions and/or penalties that were expected, that led to a lack of confidence that frauds were being effectively dealt with.

With regard to product development, the explosive growth of derivatives markets since the early 1980s eventually gave rise to political and regulatory concerns in the United States when a number of public bodies and corporations incurred heavy losses as a result of their use of derivatives. A derivative can be defined as an instrument deriving its value from an underlying security, market index or other product.

The main losses were incurred by the US affiliate of Metalgeselschaft ($1.3bn), Gibsons Greetings Cards and Proctor & Gamble although other losses (eg Orange County) were attributed by the press to derivatives even though the losses did not strictly arise from derivatives (just a wrong view on the direction of interest rates).

Politicians and regulators openly debated whether there needed to be new laws or regulations relating to the marketing of, dealing in and disclosure of financial positions arising from derivative instruments.

In March 1994, the two principal US regulators involved in the derivative markets (the SEC and CFTC) issued a joint statement with SIB on an agenda for the appropriate regulation of derivative business. On customer protection, the statement said that 'one approach would be to require providers to *ensure* the customer has sufficient information and resources to assess appropriateness including the capability of the customer to understand risk'.

Numerous Parliamentary and other committees have been set up to review the derivative business, but the conclusion of the UK regulators so far is that there is no need for further law or regulation subject to the industry itself behaving responsibly (ie there being no scandals). Furthermore, the Financial Law Panel has observed that duties of the providers of derivatives, with regard to their customers, can be ascertained under the existing laws of contract, tort and fiduciary duties.

The Barings collapse further exacerbated the fears of the press and the politicians about derivatives (in this case exchange traded). The Barings Report has concluded, however, that (notwithstanding some regulatory supervision failures) the action of one trader allied to lack of proper controls and procedures was the root cause (rather than the use of derivatives per se) of the failure. The response of the regulators has been to set up an agenda of areas where cooperation between the major regulators and markets in the futures and options business should occur (see 'International Cooperation' below).

It can be seen, therefore, that the regulators have been responsive to the problems arising from this relatively new area and have, where they think it appropriate, taken action to improve coordination between markets and regulators. Despite the political pressures, they have not regulated just for the sake of regulating. They will, however, increase their surveillance of risk management and internal controls.

The current political weakness of the Government has produced its own form of pressure on the regulators. They are determined to be and to appear to be independent and tough (no more self-regulatory descriptions) and to protect their turf (even against other regulators) lest there be major structural changes should there be a change in Government.

DISCIPLINE AND ENFORCEMENT

No regulatory system would be effective in providing investor protection without a strong and efficient system of discipline and enforcement. As we have seen, the SFA and IMRO rules apply not only to member firms that conduct investment business but also to registered persons employed by them. There is, therefore, both corporate and individual liability for transgression of the regulations.

The regulators currently have a wide range of sanctions they can apply to both individuals and member firms alike. These sanctions include reprimands, fines, suspension orders and expulsion from membership. Most sanctions must be publicly disclosed and this acts as a major deterrent for investment firms because of the damage to their reputation. The withdrawal of an individual's authorisation to conduct investment business would have particularly severe consequences because that individual may never be able to work within the financial services industry again. A ban from one SRO would be effective across the whole regulatory board.

By way of illustration, the SFA has fined individuals up to £20,000 personally, together with various suspensions and, in certain circumstances, expulsion. The principal reason for sanctioning individuals has been for conduct which is deemed to be not fit and proper. Similarly, sanctions to authorised firms have ranged from reprimands for minor rule breaches through to fines in excess of £200,000 and in certain exceptional circumstances, removal of firms' authorisation to conduct investment business. IMRO has also demonstrated a similar approach to enforcement with both firms and individuals being sanctioned. The SIB, during 1994/1995, has shown high levels of enforcement activity for example investigations have increased by 31% upon the previous year.

Notwithstanding the strong action that can be and has been taken by SIB and the SROs (but only against their own members and registered persons), the area of enforcement in the financial services industry is generally perceived to be weak and the reputation of the regulatory system has suffered accordingly.

Much of the criticism has resulted from the 'failure' of several high profile fraud cases in the criminal courts (which, of course, has nothing to do with regulators). The cumbersome nature of the criminal process and the difficulty of meeting the strict burden of proof required are identified as the main weaknesses.

In cases of misconduct which may involve a breach of criminal law, the regulators must generally await the outcome of criminal proceedings. Discussions between the regulators, the Serious Fraud Office and the Bar Association have been held with a view to trying to facilitate the choices of handling cases which are (a) capable of regulatory resolution, (b) best left to the criminal prosecutor or (c) in due course pursued by both criminal and civil authorities with a process of plea bargaining.

It has also been argued that some financial crimes (eg Insider Trading) should not be part of the criminal law (since theft or abuse of information is so difficult to prove), but that there should be civil penalties available to a central regulator (the SEC's power is the example). These issues are not easy to resolve and will remain the subject of debate. De-criminalising 'white collar crime' is politically sensitive even if a regulatory solution might be quicker and more effective.

It is generally acknowledged that there needs to be greater coordination and concentration of enforcement powers and improvements in the criminal law system and the sanctions available to the regulatory system if the public perception of enforcement is to change.

INTERNATIONAL COOPERATION/REGULATION

We have already noted the globalisation of securities markets and the ability of an investor to access a wide range of markets throughout the world. The major investment houses (many of which are divisions of the large international banks) carry on their investment business on a global basis and have established presence not only in the major financial centres, but in many other centres in which international investors have an interest.

As already noted, a high proportion of business in London involves a cross-border transaction or a foreign stock or bond. The need, therefore, is obvious both for cooperation and coordination between regulators of different countries.

Recent concerns about derivatives and the Barings collapse and the increasing integration of markets across borders and functions have caused regulators to push harder with international coordination initiatives.

The banking regulators had the BCCI affair to spur them to look at supervision across borders. The fact that many of the largest financial services groups are supervised or regulated by both banking and securities regulators makes the problem of coordination even more complex.

As SIB has pointed out in the UK Equity Markets Regulation Report 'No individual regulator or jurisdiction can achieve effective market regulation acting on its own; over time domestic regulation is likely to be an increasingly smaller part of the whole'.

There have for some time been contacts between the major stock exchanges in the world and SIB has developed contacts with securities commissions both bilaterally and through IOSCO and the importance of such contacts is acknowledged. The major stock exchanges, including the International Securities Markets Association are affiliated members of IOSCO. SIB has a working party drawn from the regulators, Bank of England, the Treasury, industry and academia to identify and address the implications for international regulation of the increasing internationalisation of securities business.

With regard to the trading of UK equities abroad, the integrity of the market depends to an extent on the regulatory reporting and transparency requirements in other jurisdictions.

SIB notes that it would be unrealistic and disproportionate to try to set up an international reporting and transparency requirement applicable to all trading in UK equities world-wide. However, in the case of the EU, the ISD sets out requirements for the reporting of trades and for information to be exchanged among regulators. Discussions are proceeding over the detailed arrangements which need to be put in place.

Other arrangements will be put in place on an 'as needed' basis such as the inclusion of ADR trading in UK stocks on the New York Stock Exchange under the UK rules for disclosure of short selling in secondary offerings. In addition, there is a category of overseas recognised exchange (including most of the major stock markets) with whom there are cooperative arrangements established.

Recently SIB established a joint initiative in connection with the supervision of futures exchanges with the US body the Commodity Futures Trading Commission (CFTC). Together with the CFTC, the SIB sponsored a high level meeting of international regulators which agreed to a work programme to carry forward issues arising from the Barings collapse referred to, rather grandly, as the 'Windsor Declaration'.[1] The work will be taken

[1] The 'Windsor Declaration' is discussed by Whittaker, infra, pp. 263–4.

forward under the auspices of IOSCO. The principal issues addressed were: cooperation between market authorities; protection of customer positions, funds and assets; default procedures; and regulatory cooperation in emergencies.

With regard to fund managers, US and UK securities regulators announced in April 1995 that they had reached agreement on reciprocal on-site inspections of fund managers located in each others' jurisdiction; the first ever such arrangement for the supervision of cross-border fund management activity. IMRO, for example, can inspect the records of a US-based subsidiary of a UK firm.

The SEC and SIB announced in July 1995 a joint initiative to improve oversight of global securities firms. This initiative builds on other cooperative efforts between the SIB and SEC such as the Joint Statement on OTC Derivatives Oversight in March 1994.

Richard Dale, Professor of International Banking and Financial Institutions, Southampton University, has commented 'The overall trend, then, is clear: financial services regulators are being pressured by events to develop an embryonic global regulatory framework. It is, of course, much too early to speak of a supranational regulatory regime presided over by a multilingual supervisory agency—but the way things are going that could be the ultimate destiny'.

CONCLUSION

The challenges to regulators in the UK are clear:

- responding to diversity, which involves proper coordination across a broader market place;
- the fragmentation of markets;
- innovation of markets and products;
- banking and securities business combining within one group;
- the global structure of major investment/banking groups.

The solutions, however, are not clear. The structure of UK regulation is once more under review. SIB has called for changes in the FSA to give it greater powers. Some SROs believe SIB is exercising too much control. There are reports that the Labour Party may want SIB to be given increased powers and for the SROs to be merged into SIB. There are calls for the power to impose civil penalties to be given to either the Treasury or SIB to give more teeth to combating insider dealing/fraud since the criminal law is generally perceived to have been ineffective in major fraud cases. Finally, the role of the Bank of England as supervisor has been questioned in the light of the Barings failure.

The Board of Banking Supervision, in its report on Barings, stated its view that there was no need for any fundamental change to the framework of regulation in the UK but recommendations were made in the supervision of banking groups involved in securities business. The style of supervision of the Bank of England has traditionally been different to that of securities regulators. Although the Bank has been moving away from its informal approach, there are pressures for it to become much more rigorous in its supervisory/regulatory approach or for the supervision function to be given to a separate body.

What we can conclude about the attitudes of UK regulation, despite the above uncertainties, are that the following objectives are being pursued:

- the principles of disclosure and fairness should underpin the system;
- greater cooperation between regulators banking and securities nationally and internationally;
- a recognition of the different requirements for regulating wholesale and retail markets/products and professional/business and private clients;
- a significant practitioner input;
- flexibility and responsiveness to change and innovation particularly given London's role as a major (if not the pre-eminent) international financial centre;
- freedom to choose for market participants ie as to what changes in market processes should happen or what mechanisms for trading are best; and
- efficiency and cost effectiveness.

12

The French View of Cross-Border Securities Offerings (Aspects of the Modernisation of French Capital Markets)

WAYNE H. SMITH

Not so very long ago the securities markets of Europe were to a large extent isolated from one another. Companies raised nearly all their finance domestically, investors seldom bought significant amounts of foreign securities (with the major exception of British fund managers) and domestic regulations tended to perpetuate this state of affairs.

A number of developments in world capital markets over the past ten or fifteen years have led to a gradual lifting of barriers, and cross-border securities offerings have become relatively common. Among these developments the most important are the virtual elimination of exchange controls (at least in the OECD), the explosion of the Euromarkets (principally for debt instruments), the influence of European law on French law, numerous waves of privatisations by an ever-growing list of countries, as well as a profound change in the nature and tastes of investors, who have become both increasingly institutional and international-minded.

France of course has not been immune to these changes. France has evolved under the pressure of market forces, as have other countries. As I present the French view of cross-border securities offerings, I shall try to emphasise how France has evolved recently—and the ground covered has been considerable—and which specialities of French practice appear to me to remain of overriding interest to non-French issuers, intermediaries, investors and their advisers.

I hope that the fact that I am not an expert on all these matters—which is obviously a shortcoming on my part—will be an advantage, insofar as it allows me to present to you a bird's-eye view of the French position. I can therefore avoid dwelling on some of the more esoteric minutiae of French regulations, and in the bargain stand a chance of making myself understood.

The most convenient way of dealing with this subject seems to be, first, to discuss offerings of foreign securities in France, then to discuss offerings of French securities abroad.

OFFERINGS OF FOREIGN SECURITIES IN FRANCE

Offerings of securities in France, whether they be French or foreign, may be either public or private. Euro-issues fall somewhere between these unrealistically neat categories.

Public Offerings

French Regulators and the Regulatory Framework

Offers to the general public of foreign securities are almost invariably made either in connection with the initial Paris listing of a foreign company, in which case existing shares are offered, or in the context of a new issue of securities belonging to the same class as those that are already officially listed and will therefore be listed once the offer has been completed. The documentation used for the offer is therefore drawn up to comply with the requirements for a listing prospectus.[1]

These requirements result from the 1980 European Directive and are implemented in France by the *Commission des Opérations de Bourse* (COB), a regulatory agency patterned after the United States Securities and Exchange Commission. In broad terms, the COB's brief is investor protection, and one of the principal means of achieving this aim is by ensuring proper disclosure by listed companies. In the context of an offering of securities, this takes the form of scrutiny and approval of the offering/listing document.[2]

I take this occasion to point out that a second body called the *Conseil des Bourses de Valeurs* (Stock Exchange Council or CBV) is France's self-regulatory market authority. The CBV, inter alia, adopts the basic stock-market regulations, licenses broker-dealers, and grants listings. The CBV delegates the day-to-day running of the securities markets to the Société des Bourses Françaises, or SBF-Paris Bourse, which is the Exchange itself.

I should point out that if the investment services bill scheduled to be laid before Parliament towards the end of 1995 becomes law, some aspects of this institutional framework will be modified in the very near future, in particular the licensing and supervision of investment services firms. Prospectus requirements deriving from earlier European legislation will not.

[1] This document is called 'listing particulars' in contemporary Euro-British parlance, though the UK Public Offers of Securities Regulations 1995 that came into force in June and implement the 1989 European Directive require the prior publication of a 'prospectus' instead of listing particulars where the offering concerns securities to be listed in London. In fact, subject to minor adaptations, a European listing prospectus (if made available on time) will generally serve as an offering prospectus, and the reverse will also hold in most circumstances.

Current French prospectus requirements are set forth in COB Regulations 91-02 for listing, and 92-02 for public offers.

[2] COB approval of a document generally takes the form of a so-called visa number.

The Practicalities of Implementation

With some 200 foreign companies officially listed in France, public offerings of foreign securities are not a rare occurrence. However, the vast majority of public offerings I have seen over the past 5 years have been European issues. This is due to two facts: on the one hand, the major Japanese companies have almost stopped issuing new equity on any significant scale because of market conditions; on the other, most North American companies have abandoned pre-emptive rights for existing shareholders in favour of book-building, where new shares are issued to all investors at a price near the current market price. In such circumstances, American issuers will wish to avoid the expense of making offers available to the French public at large, and the French authorities will not insist on such non-preferential cash issues being opened in France because French shareholders (in particular retail investors) can purchase the shares at a comparable price on the Paris Bourse.[3]

Where the issue is by a European Union company—the bulk of recent public issues in France, and which as a rule carry pre-emptive rights—the mutual recognition procedure laid down by the 1980 European Directive (as amended) will generally be used. Under this procedure, the COB, which must clear the offering document prior to any solicitation of the French public, will approve the prospectus on the basis of the approval given by the competent authority of the home country. The COB will require, however, that the full prospectus be translated into French, and that information specific to the French market (such as tax treatment of dividends) be added to the original document.

Eurolist

Perhaps in the near future, those European regulators requiring full local-language documentation—France, Germany, Spain and Italy in particular—will agree that a summary would suffice, since the local-language document is aimed primarily at retail investors who seldom need—or even attempt to fathom—all the information contained in today's hefty equity offering prospectuses.[4]

The issue of streamlining information requirements in host markets is at the heart of the Eurolist process. For the benefit of those who may never have heard of Eurolist, suffice it to say that Eurolist is a project of the

[3] The listed company will, however, be asked to publish the terms of any new issue in a French newspaper for informational purposes if the new issue involves a major capital increase (more than 10% roughly speaking).

[4] Several exchanges in Europe already accept English documents, though I doubt whether the UK regulators will ever accept that English is just another local language.

In France, it is not perfectly clear how far-reaching the scope of the *loi Toubon* on the mandatory use of the French language should be in practice in several areas, including the capital markets.

Federation of European Stock Exchanges aimed at simplifying the multi-listing of the largest, most actively traded European companies, while at the same time increasing the attractiveness of such companies in European host markets. The project may be viewed as a first step, on the part of the exchanges, in the direction of greater integration of European capital markets. Not only issuers and investors but also the exchanges and their members stand to benefit from Eurolist.

In 1994 the project gave rise to a new Directive (94/18) eliminating the requirement to produce listing particulars where a company listed in one European country seeks additional listings in Europe. At present, Member States are implementing the new Directive, and participating exchanges are completing development of a dedicated electronic mail system that will link all the European exchanges and ensure Europe-wide, real-time dissemination of company news and other important information to host markets.

Achieving all the aims of the Eurolist project—such as further regulatory simplification and the creation of a new stock index—will take time, but we shall certainly see the first tangible results before the end of 1995.

The Significance of Foreign Offers in France

The primary market for foreign securities sold to the public in France is not a very significant source of funds for issuers.[5] This is because the amount of foreign equities held by private investors—who are the additional investors reached through a public offering—while not negligible (estimated at USD 20–25 billion), is necessarily relatively small compared to the size of French institutional portfolios, and typically infinitesimal compared to the holdings of investors (private and institutional) based in the same jurisdiction as the issuer.

Furthermore, since foreign companies almost invariably have secondary listings in France, French institutional portfolios tend to be held in the issuer's home country, making it rather difficult to measure such institutions' holdings, unlike those of retail investors which are measurable because they are generally held through SICOVAM, the French central securities depository.[6]

Nonetheless, French retail investors do respond favourably to attractive new foreign equity listings. Individuals in France have long invested in foreign securities, and are not put off by exchange rate risk[7] or the fact that

[5] This is an additional argument in favor of simplifying the formalities required of foreign listed companies in European host exchanges.

[6] The SICOVAM is usually termed a securities depository. Given that French securities were completely dematerialised in 1984, however, it may be less misleading to speak of a central registry, or of a book-keeping system, since most French securities are not in registered form and SICOVAM 'holds' them in the name of financial intermediaries affiliated to the SICOVAM system. Intermediaries in turn 'hold' them on behalf of their clients.

[7] In fact, many French private investors purchased foreign securities in the past not only

the company's principal operations are overseas, provided however the company communicates well in France. As for foreign listed companies themselves, they appreciate most of all the notoriety and enhanced press coverage that accompanies their French listing, even though only the top 40 or 50 (out of 200) foreign equities can boast an active secondary market on the Paris Bourse (over FRF 1 million per day on the central order-driven market).

As for debt instruments, the only foreign issuer that regularly taps the French domestic market is the European Investment Bank (EIB).[8] It must be confessed that the only foreign debt instruments that the French population seems truly to take to heart are defaulted Russian bonds.[9] Unlike certain other European retail investors, the French public seems to be content investing in domestic bonds, perhaps because the national currency is strong and tax evasion difficult.

However, as both European issuers and investors increasingly look abroad, regulators should do what they can to accommodate this trend. The French authorities in particular do not wish to see individual investors excluded from the process of internationalisation and institutional investors reap all the benefits provided by today's expanding markets, through private offerings, for instance.

Private Offerings

Definition

An offering is considered private in France if the following three conditions are fulfilled:

- first, there is no press advertisement or other form of publicity;
- second, no individual investors are solicited; and
- third, no more than 300 institutional investors are contacted.[10]

because the French equity markets were relatively underdeveloped, but also because the chronic weakness of the French franc, combined with capital controls, made investment in listed foreign securities an attractive foreign exchange play.

[8] The EIB of course is foreign only in a narrow sense, since France is a member of this international organisation.

[9] Russian bonds coincidentally appear to have been the first global issues, well ahead of the 1990's innovations, though of course circumstances—in particular regulation—were very different a century ago.

[10] These criteria were published in the COB's 1985 annual report in connection with a British privatisation and were considered at the time to be the official position on the general concept of the private offer. The 1985 COB report also indicated that in addition to these restrictions, no order forms should be sent to institutions requesting the offering prospectus (though it would appear that they could request an order form after having received the prospectus), and unit trusts or mutual funds should not be solicited at all (presumably because of the individuals that lurk behind the veil). This position appears to have changed since the issue of COB Regulation 92-02 on the Public Offer of Securities which defines a public offer

Practice

If we ignore cases of fraud such as boiler-room operations and cases of illicit solicitation of French investors to invest in unrecognised foreign futures markets or unheard-of penny stocks, private offerings meeting these criteria seem very rarely to have given rise to problems.[11] Foreign privatisation issues, for example, may be offered to French institutions within the above limits. The offering of such issues to individual investors, however, would require the publication of a French-language prospectus.[12]

However, even institutions may not be approached freely by any member of the offering syndicate. It is necessary to ensure that the persons making the phone calls to potential French investors or visiting them are properly registered and licensed to undertake this type of professional activity, either in their home country or in France.[13] In fact, they will generally be employees of the French bank(s) present in the underwriting syndicate, and it is advisable to inform the COB beforehand to avoid any misunderstanding, especially where the securities are listed on unfamiliar markets or are marketed by unfamiliar intermediaries.[14]

(*appel public à l'épargne*) as being one which results in more than 300 persons holding the relevant securities or which is effected using either financial intermediaries or any form of publicity or direct solicitation. More importantly, for the purpose of determining whether or not the threshold of 300 is exceeded, unit trusts (*fonds communs de placement*, which lack legal personality) are considered to be a single entity; it would seem that, implicitly, investment companies (such as SICAVs) may be viewed in the same way, as a single, non transparent investor. It may be argued, however, that the definition given in the 1992 COB Regulation of a public offer, and a contrario of a private offer, is valid only for that Regulation (which only applies to unlisted securities). Even recently, the COB has stated that collective investment schemes should not be solicited. It nevertheless appears that greater flexibility than the 1985 position would suppose will very likely be demonstrated in the future as regards professional investors, in the form of confidential COB rulings on specific cases submitted by the underwriters' attorneys.

[11] A recent controversy turned on the compatibility of private offering status with a Parisian 'roadshow' where French newspaper reporters were invited. This seems allowable provided the reporters are adequately briefed on the applicable selling restrictions and refrain from using their columns to provide overly specific publicity for the offering. English-language newspapers such as the Financial Times and the Herald Tribune raise further difficult issues.

There is also the question of issuers that have a large number of employees in France. The COB limit for French-resident employees of French issuers is 500, which is combined with the limit of 300 institutional investors. As for foreign issuers, the COB appears to cite a limit of 300 for employees, though in practice specific rulings have allowed more.

[12] The principal law in this area (called *démarchage financier*) is Law No. 72–6 of 3 January 1972.

[13] Actually, for the time being, home country registration will suffice only if the Second European Banking Coordination may be invoked by the person soliciting French investors, or if such person is selling futures contracts traded on a market specifically recognised by the French authorities.

[14] For British privatisations, HM Treasury has always insisted that the COB be approached, leading to a letter stating that the proposed offer falls within the private offering exception.

Reform in the Offing?

It is not yet absolutely certain whether the implementation of the Investment Services Directive (ISD) in France will lead to any significant liberalisation of the rules surrounding the solicitation of the public—in particular by foreign intermediaries—and the placing of securities—in particular foreign securities—with investors. In law, all France needs to do to implement the ISD is adopt statutory provisions on the one hand allowing for the European passport—which means repealing the exclusivity of brokerage firms for securities transactions—and on the other determining which French markets are to be considered 'regulated' within the meaning of the Directive or determining which authority is competent for compiling such a list. However, it seems inevitable that the obligation to allow licensed European investment firms to operate in France and solicit French investors will lead to an overhaul of French regulations in this area.[15]

The direction that reform might take, however, is not yet clear.[16] In any event, it is generally expected that France will take advantage of the debate created by the need to implement the ISD to modify a number of laws and regulations that appear discriminatory or too complex and consequently unadapted to the Single Market and the liberalisation of capital flows. Among these, regulations governing investment advice and marketing will likely be made more competition-friendly and more consistent in the near

[15] This would seem so even though the provision of investment advice and therefore the solicitation of the public to buy securities is a 'non-core' service under the Investment Services Directive—like custody for example—and as such is not covered by the European passport because such services are not necessarily subject to authorisation under the ISD. Investment firms authorised by their home country authorities to furnish core services may also be authorised to furnish non-core services in which case all such authorised services will benefit from the passport provisions. Moreover, the placing of securities, even independently of their underwriting, is a core service, but the scope of this right, especially in the context of the freedom of provision of services (i.e. without an office in the host country), appears to be potentially limited by host country rules governing relations with investors. Such rules may or may not be maintainable in light of their discriminatory character and protectionist effects.

[16] Perhaps a new profession of independent investment advisors, separate from the banking and brokerage communities who have traditionally occupied the securities field alone, will be recognised and made subject to its own supervisory body; this would amount to diversifying the current organisational approach whereby banks and securities houses are supervised by their own authorities. This does not seem likely, however, given the French tradition of universal banking and the strong positions of the established banking and securities players (the latter often belonging to a banking group since the 1988 reform). Probably, a new functional approach will be adopted, under which all investment services providers, including firms and individuals whose occupation comprises the giving of investment advice in securities, regardless of whether they are employees of financial institutions or independent professionals, would be authorised and supervised by a single authority. In the same way, it seems likely that the prudential supervision of both banks and securities firms will be entrusted to a single body, though separate banking and securities licenses may be granted by different authorities and banks may well in the end preserve their regulatory specificity.

future, perhaps through the recognition of greater freedom for transactions targeted at professional investors as the ISD itself provides.[17]

The Special Case of Euro French Franc Issues

Some of the questions arising from today's interpenetration of markets—in particular retail and professional; domestic and overseas markets—may be highlighted by examining the situation of Eurofranc debt securities (Eurobonds and Euro Medium Term Notes). It may seem incongruous to do so under the general heading of offers of foreign securities in France. However, though such issues are denominated in French francs, issued predominantly by French companies, purchased in very substantial amounts by French investors on the primary market,[18] listed in France and generally subject to French law, they are not fully French in several important aspects.[19]

Distinguishing Euro-issues

In France the market for domestic franc debt issues and the market for Eurofranc issues have grown closer in certain respects, but are still sepa-

[17] Until very recently, it appeared likely that the implementation of the ISD per se would be one small piece of a much wider Big Bang crowning ten years of constant, far-reaching reform of French capital markets. It now seems generally agreed, however, that the present organisation and regulation of the markets is largely satisfactory. The forthcoming investment services law will therefore likely concentrate on simplifying the legal structure and tidying up a few loose ends.

[18] The Euro-franc rules indicate that Euro-franc debt instruments are 'destined' to be placed with non-resident investors and 'as such' cannot be offered on the primary market to 'the public in France'. This is not entirely devoid of ambiguity—one reads elsewhere in the same rules that such issues are addressed '*inter alia*' to non-resident investors—but in any event the situation in France is quite unlike the situation in certain other countries whose residents are explicitly denied access to Euro issues denominated in the national currency, at least temporarily (often 2 or 3 months). It should be pointed out, however, the definition of private Eurofranc issues—which must be listed in France only if they are listed elsewhere—is much stricter: 'issues durably placed with a small number of pre-determined non-resident investors'.

[19] It is often maintained that Eurofranc instruments are foreign securities from the point of view of French law. This, it is said, explains why they are documented in English and listed in the international section of the Paris Bourse. However, the Eurofranc rules state that the 'issue contract' (i.e. the terms and conditions of the bonds supplemented by the fiscal agency agreement, as opposed to the subscription agreement) is 'preferably' subject to French law, and this is generally the case in practice. Another school of thought, which appears to be on more solid ground, maintains simply that Eurofranc instruments are issued outside France, delivery and payment being performed abroad, in accordance with the withholding exemption of French tax law. In most cases, furthermore, French law will apply in order to settle any issues arising under the bonds (though this will not always be true even of a French law-governed issue, for instance where the guarantee is subject to the law of the guarantor). In any event, my classification, for the purposes of this paper, of Eurofranc issues as 'offerings of foreign securities in France' must be considered arbitrary to some extent, just as my classification of Eurofranc global issues under the general heading of 'offerings of French securities abroad' is not immune from criticism from a legal standpoint. All of which tends to show how internationalisation has eroded not just borders, but even the sureness of definitions.

rated by a number of significant differences, despite the complete lifting of exchange controls in 1989.[20]

The main differences are the following.[21]

First and foremost, Eurobonds may not be offered to the French public, i.e the retail segment of the French market. A Euro-issue is therefore a private issue on the primary market from the point of view of the French authorities and must therefore qualify as such by reference to the criteria stated above.[22]

Second, Eurobonds are usually certificated,[23] whereas French domestic bonds, as required under French law, are invariably dematerialised, no paper certificates ever being printed.

Third, a Eurofranc bond issue, if it is either syndicated or listed outside France, must be listed in France as is the case with domestic franc bonds, but the formalities are much simpler. In particular, since the offer is not made to private investors in France, no documentation need be published or approved until the date for first trading on the Bourse—which is generally the closing date for the issue[24]—whereas for a domestic issue both COB approval of the offering document and publication of the terms of the issue in a legal gazette (the BALO) must be secured no later than the start of the offering period. Moreover, for listing purposes, the Euro prospectus may be in English[25] and often contains much less information than the document used for offering bonds to domestic retail investors.

Fourth, domestic bonds must have a minimum maturity of 3 years while for Eurobonds the minimum is one year, and the size of a syndicated Eurobond must be at least FRF 300 million while on the domestic market the minimum is only FRF 100 million.

[20] The continuing power of the French Finance Minister (acting through the French Treasury) directly to regulate new issues on French securities markets appears to be founded in article 82 of Law No. 46–2914 of 23 September 1946. Although this law, which is extremely strict and wide-ranging, has never been repealed, the authority it grants has been gradually waived for certain types of transactions by the issuance of a French version of 'no-action' letters.

[21] The discussion which follows is concerned only with long-term debt instruments called *obligations*; typically short-term instruments called *titres de créance négociables* (which may in fact be long-term, especially the French version of medium-term notes called BMTNs) are dealt primarily on the domestic interbank market and obey different, generally more flexible rules. In particular, they are subject to Banque de France supervision, and are issued without many of the legal formalities of bond issues.

[22] The offering documentation always incorporates a reference to this French selling restriction.

[23] As a general rule, certification takes place after the 40-day 'seasoning' period imposed by US regulations. However, some eurobonds are not certificated in the usual sense, since they are represented exclusively by a permanent (or semi-permanent) global bond, no definitive bonds ever being issued. This in reality is very close to dematerialisation.

[24] In practice the COB visa is given a few days before the closing/first quotation date.

[25] Summary terms of the issue in French must be provided at the back of the prospectus, however.

Fifth, the underwriting commitment of a bank in a domestic issue goes no further than its accepted allotment of bonds, whereas all members of a Eurofranc offering syndicate are jointly and severally bound to transfer the full money amount of the bonds to the issuer on the settlement date.

Sixth, whereas only licensed French-owned banks, i.e. to the exclusion of French subsidiaries of foreign banks, may lead-manage a domestic debt issue (bar a recent and so far unique exception mentioned below), lead management of Eurobond issues has for years been open as a matter of principle to French subsidiaries of foreign banks. However, lead management of Eurobond issues is only open to such institutions who show a substantial and lasting commitment to the French franc market through a significant and active presence in Paris and accordingly receive specific authorisation from the French Treasury.[26]

Seventh, the tax treatment, though similar, is not identical. No tax is withheld at source on either Euro or domestic bonds, but Eurofranc bond income may more easily avoid the French tax net, and non-resident investors who wish to remain anonymous tend to prefer Eurobonds because foreign holders of domestic bonds must identify themselves and certify that they are not French residents to escape withholding tax.

Current Practice and Recent Rule Changes

Given the tax and regulatory advantages peculiar to the Eurofranc market, as well as often keener pricing, many French issuers had begun developing a clear preference for Euro-issues. This was most evident in 1993, when for the first time more money was raised on the Euro than on the domestic market (excluding French government borrowings), admittedly in great part due to a record number of non-French issuers.[27] In reaction to the perceived threat of an inexorable decline of the French debt market, the French authorities have considerably liberalised the rules under which the domestic bond market functions.

For example, the constraints of advance notice and prior consent by regulators are less acute than formerly. Though lead managers must still notify the French Treasury,[28] prior to the launch of all French franc bond issues

[26] French branches—as opposed to subsidiaries—of foreign banks are barred from lead managing Eurofranc issues. When Barclays France SA merged with Barclays PLC a couple of years ago, the group was obliged to appoint another French subsidiary for this purpose.

Naturally, no such additional conditions are imposed upon dealers for the private placing of Euro Medium Term Notes. As for public, i.e. syndicated Eurofranc issues, the Treasury has used its leverage in this area to obtain reciprocal treatment for French banks in other countries.

[27] 1993 was the most active year to date for French franc debt issues. Domestic non-government issues totalled FRF 153 billion, and Euro-issues totalled FRF 255 billion. During the same period, the French State issued FRF 352 billion in OATs (*Obligations Assimilables du Trésor*, fungible bullet bonds having maturities between 10 and 30 years).

[28] Through the *Comité des émissions* (New issues committee) which is made up of the major French banks and chaired by a Treasury representative.

and obtain the Treasury's consent, this has for some time been a pure formality for Eurofranc issues[29] regardless of the lead manager's proposed launch date—which could be the following day—whereas a much stricter timetable has always prevailed for domestic debt. Until last year, a domestic issue of more than FRF 1 billion had to be notified three weeks in advance.[30] Now the queuing system is limited to issues to be launched on Mondays and Tuesdays,[31] leaving the rest of the week open for unscheduled issues—of any size—which can come to market at 24 hours' notice whenever market conditions offer a window of opportunity (such as a favourable swap rate).

A series of other steps has been taken over the past two years to render the domestic franc market more issuer-friendly. On the one hand, the cost of issuing domestic debt has been reduced,[32] and issuers now receive their funds the day the lead manager is paid, rather than the following day (which was the quaint tradition in France termed '*le jour de banque*'). On the other hand, the COB has adopted a shelf registration procedure for frequent issuers of domestic fixed-rate 'bullet' bonds,[33] the placing of which among professionals may begin as soon as the principal terms have been transmitted to the COB,[34] and Eurodebt issues, until recently exempt from registration fees, now give rise to a COB fee of FRF 50 per FRF 1 million issued.[35]

A further sign of the liberalisation of the domestic franc market is the agreement reached by French banks in March of this year to put an end to the cartel-like arrangement whereby the largest French underwriters were guaranteed a certain percentage of bond issues over FRF 1 billion.[36] Such restrictive practices of course have never prevailed on the Eurofranc market, where competition is keener (to use a mild expression). The only allotment 'rule' remaining today is that the lead manager may receive no more

[29] At least as far as previously accepted issuers (BBB minimum, though almost all issuers are rated much higher) are concerned.

[30] Smaller issues required three days' advance notice.

[31] This mechanism ensures priority access for large, regular issuers on these days.

[32] Standard underwriting and paying agent fees have been negotiated downwards under the aegis of the French Treasury, and the VAT heretofore applicable to part of domestic underwriting fees (the so-called management and placing commissions) has been completely eliminated.

[33] That is, redeemable in full at maturity.

[34] The COB visa must still be obtained, however, before the bonds may be offered to the public, which is usually the following day.

[35] Which is nevertheless only one-third the fee charged for domestic issues, which remains unchanged. As for the Paris Bourse, since SBF charges listing fees on a flat-rate basis for Eurobonds and according to outstanding par value for domestic bonds (which makes the listing of domestic debt almost always more expensive), you may conclude that we are the only party involved not to have done its duty in trying to deter issuers from the Eurofranc! In fact, listing costs are marginal, though SBF would be happy to raise Eurobond listing fees if everyone insists!

[36] The breakdown was 83% for the Big Seven and 17% for the others including a maximum of 5% overall going to any foreign members of the syndicate.

than 35% of the issue. The domestic market is therefore now as free in this respect as the Eurofranc market, and foreign banks are entitled to equal treatment, ahead of implementation of the Investment Services Directive.[37] Proof of the trend towards opening the debt market to foreign institutions was provided in December 1994 when for the first time a bank not controlled by French interests co-lead-managed a domestic French bond issue.[38]

The authorities have also reacted to the surge in Eurofranc issues by trying to clarify the boundary between the domestic and Eurofranc markets. The current position of the French Treasury is that at least half the total amount of a new Eurobond issue must be sold to non-resident investors.[39] This forces French issuers to use the domestic market when demand is shown essentially by resident investors.[40]

Also, the requirement that the lead manager of all French franc issues be either a French bank or a specially authorised French subsidiary of a non-French bank, which is a trait common to both domestic and Eurofranc issues, appears doomed under the ISD which is due to enter into force in January of 1996.[41] Banks authorised to underwrite and manage debt issues in their home country will doubtless be allowed to manage French franc issues whether in France or on international markets.[42]

Further rapprochement to come?

On the whole, it appears inevitable that the distinction between domestic and Euro issues will continue to grow slimmer, and probably disappear

[37] Still another sign of liberalisation was the authorisation given two years ago to include the French franc option in Euro Medium Term Note programs.

[38] It should be pointed out that the bank involved, JP Morgan, is authorised to manage Eurofranc issues (and has been present in France for more than a century). It remains to be seen whether—or when—a bank not so authorised will be permitted to lead-manage domestic debt issues, or for that matter whether the requirement for special authorisation to manage Euros can be maintained.

[39] By contrast, until the coming into force of the UK Public Offers of Securities Regulations 1995, the primary market for sterling bonds of UK issuers was openly treated as a Euro-market from the standpoint of prospectus requirements although gilts are distributed almost exclusively in the UK. However, the new Regulations (which implement the 1989 Public Offers Directive more than four years late) contain new 'professionals' and 'restricted circle' exemptions which, when taken together, should allow gilt offerings to continue in much the same conditions as before.

[40] However, it is impossible to predict how a given issue will be placed until it is launched, and difficult for the authorities even to know precisely who the investors are post facto. Furthermore, nothing other than market conditions will prevent a major French issuer from issuing in dollars and swapping the proceeds into francs.

[41] This is the short-term outlook, based on the ISD. In the medium-term, of course, the French franc will probably be replaced by a common European currency.

[42] The same will be true of French franc warrant issues, the special rules for which (as amended) were published in an SBF notice on 29 June 1994 and in the COB's August 1994 Bulletin. Warrants have become a very important part of the Eurofranc market, and generate increasingly significant trading on the Paris Stock Exchange.

altogether in the medium term. Perhaps this distinction will be replaced by a new distinction which would seem to better reflect the needs of investors and the realities of today's market, i.e. the distinction adopted elsewhere between institutional and retail investors.

Dealings among professional investors certainly do not require the same degree of regulatory safeguards as transactions involving the retail sector. Yet in France, where the policy of the authorities is to encourage the direct participation of private investors in the securities markets and to provide access thereto in conditions as equivalent as possible, and where many institutional investors appreciate the level of protection currently afforded to all investors,[43] it may appear more difficult than in certain other jurisdictions to adopt a double standard that inevitably carries with it certain disadvantages, in particular the difficulty of defining suitable levels of regulation for two very disparate groups of investors (and building watertight walls between them), as well as the potential frustration of retail investors who may feel shut out of transactions reserved for the happy few.

Situations illustrating the difficulty of reconciling such different needs may arise in the context of an offering of French securities abroad, for example where a French company wishes to offer convertible bonds to new, usually foreign, institutional investors.

OFFERINGS OF FRENCH SECURITIES ABROAD

The issues arising in the context of an offering of French equities abroad may be grouped under two headings. First, I shall look at the way in which offers are structured, in particular as between the banks managing the transaction and the various target investor groups, in particular the 'privileges' granted to certain privatisation shareholders. Second, I shall examine the way in which offers are documented for investors through the prospectus, as well as the specific problem of anti-dilution protection in new issues by French companies.

It also behoves me to say a few words about the recent inaugural French franc global bond issue, which bears some not-too-remote resemblance to global offerings of French equity.

[43] Even professional investors require objective and accurate information to assess an investment opportunity.

The Structure of Issues and Relationships Between the Managers and the Issuer/Vendor

The Importance of the French Privatisation Model

I shall take the example of French privatisations as being not only a phenomenon of unparalleled importance in French capital markets but also as a model which shows more clearly than any other the direction of change in recent years. However, I do not wish to create the impression that outside the privatisation sphere nothing much of importance involving French equities ever occurs. This would be far from the truth. Over the past 4 or 5 years some 50 or 60 non-privatisation transactions involving a significant international distribution have taken place.[44]

First, I shall deal with the size of the French privatisation programme. During the first wave, which took place between December 1986 and October 1987, the privatisation of twelve state-controlled groups generated FRF 84 billion (USD 17 billion at today's exchange rates). If we look at the second wave, which was kicked off in September of 1993 with BNP,[45] 7 transactions worth FRF 127 billion (over USD 25 billion) have been brought to market, and 2 or 3 transactions totalling perhaps FRF 30 or 40 billion will in all likelihood take place between now and the first few months of 1996.[46] When the process is completed, say in two or three years' time, it is estimated that the stock market capitalisation of the Paris Bourse will have grown by 15 to 20% and should approach FRF 3,000 billion (USD 600 billion).

Evolutionary Changes in the French Privatisation Process

How has this huge process been carried out? Each privatisation transaction is unique, but with hindsight it is possible to distinguish a clear evolutionary trend between the first wave and today's second wave.

Looking back seven or eight years ago, during the first wave of French privatisations, it is clear that the French financial services industry was significantly weaker, especially internationally, than it is today, and the way in which the privatisation offerings were sold reflected this lack of strong international investment banking operations. The lead managers of the international tranche of all the major privatisations in 1986–7 were either American or British firms, the international syndicates functioned under English or American law, and the French input was largely limited to the offer for sale on the domestic market, which was predominantly directed at the French retail investor.

[44] That is, including a Euro-type offer and/or a distribution in one or more domestic markets subject to that market's national regulations (such as the United States).

[45] When the State offered Total shares in 1992 and CLF shares in the first half of 1993, it had already surrendered majority control of these two enterprises, so the transactions prior to the BNP offer do not qualify as privatisations in French law and terminology. The second true privatization of the new wave was Rhône-Poulenc.

[46] These figures exclude offers to employees.

It should be recalled, however, that in the 1986–7 context, the limited international distribution capability and expertise as advisors of French intermediaries was not an acute problem because of the very strong French demand for privatisation issues. Also, until 1990, numerous countries in Europe, including France, still had exchange controls of varying importance and effect, which complicated cross-border distribution significantly.

Today, the size of the French privatisation programme—as well perhaps as greater attention given by French privatisation candidates to their international image and exposure—makes broad international distribution essential. Today's privatisations are therefore rather different from yesterday's, and the evolution undergone by the French privatisation process speaks volumes about the osmosis between French and Anglo-American law, methods, markets, and intermediation.

Since the first privatisation of the latest wave, which began two years ago with the BNP, French banks have always won the lead management role, despite the crucial contribution of foreign institutions as advisors and placers—especially in the United States.[47] This has been commented upon at length in the press. What may be less well understood is the profound change in the way the privatisation issues are structured and managed.

In 1986–7, privatisation offerings generally comprised two tranches. One was an international tranche offered outside France, and which was often subdivided into regional tranches.[48] The other was a domestic tranche placed as an undifferentiated offer for sale during a three-week period to all French investors. This structure presented three major drawbacks. First, since French institutional investors had access only to the offer for sale which gave high priority to individual investors, strong demand meant that they received literally no shares. Second, the 1986 structure left the underwriters exposed for a long period of time, which constituted both an argument in favour of raising the cost of their services and a deterrent to maximising the offer price.[49] Third, it delayed the beginning of official trading on the Paris Bourse, thereby allowing a grey market to develop in London which could be detrimental to the success of the distribution should the grey market price ever go below the offering price. Complicating

[47] Other than the French lead manager, there are often nowadays both a French and a non-French 'global coordinator' or 'global lead manager' (this second expression refers to the global institutional tranche whereas the first expression appears to encompass other elements of the offering). BNP, however, acted as global coordinator for its own privatisation offering, with Merrill Lynch in the role of US lead manager. Further, it is not at all inconceivable that in the future, for certain offerings, the international placement—and not just the US tranche—may be lead-managed by a non-French institution.

[48] Then, as now, the international tranches have usually been offered privately to institutions. The only public offers to date—in the US and Japan—have been the 1993 Elf and Rhône-Poulenc transactions.

[49] This also made such transactions particularly unattractive to potential foreign underwriters unaccustomed to such practices, e.g. US firms.

matters further, the international and domestic tranches were sold under separate underwriting agreements, the domestic tranche being subject to French law and the international tranche subject to English or American law.

Also during the first privatisation wave, the contracts between the French State and underwriters were of traditional French inspiration. They were very short, with little or no legal boilerplate or detailed terms and conditions. For example, the French underwriters generally guaranteed the success of the distribution in unconditional terms, without any escape clause (force majeure) they could fall back on if market conditions deteriorated seriously. The experience of attempting to place large issues of British Petroleum and Indosuez during the 1987 market crash has since made all underwriters insist on American-style escape clauses allowing the lead manager to renounce syndicate undertakings upon the occurrence of events seriously jeopardising the transaction.[50]

Main Features of Today's Privatisations

A general understanding of French privatisations may perhaps best be conveyed by concentrating on the most important innovations introduced into the process during the last two years.

One innovation, strictly regulatory in nature, is the use of a preliminary prospectus. Such a document, referred to as a pathfinder prospectus in the UK and containing neither the actual offer price, nor the exact number of shares to be offered, nor the timetable, was accepted by the COB for the first time with the BNP issue.[51] I shall return to this development later under the heading of investor information.

The four other major innovations introduced during the second, current privatisation wave are:

[50] Perhaps a word of caution is appropriate here. Osmosis between legal systems can lead to strange and sometimes dangerous mutations. One may rightly wonder whether all the parties to a privatisation transaction really understand what they are signing when the underwriting document, for example, is a model contract imported from the United States (or England), translated into French and subject to the jurisdiction of French courts. Terms used in the American (or English) legal system with a specific meaning may have an entirely different meaning in the French legal system, or no apparent meaning whatsoever (thus 'affilié' for 'affiliate'). No one knows what a French judge would make of such language that the parties have expressly submitted to his jurisdiction.

[51] BNP was the first true privatisation transaction to have benefited from the preliminary prospectus, though previously the 1992 Rhône-Poulenc offering had made use of the new procedure, and even before this a technique incorporating a press release approved by the COB was employed, in particular for the 1991 Elf and Total transactions. These latter transactions were highly unusual issues from more than one point of view, since they were made in the context of the listing of these two companies on the New York Stock Exchange, and the 'green shoe' clause was used to satisfy excess demand from new foreign investors rather than existing French shareholders, who furthermore enjoyed no form of preferential access to the new shares.

- the creation of separate tranches for different segments of the market, specifically reserved for either private or institutional investors;
- the introduction of the book-building procedure in France;
- the shortening of the offer period; and
- the development of a highly original pricing scheme.[52]

The second innovation relates to the structuring of offerings by tranches. A French privatisation transaction is now generally made up of two tranches, one for institutions and another for French individuals.

For French retail investors, the traditional offer for sale—*offres publiques de vente* or OPVs—has been enhanced and a broad distribution secured through the creation of a higher priority for orders of a small number of shares.[53] Moreover, individual domestic shareholders who hold their privatisation shares for 18 months will receive 1 bonus share for every 10 shares held up to a maximum per issue holding of FRF 30,000.[54]

Offers for sale are not reserved exclusively for French private investors. In law, this would be impossible. All individuals who are either French nationals or residents, or nationals of a Member State of the European Economic Area[55] are in theory entitled to participate in a French privatisation offering on exactly the same footing. However, the rule whereby each individual may place a single A-order (top priority), coupled with the bonus entitlement for investors who hold their shares for 18 months and the mandatory dematerialisation of French securities, leads to the requirement that investors must have a cash account and a stock account with a French intermediary through which their orders are placed and their shares held in custody. This obligation to use a French intermediary, which entails disproportionately high costs and novel administrative burdens for non-resident investors, combined with more or less strict national regulations governing the marketing of securities to the public in Europe, means that

[52] It is interesting to emphasise that all these innovations are market-driven, and that laws and regulations have adapted—slowly but surely—to market pressures.

[53] This so-called A-order, combined with a specific priority for investors proposing to pay in Balladur bonds and the policy of guaranteeing both a 100% fill rate to the smallest orders and equivalent fill rates to orders of a size greater than the uniform minimum number for the highest priority tranches, has led to considerable complexity as regards allocation rules for the offer for sale. Equal treatment and strictly proportionate scale-back of orders are however guaranteed in the offer for sale, unlike the book-building process where the underwriters—in conjunction of course with the vendor and/or issuer—enjoy broad discretion in filling institutional orders.

[54] The bonus share terms indicated are the maximum allowed by the law, but have in practice been precisely those adopted to date. The terms of privatisation issues have apparently been deemed favourable by the French retail sector, for each transaction has so far attracted between one and three million individuals, and between 40 and 50% of the total number of shares changing hands have been absorbed by the offer for sale. The BNP still holds the record for oversubscription of the offer for sale with more than 5 times as many shares requested as were available (though for A orders the proportion was only 2,8 and for A1 orders only 1,6).

[55] European Union plus Iceland, Norway and Liechtenstein.

nearly all the shares allotted under the most recent offers for sale have gone to French resident individuals.[56]

As for French institutional investors, who had complained loudly during the first privatisation wave of receiving nothing but leftovers from the domestic offer for sale,[57] they now typically have access to the same tranche as international investors and consequently benefit from a comparable fill rate for their orders.[58] However, demand has been such that the global institutional tranches offered during the second privatisation wave have been oversubscribed between two and fifteen times.[59] On average between 25 and 30% of the total number of shares sold during each privatisation[60] have gone to the underwritten institutional tranche, and within this tranche French institutions typically account for about one-third and foreign institutions two-thirds.

The terms of each privatisation to date have allowed the French State to cut back the number of shares initially earmarked for the institutional/international segment (and in some cases the core shareholder group) in the event of excess demand from the French retail segment, and in practice the claw-back clause has been used to provide additional shares to every offer for sale,[61] with the sole exception of Renault. Moreover, the State has frequently granted the underwriting syndicate an option to acquire additional shares in the event of strong institutional demand (greenshoe option), which has in fact always proved to be the case and has therefore offset, at least in part, the scaling-down of the institutional allotment resulting from the claw-back.[62] No general 'flowthrough' however is allowed; in particular, no claw-back from the offer for sale is ever allowed. The size of the tranches is fixed, subject to these two possible exceptions, at the same time as the price by the Finance Minister, the day before the offer opens. In the preliminary prospectus, moreover, both the approximate size of the tranches as well as an indicative price spread are indicated.[63]

[56] It appears that most UK private investors who choose to participate in French privatisations buy into a specialised investment trust. This route has obvious attractions, chief among them being less bother, though such funds must pay the institutional offering price which is higher than the price available to individuals.

[57] For example, French institutionals other than the selected core shareholders received less than 1% of the CLF shares they applied for in 1993.

[58] Because demand for an issue always exceeds supply, C-orders in an offer for sale, which may be placed by EEA-controlled legal entities, are in fact never filled. In some earlier privatisations (for example Elf and BNP), a specific tranche of the underwritten offer targeted at institutions (French only at that time) was created.

[59] The record is still held by Renault.

[60] Public offer for sale, offer to employees and private sale to core shareholders included.

[61] Generally between 10% and 20%, the latter figure having been to date the maximum provided for by the implementing executive order.

[62] The maximum over-allotment option allowed by Paris Bourse rules is 25%, but in practice the number of extra shares made available is nearly always 10–15%.

[63] No indicative prices are given, however, where the shares to be offered are already quoted on the stockmarket, as was the case for the most recent Elf and Rhône-Poulenc offerings.

The institutional/international global tranche, unlike the offer for sale tranche, is priced using the book-building procedure and placed by an international syndicate of investment bankers led by a French bank.[64] For the latest privatisations, the US market has been solicited under SEC rule 144A, which allows a private offer to be made to certain institutional investors who are authorised to re-sell their holdings under certain conditions, rather than in the context of a listing on the New York Stock Exchange.[65]

Not only are the two tranches separately priced and placed, but also the placing of orders is quite different. Firm institutional orders are placed only when the pricing is final, and once placed are—at least in theory—irrevocable. French retail investors, by contrast, are encouraged during the pre-offering phase to sign up for the offer for sale to the extent of a given money amount, and remain committed accordingly unless they cancel their orders shortly after the publication of the final offer price.[66] As for orders placed by individuals during the offer for sale itself, they are—in theory and in practice—irrevocable.

The third major innovation introduced in 1993[67] is the adoption in France, following the 1986 British Telecom I example,[68] of the book-building procedure.[69] Using the preliminary prospectus, the syndicate inquires into the state of potential demand at different price levels, especially interest originating from institutions. This certainly facilitates price optimisation and tends to lessen the exposure of the underwriters,[70] and

[64] There may be several separate regional sub-syndicates, who receive allotments based on demand in their particular region.

[65] These investors are termed QIBs, for Qualified Institutional Buyers, in US law. Approximately 11% of the Renault institutional tranche was placed with US investors in this way, against 31% going to French institutions.

It seems likely one or more future privatisation transactions will include a full public offering in the US with a NYSE listing.

[66] Such revocable orders have only been allowed for privatisations thus far.

[67] For the Rhône-Poulenc privatisation.

[68] British Telecom II and Wellcome served as direct sources of inspiration for the Elf privatisation offering in early 1994. In addition, BT II is regarded as the first truly global offer of shares, though by this time—1992—the book-building procedure was no longer a pioneering feature.

[69] This procedure was at first called *préplacement* in French but is now translated word-for-word as *construction du livre d'ordres*. The first term is used to describe the rather different procedure used with regard to French retail investors, who prior to the determination of the final offer price may mandate their intermediary to purchase shares on their behalf up to a specified money amount—they are not allowed to express their price preferences—subject to withdrawal before the end of the actual offer period. This was contrasted with book-building institutional orders above.

[70] The underwriters assume their obligation to find buyers on the basis of a price that, though it is set by the French authorities, is determined after consultation with these buyers. Once the final pricing is determined, the underwriters need only request confirmation of the interest already shown. However, the agreement on the part of the investors to purchase the securities only becomes binding at the end of the process, when the underwriter itself has received notice of its allocation and consequently is able to confirm to its clients the exact number of shares in fact purchased. Underwriting risk is therefore significantly reduced with the

also in theory allows the vendor to choose the purchasers considered to be most desirable, since the underwriters will undertake to transmit to the lead manager the identity and indications of interest of every potential investor exceeding a set amount, for example FRF 1 million.[71]

The fourth major innovation in current transactions is much quicker completion. Privatisation timetables have been tightened up considerably over the past few years. This is due in large part to the shortening of the offer period (from three weeks for a 1986-1987 offer for sale to a typical period today of six business days), but also to the improvement of back-office procedures made possible by the full dematerialisation of French securities since 1984. The transaction process has been gradually speeded up to the point that for today's privatisations, the total time that elapses between launch and final delivery of shares (with simultaneous payment therefor) is now just fourteen business days,[72] and trading on the Paris Stock Exchange begins on the tenth business day after the start of the offering.[73]

The fifth major innovation lies in the highly original pricing structure of recent French privatisations. By far the best terms—price, credit facilities, bonus shares—are those available to employees of the company, who receive on average 6–8% of each privatisation issue[74] and benefit from generously preferential treatment and in particular a 20% discount on the base price, which is the offer for sale price.[75] The next best price available is that of the domestic offer for sale, generally very near the minimum price set by

book-building process; however, the exposure period will nonetheless last 10 to 12 days on average.

[71] In addition, the high degree of uncertainty as to the timetable, price, and number of shares to be offered makes the creation of a significant grey market nearly impossible during the book-building process. This is another advantage of book-building in that it helps to ensure the success of such distributions.

[72] For all investors with accounts in France, regardless of whether they are individuals or institutions.

[73] Also, it may be of interest to know that typically, for the most recent privatisation issues:
- the launch including the announcement of the final terms is made the day before the offering begins;
- negotiations with potential core shareholders extend over 5 weeks;
- the book-building process takes 2 weeks;
- the offer for sale lasts 6 full business days;
- the institutional offer is made over a period no longer than the offer for sale and may be closed at any time with 24 hours' advance notice. (It has typically closed after 3 or 4 days for the latest transactions, though in several earlier privatisations—Rhône-Poulenc, Elf, UAP—the book-building process extended beyond the close of the offer for sale and the institutional price was therefore determined subsequently, generally just prior to the publication of the results of the offer for sale.)

[74] Under the law, 10% of the total amount of shares to be placed on the market, i.e. excluding the core shareholder transaction, must be offered to employees, though they will seldom take up their full entitlement.

[75] Although domestic regulations governing the offer of securities in countries of location of subsidiaries may forbid an offer being made to employees in the absence of a public offering in such countries, and employees must hold their shares for two years.

the Privatisation Commission, which performs an independent valuation of the company prior to the determination of terms.[76] The institutional offer is typically priced 2–5% higher than the offer for sale,[77] and the price offered to potential core shareholders is typically 2–3% above the institutional price.

Stabilisation vs Manipulation

On the subject of issue price a few words should be said about stabilisation rules and anti-manipulation regulations. Under French rules, stabilisation may start as of the public announcement of the offer and may continue until one month after listing of the securities offered, provided only that stabilisation transactions are carried out against the market and do not exceed 25% of average market volume.[78]

International Primary Market Association (IPMA) rules are rather different and this may give rise to conflicts where stabilisation transactions are effected on SEAQ International. The principal difficulty for French issues, however, has originated in US regulations. The SEC has traditionally considered that its anti-manipulation rules, which are designed to ensure that only market players independent of the issuer or its agents contribute to the formation of the price of securities offered,[79] should apply, even outside the US, whenever shares are to be distributed in the US. This policy has in the past created serious problems for non-US issuers and their underwriting syndicates. In particular, market-makers, such as MONEP market-makers in France who happen to be affiliated with a member of the underwriting syndicate, were not authorised, under SEC rules, to honour their commitments to the Paris equity options market.

This type of situation created by conflicting rules of different jurisdictions, was at first dealt with case-by-case by the issuance of no-action letters by the SEC on the basis of commitments made by such market-makers to engage exclusively in 'passive market-making' during the relevant period, but has now been resolved through an exchange of letters in 1994 between the COB and the SEC as regards distributions of shares that are component

[76] The Privatisation Commission examines the proposed privatisation terms—and in particular evaluates the company concerned—during the book-building period. Should the transaction not be launched within one month of the setting of the minimum price, the evaluation process must be renewed.

[77] Though for BNP the price was the same because the institutional tranche was not priced using the book-building technique. This technique, which was first used for Rhône-Poulenc in November of 1993, has in the past led to a price as much as 10% higher than the offer for sale price. The question of whether core shareholders, who pay even more, should be considered 'privileged' in such circumstances therefore arises (see below).

[78] In addition, the authorisation for such *règularisation des cours* must be granted by the shareholders in general meeting insofar as the issuer is deemed to be purchasing its own shares.

[79] The reference here is to SEC Rule 10b-6.

stocks of the CAC 40 index. The blanket exemption, which covers all transactions performed on French markets[80] for such issues, is subject to three conditions: first, prior notification of the SEC before any distribution; second, disclosure in the US prospectus of transactions allowed under French law that US law would prohibit; third, the keeping of records for two years of all significant transactions undertaken by all parties involved in the offering during the relevant offer period.

'Privileged' Privatisation Shareholders

The international press has discussed at great length a peculiarity of French privatisations: the *noyaux durs*, or a hard core of shareholders in newly privatised companies.[81] The explanation of this phenomenon is simple. France lacks big pension funds to act as stable, long-term investors,[82] and the French government fears that newly privatised companies might be an easy target for foreign raiders. Such fears may or may not be exaggerated, but in any event the device employed—sale by private agreement rather than an offer to the market as a whole—to ensure that companies have a sizeable,[83] coherent, active group of friendly core shareholders when they come to market has only temporary effect, and such shareholders are not arbitrarily selected and privileged.

First, they are attracted by public invitation to tender; second, they and their terms of purchase must be cleared by the Privatisation Commission, which is accordingly notified of all offers before the transfer of the shares;[84] third, they pay extra for their stake (approximately 4–10% more than retail investors for example); fourth, they must bid, typically, for between one-half and one percent of total equity; sixth, they generally must maintain the majority of their holdings for two years, only thereafter being able to divest.[85]

Furthermore, the core shareholders, who may or may not win a seat on the board of directors depending on the particular company's circum-

[80] US transactions must still comply with SEC anti-manipulation rules.

[81] *Groupements d'actionnaires stables*, abbreviated unfortunately as GAS, is now the officially sanctioned term.

[82] French institutions as a whole own only 18% of total market capitalisation.

[83] In general, 10–15% of the total capital stock which translates roughly into 15–20% of the total shares sold in a typical privatisation transaction, where 100% never changes hands immediately.

[84] In 1986–7 the selection of core shareholders rested exclusively with the Finance Minister.

[85] The gradual breakup of the friendly core shareholder groups in newly privatised companies and other cross-shareholdings, which are notoriously widespread in France, is to be expected, given the generally very low returns on such holdings, the new mood in France characterised by the heating-up of the great debate on corporate governance, and the forthcoming emergence of private pension funds. Already, these core groups do not necessarily present a united front.

stances,[86] also generally grant each other a right of first refusal on the sale by any one of them of all or part of its holding for three years following the close of the offer, though each investor's stake is often capped contractually.[87] In the case of BNP, its core shareholders were precluded from selling any of their holdings for three months, thereafter at most 20% was available for disposal over the following twenty-one months. Two years after the completion of the offer they were free to divest all their holdings, subject however to a mutual right of first refusal over 80% of each investor's holdings for 3 further years.[88]

As for the golden share, which allows the Finance Minister to counter a hostile takeover[89] or veto the sale of strategic assets[90] for as long as such share exists,[91] it has been used only in the case of Elf.[92] Moreover, the creation of the golden share must necessarily precede the evaluation of the company by the Privatisation Commission so as to allow for the market impact of the State's specific prerogatives.

I should also like to point out that the 20% cap on the number of privatisation shares that may be acquired by non-European Union investors (taken together) applies only to the privatisation offering itself and does not limit the number of shares that may be acquired on the secondary trading market, and moreover may be waived in the context of a partnership with a foreign group, such as was the case with the ill-fated Volvo-Renault alliance.[93]

[86] In particular, the presence or absence of other large long-term shareholders not party to the agreement among core shareholders, e.g. UAP holds 15% of the equity in BNP which itself holds an equivalent portion of the equity in UAP.

[87] I should point out that such shareholder agreements have raised novel, difficult issues from the viewpoint of regulations employing the notion of concert party such as those requiring the publication of shareholdings exceeding 5% or the launch of a takeover bid by shareholders holding more than one-third of a company's voting rights, since the lock-up clause is imposed by the State. Each shareholder agreement is submitted to the Conseil des Bourses de Valeurs, which has to date always concluded, save a single exception, that no concert party was constituted. For SEITA, the special provisions concerning voting and other matters were considered to demonstrate the existence of a concert party.

[88] For SEITA the restriction period is longer because such a relatively small company could be easy prey for foreign tobacco giants. As a further measure to deter potential predators, the French State has also retained 10% of the share capital.

[89] Through the requirement to secure official approval for any holding greater than 10% under pain of having all shares acquired in breach of the rule compulsorily sold.

[90] Where this could harm France's 'national interests', under pain of the disposal being deemed null and void.

[91] Unlike the 1986 law which limited its duration to five years, under the 1993 privatisation law the golden share is a permanent feature unless removed by ministerial order. The result, curiously, is identical to that in English law where only a qualified majority of the shareholders concerned by any proposed change can modify the rights attaching to their shares!

[92] In which the State, in addition, still holds 13% of the stock. In the first wave only two companies were concerned by the creation of a golden share, which has since lapsed.

[93] In the 1986–1981 privatisation issues, the 20% cap applied to all non-French investors, including European investors, which was of doubtful legality under the Treaty of Rome's provisions in favor of equal treatment.

It is by no means the intention of France to create disincentives to investment in French stocks. On the contrary, the French State has in particular tried to make the trading and holding of French equities as fiscally attractive as possible, by first (in 1993) exempting foreign investors from the stock exchange transaction tax and then (in 1994) improving the tax treatment of dividends paid to shareholders established in countries having a double-taxation treaty with France.[94]

Shareholder Rights and Information

I shall once again take the example of French privatisations, but my remarks remain generally valid for new issues by private sector firms.

Prospectuses

Because of the high proportion of English-speaking fund managers in the world and the necessity to cater for their exacting requirements in terms of disclosure, prospectuses for any very large securities offering must today contain extensive information on the issuer and be written in a language understandable by the majority of potential investors.

Furthermore, as I pointed out earlier, French practice, especially in the field of privatisation, has adopted the US technique of book-building which requires making available to a large number of investors detailed information in order to obtain the best price possible for the vendor whilst ensuring the success of the distribution in a number of markets.

To take into account these constraints, French prospectuses and procedures have been adapted to a considerable extent, so that investors receive more detailed, officially sanctioned information earlier and in the English language.

Whereas prospectuses a few years ago were relatively lightweight, their length, precision and sophistication have grown to the point that most investors are unlikely to be able to scrutinise the entire document in any depth. Yet this level of disclosure has become indispensable for any major international offering.

In the past the level of disclosure required by international investors led to the issuing of a prospectus in English that was as a rule superior to the French-language document used for the French market. As a matter of fact, the two prospectuses had little chance of being similar since they were

[94] The tax credit paid by the French Treasury as well as the dividend paid by the company are now subject to the relevant treaty withholding rate directly upon payment of these amounts to non-resident shareholders (rather than the application of such lower rate being achieved the following year through the submission of tax reclaim forms), and certain foreign investors previously denied the benefit of the tax credit are now entitled thereto under the new rules (specifically, tax-exempt US pension funds now receive payment of the tax credit up to the amount of tax withheld on their French-source dividends).

drafted separately by different teams. The international team would organise a series of due diligence meetings in accordance with Anglo-American practice and consequently produce a document containing some information that was not to be found in the official French prospectus approved by the French authorities.[95]

This situation, where French investors in French companies were treated poorly compared to foreign investors, was obviously not acceptable.[96] Under pressure from the COB and leading French underwriting banks alike, the parties involved have now agreed to make the two versions of the offering prospectus consistent to the highest degree practicable. French issuers and their advisors have learned the ropes and now use the due-diligence techniques that international disclosure standards require. Today, the information contained in the French offering documents approved by the COB is nearly identical[97] to that contained in the prospectus drawn up to international standards, except for a few items that would not be of particular interest to one or the other groups of investors.[98]

Another recent development designed to ensure that all investors—private or institutional, French or foreign—are able to assess the merits of an offering on the basis of equal information, is the new procedure adopted by the COB for the approval of documentation. The new COB procedure allows—indeed encourages—the splitting of documentation concerning the

[95] Among the differences between the two sets of offering documents prepared for certain earlier privatisations, especially those incorporating a US tranche, the most remarkable inconsistency was often the fact that the US and international circulars contained a rather different—and in some respects more detailed—Management Discussion and Analysis.

By contrast, it appears normal that the international offering circular (which unlike the French offering documentation was and remains a single document in its final form) should explain the main differences between US and French Generally Accepted Accounting Principles as they affect the issuer's consolidated financial statements, whereas the French documents merely summarise in general terms the issuer's accounting policies.

[96] The fact that the two offering documents were very different may help to explain why the international offering circular may not be used in France. Nonetheless, the recent convergence of the two versions has not changed this prohibition since only the French prospectus is subject to the clearance procedure of the COB and may therefore be legally distributed in France, despite the fact that the Republic of France itself, in addition to the issuer of the shares being offered, states in the international offering circular that it is aware of no material facts not contained therein.

[97] A distinction should be made here. In most cases today, the level of disclosure is almost identical, but the presentation of the information is often different. This is because French prospectuses are required to follow the layout provided by the COB in its *Instruction* or implementing guidelines. The current trend, exemplified by SEITA, appears to be toward even greater harmonisation. Not only is the content of the SEITA business description identical in both versions, but also the layout. This is achieved by first drafting the prospectus in French according to COB rules, and then having it translated into English with no other modification than the re-arranging of certain headings.

[98] For example, information on French company law or securities settlement periods is not reproduced in the French prospectus, and the tax regime for French residents is not detailed in the international prospectus, which on the other hand explains selling restrictions and tax treatment of dividends in various jurisdictions.

issuer and its securities into separate pieces. An annual shelf registration statement (*document de référence*) containing a detailed description of the issuer, its securities, shareholders, management, activities and latest financials may be submitted for approval and used for any new issue—debt or equity—until the following year's accounts are published; only the terms of the new issue as well as any more recent published financial statements need be included in the actual issue prospectus (*note d'opération*) which the COB undertakes to approve in forty-eight hours. This new procedure, which is voluntary, was adopted by the COB in 1992, and today some 60 companies register a comprehensive reference document on an annual basis.[98a]

As I pointed out earlier, a slightly different procedure has been adopted for the current wave of privatisations, and is now available for all new offerings using the book-building procedure (which in fact is indispensable for any sizeable international tranche). For the BNP issue, a preliminary prospectus (*note d'opération préliminaire*) was approved for the first time. On the basis of this new document, which in addition to any update of the information contained in the shelf registration statement indicates the approximate number of shares to be offered and the structure of the various tranches (including their priority status if any), as well as an indicative price spread, the syndicate builds the institutional book and the French public may place revocable orders. Then, once the pricing is completed, a final prospectus or offering circular (*note d'opération définitive*) is approved and issued (and published in the press), containing the final price and timetable of the issue.[99] During the offer period strictly speaking, institutions may confirm or abandon their orders to members of the syndicate. As for private investors who have sent in orders prior to the pricing, they may elect to cancel them, failing which they become firm.[100]

The COB has also encouraged—indeed made mandatory since 1994—the use of a two-page summary of the full offering documentation (issuer reference document and issue prospectus), so as to facilitate and accelerate the information of private investors, largely through France's retail banks.[101]

The end result of this adaptation of French procedures is to allow a greater degree of flexibility for issuers whilst ensuring adequate information, regardless of the type of issue or the target group of investors. In France,

[98a] For the use of a similar shelf registration in the United States, see Greene, Braverman and Schneck, supra, pp. 175–7.

[99] As well as the make-up of the stable shareholder group, the size of the various tranches and any claw-back or greenshoe clause.

[100] It should be stressed that private shareholders may place orders prior to the offer period per se only in the context of a privatisation issue, and that such orders may be cancelled up to the last day of the offer period.

[101] There are now more than 6 million individuals in France who directly hold securities, mostly equities. This makes widespread publicity vital. For major issues such as privatisations the full prospectus is published in the press, and up to 3 million copies of the two-page summary are made available to intermediaries for distribution to their customers.

as elsewhere, the privatisation process has greatly contributed to the modernisation of capital markets and in particular the way in which securities are marketed and sold.

Accounting Standards

On the subject of disclosure, I should also mention the matter of accounting standards. Historically, the accounts of French companies have always largely been driven by tax considerations, and this is still true today as far as corporate accounts are concerned. However, an increasing proportion of the largest listed French companies use a less biased benchmark than French tax rules to report their consolidated accounts, where considerably more latitude is available under the law. Groups such as Elf, Total, Alcatel Alsthom and Rhône-Poulenc, which are all listed on the New York Stock Exchange, as well as a half-dozen others, report under US GAAP standards, while an additional 25 major French companies report their consolidated accounts under international (IASC) standards.[102]

At the risk of belabouring an obvious point, I would say that this demonstrates two very different things: on the one hand, the need for major French companies to report in an accounting language understood by foreign investors; on the other, a degree of disharmony, resulting from the use of a variety of accounting languages, that makes comparison—and therefore the disclosure of truly useful information—in many cases impossible.

The recent agreement between IOSCO (International Organisation of Securities Commissions) and IASC (International Accounting Standards Committee) to develop a comprehensive set of standards for companies seeking a listing in foreign markets or wishing to raise capital outside their home jurisdictions is very encouraging. Should such efforts, which are fully supported by all the relevant French authorities, come to fruition, universally recognised standards may emerge by the turn of the century, which would be a considerable achievement. In particular, the registration of French and other non-US securities with the SEC and their distribution into the United States would be greatly facilitated,[103] to the benefit of both non-US issuers and US investors.

[102] In theory, of course, French companies listed in France must abide by French accounting standards. In fact, differences between French and US and IASC rules only seldom give rise to significant problems. US standards are almost always deemed compatible with French rules, and the broad choice of options under current IASC standards makes it possible in almost any situation to choose an 'international' treatment that French standards will endorse (though an alternative IASC treatment might run foul of French law).

[103] As for incoming offerings and listings, the French authorities accept US GAAP, IASC and European accounting standards. Where the issuer's standards differ notably from French rules, however, the COB will require that those principles be explained and the impact of the application of French accounting standards on shareholders' equity and net income be estimated (this has often been the case with the treatment of goodwill by UK companies for example).

Anti-dilution Provisions

One of the major obstacles to international distributions of French equities has been the anti-dilution protection provided under French company law. The desire of issuers to diversify their shareholder base outside France and tap the international capital markets in better conditions has led to a gradual relaxation of the relevant rules, under the guidance of the COB which has deliberately chosen to accommodate the internationalisation of French issuers and seek practical remedies within the constraints imposed by the law.

Traditionally in France, it has been judged essential to preserve the interests of existing shareholders by giving them a pre-emptive right to subscribe for any new issue of shares. Under these circumstances, non-shareholders must either purchase subscription rights on the market from shareholders who do not wish to provide additional funding, or else hope that some shareholders will let their rights lapse so that outside investors may have access.[104] This anti-dilution protection is still very much alive today in France, as it is in most European countries. Market forces have nonetheless led to a significant weakening of the principle of pre-emptive rights. The Elf and Total transactions of 1992–3 may be considered turning points in this area.

Any new issue of securities by a French company must in the first place be approved by the shareholders by resolution in an extraordinary meeting.[105] Furthermore, when shareholders delegate to the board of directors the power to go forward with a new issue, the delegation must specify the maximum amount of new shares to be created and whether or not current shareholders will be granted pre-emptive rights.

Where shareholders authorise an issue without pre-emptive rights, the COB will require that shareholders nevertheless be accorded a time priority. Unlike a (pre-emptive) rights issue which is characterised by a listed, tradeable right (*droit préférentiel de souscription* which is generally in certificated form in paper-based systems such as the UK where it takes the form of a 'renouncable letter of allotment'), a new issue of shares with time priority rights (*délai de priorité de souscription*) is characterised by the necessity for shareholders to carry out any subscription they wish to make within the allotted period, their right being evidenced exclusively by their holding

[104] Here we have momentarily left the area of privatisations since no new shares are generally created when the State transfers all or part of its holdings to the private sector. Even where new shares are issued, as was the case in the Renault and Usinor Sacilor offers, the issue of pre-emption rights does not arise where the State itself as exclusive shareholder (directly or indirectly) either waives its rights or takes them up only to re-sell the new shares immediately to investors. The 1991–2 Elf and Total offers, as it was pointed out earlier, involved the issue of new shares but by entities that had already left the public sector (more than one-half of their share capital being held by outside investors at the time of the respective offers).

[105] Such a meeting requires a two-thirds majority of shareholders present or represented.

the relevant securities throughout the subscription period. The priority right is neither negotiable nor transferable in any way.

Since French company law imposes conditions upon rights issues—in particular early publication requirements[106] and a rather long subscription period[107]—that are felt to be increasingly burdensome in today's global, fast-moving markets, more and more capital increases are carried out today where shareholders are granted only a time priority. Furthermore, this period during which current shareholders are entitled to subscribe prorata to their holdings is always shorter than the subscription period for pre-emptive issues,[108] and green shoe clauses allowing a 10 to 15% increase in the issue size have been authorised to respond to excess international demand. Moreover, the open tranche of the issue, not requiring prior share-ownership and generally directed towards international investors, is offered simultaneously, and any part of the priority offer left unsubscribed may be immediately recycled to the international tranche.[109]

I should like to recall here that one of the top priorities of the SBF-Paris Bourse and the French authorities in general is to make equity investment and trading responsive to the needs of private investors.

It seems possible to take adequate account of these needs without granting current shareholders privileged access to new issues through pre-emptive rights.[110] The way in which issues without pre-emptive rights are priced may be thought to provide sufficient anti-dilution protection. Whereas rights issues in France generally carry a 10–20% discount to market price, French law determines a floor price for issues without pre-emptive rights. The price must be no lower than the average of any ten consecutive day's closing prices out of the twenty trading days immediately preceding the offer. In the future this rule, which until one year ago was '20 out of 40' rather than '10 out of 20', may be further relaxed so that the new issue price is based simply on the closing market price of the day just prior to the offer.[111]

[106] No later than six business days before the beginning of the offer.

[107] Formerly 20 calendar days now reduced to 10 trading days (since 1994).

[108] Generally four or five trading days.

[109] Though it is perhaps more common for the priority tranche to benefit from a clawback of shares initially earmarked for foreign investors.

In the future it appears possible that instead of the time priority, issuers may be allowed to issue a specific tranche for retail investors who otherwise might find themselves unable to subscribe in the face of overwhelming institutional demand.

[110] And perhaps even without using the time priority mechanism in some circumstances, though this latter proposition is hotly contested by many minority shareholders unwilling to accept, for example, free equity warrants instead of immediate access to a new issue of shares.

[111] This may take time, though, since the rule—newly amended in 1994—is statutory and requires an Act of Parliament to be modified.

The Special Case of French Franc Global Bond Issues

In many ways the recent global bond issue by the Republic of Portugal, the first ever to be denominated in French francs, demonstrates how far the interpenetration of French and international markets has progressed to date.

Structure of the Offer and Clearing Arrangements

Two French banks and an American investment bank managed the issue (as global co-ordinators). One third of the issue was underwritten by an exclusively French syndicate, two-thirds by an international syndicate composed of French and non-French institutions. However, the international syndicate was free to sell in France, and the French syndicate was free to sell abroad. Both tranches were underwritten severally,[112] sold concurrently and were fully fungible. A very large proportion of the international tranche was sold to US investors on the basis of an SEC registration.

The bonds were governed by French law in accordance with the Treasury's wishes.[113] To comply with French law, the issue was fully dematerialised. All the bonds were created electronically in SICOVAM, the French central securities depository. All deliveries took place exclusively in book-entry form throughout the world, whether it be in DTC in the United States, SICOVAM in France, or Euroclear or Cedel. No definitive (i.e certificated) bonds will be issued. All transfers of beneficial interests would be effected through book-entry accounts of financial institutions acting on behalf of bondholders as direct and indirect participants of SICOVAM, though investors may elect to hold book-entry interests through another clearing system. Only SICOVAM participants, however, directly hold beneficial interests in the bonds.

All aspects of the issue were governed by French law, except the depository receipt, issued by Citibank NA and subject to New York law, which represents in the United States the interests of American investors in the issue, through a nominee of DTC in whose name the depository receipt is issued. The procedure was somewhat convoluted but may be summarised as follows.

Investors holding bonds through DTC delivered them to the account that

[112] This means that each underwriter assumes no obligation with respect to the allotments of the other underwriters and is consistent with French and US practice. Only the international—e.g Eurobond—practice differs.

[113] The fact that French law governs French franc global bonds does not suffice to make them fully French (see the discussion above about Eurofranc bonds). For the inaugural French franc global bond issue, the issuer was not French, the issue was managed by two syndicates one of which was not French, and a depository receipt governed by New York law was created. A number of different jurisdictions could conceivably have to judge upon this bond, depending on the nature of the issue at stake.

Citibank (New York) had with Paribas (Paris) acting as registrar for the issue; such bonds were registered in Citibank's name. Citibank then issued to DTC (and registered in the name of DTC's nominee) the depository receipt (termed 'global receipt') which represented a 100% interest in the bonds delivered from time to time to such account, and DTC credited its own participants on its own book-entry transfer system. Thus, the bonds belonging to American investors were registered in the name of Citibank and held in custody in the SICOVAM account of Paribas.[114]

Unequal Information?

The prospectus for the international offering of Portugal's global bonds could scarcely be more different from the prospectus for the French offering. The international prospectus contained only two pages of information on the issuer, while the French document contained no less than 44 pages about Portugal. That difference was to be expected, since Portugal files its annual report (on Form 18-K) with the SEC every year, so that detailed up-to-date information on the issuer was available in the US and may be incorporated by reference into the international prospectus. This was not the case in France, hence the lengthy description required in the context of a public offering to French investors.[115]

The international prospectus contained two types of information (other than the naturally different information on tax regimes) not to be found in the French prospectus:[116] on the one hand, a relatively clear explanation of the DTC/depository receipt arrangements, which was of course of great interest to American investors and their advisors, and on the other the portion of the issue allotted to each underwriter, which should be of interest not only to the issuer but also to investors given the lack of a joint underwriting commitment.

The interpenetration of markets obviously remains less than complete in view of the numerous complexities that arise in the context of cross-border offerings nevertheless termed 'global'. Furthermore, it has not yet been convincingly demonstrated that such global bond issues rightly command the liquidity premium that investors pay. This, going beyond the familiar regulatory and settlement difficulties in respect of global offers, would tend to call into question the efficiency of markets conceived to be transnational in scale.

[114] A further peculiarity of the back-office arrangements put in place for American investors is that bondholders through book-entry interests in the depository receipt issued to DTC will receive payments of principal and interest in USD unless they elect to receive such payments in FRF.

[115] International prospectuses relating to sovereign issues generally do not contain a description of the issuer or its financials. US prospectuses do, and likewise French prospectuses (except that no prospectus at all is produced when the French State offers bonds, these always being domestic FRF offers to designated primary dealers).

[116] The French prospectus follows the COB format for sovereign public bond issues.

CONCLUSION

Before concluding, perhaps it would be salutary to make one more observation in order to temper media hyperbole about global markets. In fact, the world is very far from having a single capital market. There may be, arguably, something approaching a global shareholder base for the world's bluest-chip issuers, as there are certainly a few investment groups with a diversified global portfolio and a few banking and brokerage groups with global reach (as the marketing departments put it). Yet the vast majority of money, especially long-term money, is still invested domestically, almost all companies still predominantly fund their businesses locally, and investment rules are still largely national and extremely disparate. Though it is true that the London markets and fund management are highly international, the City remains a glaring exception and will probably remain so for the foreseeable future.

French privatisations are officially termed 'global offerings' despite the very different conditions in which French and foreign, private and institutional investors have access to the issues, as I have tried to demonstrate in this paper.[117] This diversity is obvious not only on primary capital markets but also on secondary trading markets, whether one looks at exchange membership requirements, listing requirements, company research, trading techniques, settlement rules or anything else.

If the media go on tirelessly about the globalisation of markets, it is of course because the trend is clear. Markets remain segmented overall today, but they are becoming rapidly more integrated. Businesses require access to larger pools of capital to finance expansion, and investors seek greater portfolio diversification to maximise their risk-adjusted return on capital.

In these circumstances domestic regulators have little choice but to relax unnecessary restrictions on cross-border fund-raising and portfolio investment. In particular, international equity offerings will become more and more common, and doubtless significantly easier over the medium term, under market pressure.

Given the relative weakness of French institutional investors—compared to the Americans, the British, the Swiss and the Japanese—the impetus behind securities reform in France over the past ten years has naturally come from French issuers and their advisors. As regards debt markets, the driving force has been the French State itself through the Treasury Department of the Finance Ministry which has created one of the world's most modern, efficient and liquid government debt markets. As regards equity markets, the drive towards liberalisation and innovation has been led by the largest listed French companies. Yet even here, since the largest, trail-

[117] In reality only the institutional tranche of a French privatisation offering is truly global.

blazing transactions have concerned newly privatised companies, the role of the French Treasury has been paramount,[118] though the contribution of the COB and the many privatisation advisors should not be underestimated.

Another vital aspect of the modernisation of French capital markets should be mentioned in closing. It is fair to say that the Paris Bourse is today one of the world's most advanced stock exchanges in terms of fairness, transparency, efficiency, regulatory supervision and safety. From the moment an investor decides, in view of the real-time pre-trade and post-trade central market information made available to him by the Bourse itself (directly or indirectly), to transmit an order to the state-of-the-art screen-based trading system, until cash and securities change hands on a T + 3, delivery-versus-payment, totally automated, electronic book-entry basis, market trades in France are executed, settled and reported in a fully integrated process that is one of the great success stories of modern exchanges.[119] And our recently modernised systems will allow the Paris Bourse to go beyond the record FRF 1,100 billion (USD 220 billion) traded on the CAC system in 1994, which volume shows growth by more than two-thirds since 1992.[120]

Looking ahead, French issuers, their advisors, and the French authorities will continue to work together to facilitate cross-border securities offerings—and efficient secondary trading markets—that have become vital for ensuring cost-effective financing for French businesses.

[118] The continuing role of the Treasury shows that France remains a largely *dirigiste* country, at least in the financial area.

[119] The Paris Bourse may be characterised as a centralised, order-driven, electronic continuous auction market. The new trading system introduced in 1995 is called SuperCAC. RELIT is the fully automated delivery vs. payment system, integrated into the SuperCAC trading system, and operated by SBF and SICOVAM.

[120] I should perhaps add that France is the only country I am aware of—there must be others—where the Stock Exchange itself plays an important role in the privatisation process. In fact, the SBF-Paris Bourse not only is responsible for informing the market of the detailed conditions of the offer in a notice it publishes, but it also centralises orders for the offer for sale and informs each bank and brokerage of the total number of shares to be allotted to the intermediary's clients in response to their orders (as pointed out earlier, only private investors actually receive shares in the offer for sale).

13

Competition Between Securities Markets: Good or Bad?

EDMUND W. KITCH

The regulatory and institutional structure of securities markets is one of the ways that they compete with each other for business. London competes with New York and the continental markets. The over-the-counter markets compete with the exchange markets. The structure of a market may offer superior features such as greater depth, faster execution, less price impact, more confidentiality, more reliable clearing. Or it may offer lower costs. This competition is a factor that no regulator and no market can ignore. As a result it is an important determinant of the structure of securities regulation in every country. Is this a good or a bad thing?

To the extent that regulators and legislators are influenced by the answer to that question it is one of practical importance. If they believe that the competition produces undesirable results, they can attempt to suppress it by cooperating with other national regulators to adopt uniform rules and procedures. They can insist that the over-the-counter markets resemble, as closely as possible, organized exchanges. If they believe that the competition produces desirable results, they can facilitate it by permitting the entry into their markets of securities and securities salesmen from other jurisdictions.

It is possible, of course, to view the regulatory issues as reflecting nothing more than a struggle for advantage between competing political and market centers in which concerns about what is better or worse are of no importance. It is easier, for instance, to explain the provisions of US state blue sky laws which automatically qualify securities traded on the NYSE or NASDAQ, but do not accord the same status to securities traded on any non-US markets, as reflecting the successful exercise by US political actors of their clout rather than as the result of a view that an automatic qualification rule limited to US exchanges is the best rule. The importance of economic and political power in shaping securities regulation is more likely to be important to the extent that the concept of better or worse as applied to securities regulation has no compelling content. For purposes of this

Chapter, however, I will adopt the convention that regulators and legislators are, or at least should be, concerned about what is the best institutional arrangement.

It is also relevant to note that discussions about the regulation of securities markets focus on the structure of markets for equity securities.[1] The much larger bond markets proceed without apparent difficulty and little controversy as over the counter markets in which billions of dollars of securities are traded daily without much concern by anyone as to whether the market is sufficiently or properly regulated. The emphasis on equities suggests that the real concerns about market regulation may not be concerns about markets for the purchase and sale of securities, but rather the interaction between those markets and the power to control entities that are everywhere important economic and social institutions. For instance, one of the most distinctive features of US securities regulation is that it prescribes the disclosures that issuers whose equity securities are publicly traded must make, a subject that can just as easily be considered part of corporate law. I will ignore this dimension of securities regulation.

The issue of whether regulatory competition in securities regulation is good or bad cannot be addressed without considering the objectives of securities regulation. Only if we identify what the objectives of securities regulation are can we begin to analyze whether those objectives are furthered or hindered by competition between regulatory regimes. Because securities regulation has multiple objectives, the issue of the impact of regulatory competition is complex. The attainment of some objectives is hindered by regulatory competition, the attainment of other objectives is furthered.

Securities regulation has its origins in two quite different bodies of law and practice. One of these is the organization and practice of the stock exchanges, private organizations with regulatory aspects that emerged prior to the regulation, and whose successful operation is one of its principal objectives. The other is the effort to use the legal system to combat fraud.

In most systems of securities regulation, the private exchange organization remains the front-line regulator. Along with sister organizations structured by analogy to the exchanges, the 'SROs' or self-regulatory organizations are then themselves regulated by a public body. Because the exchanges and analogous bodies are at the heart of securities regulation, both chronologically and conceptually, it is helpful to begin by asking what exchanges do.

[1] Historically, the Exchanges were places for transactions in bonds, and originally that meant government bonds and closely related obligations. It was only after Exchanges became places mostly for transactions in equities that demands for more extensive public regulation arose.

THE FUNCTION OF THE EXCHANGES[2]

1 *Establish and modify trading rules.* The central purpose of these rules is to establish the conventions within which transactions will take place on the exchange. Historically, these conventions arose from custom, but as the Exchanges evolved into formal organizations they became more self-conscious about shaping these conventions through rules. The purpose of the trading rules is to provide a standardized form of trading which covers all issues except the price at which the transaction will take place.

2 *Protection against counter-party insolvency.* In order to generate transactions in which the price is determined without consideration of any risks due to the insolvency of a particular counter-party, the Exchange limits access to trading to those who meet qualifications, most importantly, minimum financial qualifications. In addition, there are deterrents, if only in the form of social persuasion, to the use of any available insolvency mechanism to avoid obligations incurred on the exchange.

3 *Dispute settlement process.* Because the slow pace of legal proceedings is inconsistent with the need of parties on the exchange to be able to determine their position, the Exchange provides dispute settlement procedures. When disputes arise over particular transactions, the internal exchange mechanism provides a quick answer as to the consequences of the transaction so that the parties can quickly know their exposure and take appropriate action. Because the parties are repeat players on the market, random inaccuracies resulting from the quick and informal procedure cancel each other out over time.

4 *Attract a 'crowd.'* A distinctive feature of securities markets is their continuity on both the buy and sell side. When the market is open, either a buyer or seller can find someone to transact with. This quality is made possible by the presence 'on' the exchange of a group of people interested in profiting from short-term transactions. 'Crowd' is my own term, adapted from the terminology of commodities trading where it is used to describe the traders present in the pit, to indicate the presence of a group of traders with a continuous interest in taking positions in the market. 'Crowd' in my usage includes anyone who assumes a dealer position, either formally or de-facto, as, for instance, a NYSE specialist or a NASDAQ market maker, and includes anyone else who makes a regular business of being present as a buyer and seller in the market.

[2] I know of no literature that attempts to analyze the function of the exchange institution. Most of the extant literature is promotional, elegiac, or biographical. Among the more thoughtful I have found is E. Victor Morgan & W.A. Thomas, The London Stock Exchange (New York: St. Martin's Press, 1962). The finance economists, who might be expected to be interested in the institution, treat it as a given in the environment.

Before the advent of telecommunications, it was necessary to attract the members of the crowd to the physical floor of the exchange. Nineteenth century exchanges would, for instance, improve the quality of the amenities to help attract a 'crowd,' for instance by offering free coffee and snacks. It is no accident that the London Stock Exchange (LSE) originated in informal trading practices in and around the coffee-houses. The old-time floor traders on the New York Stock Exchange, who made their living on the floor by taking advantage of opportunities for short-term trading profits are a classic example of a 'crowd.'

In the long run the members of the 'crowd' come not for the coffee but for the opportunity to make a profit. The definition of the proper role of the 'crowd' on an exchange has been an endless source of regulatory and political difficulty. To the extent that members of the 'crowd' also assume agency duties for others, there is a conflict of interest. The old rules of the LSE that required a separation of dealer and broker functions was one attempt to deal with this problem. Another is the complex provisions of §11 of the Securities and Exchange Act of 1934, designed to regulate the precedence of public vis-a-vis member orders.

It is the presence of the 'crowd' that makes it possible to use market orders, orders that do not specify a price but simply provide for a purchase or sale at the 'market,' which in practical terms means an order to be executed at a price that someone in the 'crowd' is willing to offer for it. At least before the advent of modern telescreen trading, market orders had significant advantages. They required only one communication to the market, and avoided the need for further communication between the floor and the principal. A principal, of course, will not enter a market order unless he has reason to believe that there is in fact a 'market' price.

It is easy to characterize the profits of the 'crowd' as being made at the expense of the public, as any dealer's margin is frequently characterized. ('Buy direct from the source, save on the middleman's markup.') The critical issue is not that the 'crowd' makes a profit, but whether that profit is an appropriate reward for the provision of immediacy to the market. In addition, the members of the 'crowd' have never been a particularly appealing lot. Spending much of their time in idleness, responsible for no clear productive activity, sometimes loutish in their behavior and manners, they are the essence of the unattractive face of capitalism: pure speculation with no productive function. Yet without them securities markets would be no different from any other resale market.

5 *Support an objective price reporting mechanism.* Once an exchange has evolved to the point that it is possible to think of the transactions on the exchange reflecting the market in the securities, there appears a price reporting mechanism. At first the price reporting is done by third parties who report the prices, but eventually the function is taken over by the exchange

organization itself. Trading rules, such as the requirement that members execute transactions on the exchange, support the price reporting mechanism.

The price reporting mechanism has two important features. First, it operates to help principals deal with principal-agent conflict problems. The principal no longer must rely solely on the agent for information about the 'market,' but can check the agent's reports against the prices reported by the exchange. Second, once the price reporting becomes credible, it becomes a powerful tool for fraud. Anyone who can get control of the price reporting mechanism to create the appearance of value is in a position to profit handsomely.

6 *Promote the market.* Exchanges make efforts to promote the use of their market facilities through collective promotion efforts, and by attempting to establish a reputation as a desirable place to do business. This will include standards for member handling of customer accounts, standards for securities listed on the exchange, and dispute resolution facilities for customers with a grievance against a member. Since the reputations of all members of an exchange are linked to the reputation of every other member, the Exchange as an entity and each member individually has an interest in joint efforts to reduce the incidence of conduct that would deter customers from dealing with them.

Part of the effort to promote the market will include efforts to convince potential users that the market is a fair place to deal, that prices are not subject to manipulation, and that some traders do not have an unfair or improper advantage. The ability of the Exchange to act in these areas, however, is limited since its powers are only over exchange members.

One of the ways in which exchanges attempted to control the manipulation of prices of equity securities, and particularly the manipulation of their prices in connection with initial offerings, was to prescribe a listing procedure and information disclosure requirements whose objective was to reduce the ability of potential manipulators to spread baseless rumours among market traders.

7 *Create Incentives for Members to Support and Promote the Market.* In order to give its members an incentive to comply with Exchange requirements and an interest in promoting the market as a whole, the Exchange will be structured so that Members individually will gain from the success of the market as a whole. Exchange memberships can be limited in number so that they will gain in value if the Exchange becomes more successful. Agreed minimum commissions help to ensure that attracting increased business to the Exchange will in fact be profitable to members, that members will not simply compete away the gains from their own success.

8 *Adapt to new technology.* Over time exchanges and regulators have been forced to adapt their practices to new technology. In the nineteenth century,

the development of the ticker with its ability to provide nearly-contemporaneous transaction reporting to locations away from the exchange floor presented the exchanges with numerous challenges to their established ways of doing business. As the communications revolution continues, the exchanges continue to have to adapt. At the present time it appears that the technology has developed to the point where a physical trading floor is obsolete, and that regulatory techniques based upon the existence of a physical trading floor are no longer relevant. The increased ability of modern communications technology to store and transmit information raises the question of whether these capabilities can be utilized to improve markets.

USING THE LAW TO DETER AND REMEDY FRAUD

Fraud has always been both a tort and a crime, and the securities markets have always been the venue of choice for sophisticated swindlers. Securities routinely involve the payment of large sums of money and the equity product is a simple combination of a piece of paper with hopes and dreams that need not be grounded in reality.

Whether or not the legal system has in fact had an impact on the incidence of securities fraud is a difficult empirical question. Even a casual reading of the Wall Street Journal or the Financial Times confirms that fraud is a flourishing activity today, and my impression from some reading of nineteenth century newspapers is that there has not been much change in either the frequency or the basic strategies of the swindlers. Viewed with the benefit of hindsight, the gullibility of the victims is always surprising.

The first line of defense against fraud is the precautions taken by the potential victims. To the extent that they can be persuaded that the law and the regulation makes fraud less likely, they will let down their guard. Swindlers drape their efforts in the clothing of legitimate transactions to make their swindle credible. Thus it is possible that the effort to use the law to deter fraud has no effect: the reduction in the incidence of fraud resulting from legal sanctions is simply offset by the increased susceptibility of potential victims.

Whether or not the law can in fact reduce the incidence of fraud, the securities industry has always supported anti-fraud efforts. Swindlers have an impact on legitimate firms because their presence increases the wariness of potential customers, and thus the difficulty of selling to them. Legitimate firms welcome help from the government in overcoming the wariness of their potential customers.

In the early twentieth century in the US, beginning with the state blue sky laws, the anti-fraud effort was taken beyond the imposition of criminal penalties and civil liability to include a number of preventive strategies. The strategies include licensing of securities firms and securities personnel and the registration of securities issues before they are offered for sale. In theory, these regimes can separate the good from the bad before the bad have a chance to injure prospective investors. In practice, the bureaucracies created to enforce these laws have shown no ability to systematically identify the trouble makers before they have a chance to do harm. They are handicapped by limited staff and sophistication, the need to rely on objective criteria, and the sheer weight of numbers.

The US federal securities laws of the early 1930's can be viewed as an amalgam of these precedents: Recognition of the exchange as the critical institutional tool, with the addition of formal public oversight and access to governmental powers by the regulatory structure such as the ability to impose penalties on non-members, stronger civil and criminal remedies for fraud, and preventive licensing and registration strategies applied at a national level.

THE NEW AGENDA: PLANNING AN IMPROVED MARKET

As the regulation matured it evolved so that by the 1970's it is possible to identify a whole new regulatory agenda. That agenda, most prominently characterized by the 'big bang', was an agenda of market design, in which the regulator assumed the role of determining the best market structure. The Securities and Exchange Commission (with prodding from the Antitrust Division of the US Department of Justice) would determine how markets ought to be structured. The two principal features of this program in the US were the elimination of fixed commission rates and the adoption of amendments to the Exchange Act in 1975 at the urging of the SEC designed to foster the 'National Market System.'[3]

I believe that the first important initiative in this mold was to make 'insider trading' illegal. The US Securities and Exchange Commission began this initiative in the early 1960's. It shares with the 'big bang' and the 'National Market System' a central idea: the elimination of the right to profit from exclusive positions and from superior information, that the market should be 'fair' and 'level.' By the early 1980's the National Market System initiative was pretty much over, although in its recent Market 2000 study[4] the SEC treated it as an ongoing and still continuing process. The prohibition of insider trading, the elimination of fixed commission rates and the intermarket trading system (ITS) are still very much with us today.

[3] In Securities Acts Amendments of 1975, Pub. L. No. 94-29.

[4] Division of Market Regulation, United States Securities and Exchange Commission, Market 2000: An Examination of Current Equity Market Developments (Washington, D.C.: U.S. Government Printing Office, 1994).

It is not a coincidence, I think, that the high tide of market design initiatives came when it did. In 1964 the SEC gained full jurisdiction over the over the counter equity market, so that its regulatory initiatives could affect both markets equally, removing the threat that issuers and traders would move off the exchanges. At the same time, exchange controls remained important in the world so that movement between securities markets was impeded. This left the SEC free to control US securities markets without fear of competition from other markets. In the early 1980's, with the general disappearance of exchange controls, US markets faced competition from abroad and the new market design initiatives came to an end.

The National Market System was never a well-defined concept.[5] The idea, which still permeates discussions of market reform today, is of a centralized, computerized, order-driven market in which all traders enter orders into the system on the same basis, and information about all the orders in the system are transparent to everyone. The computerized software then simply matches opposite side orders by use of known algorithms and the market transactions result. The 'crowd' has no advantage over everyone else.

The central idea of the 'big bang' was that the special arrangements and incentives necessary to motivate members of a collective organization are anti-competitive and undesirable. Along with the elimination of minimum commissions and similar restraints came a weakening of private exchanges and their ability to motivate their members to support competitive success for the exchange as a whole.

On the surface, the National Market System and 'big bang' were a success. Commissions fell substantially and trading volumes soared. The Intermarket Trading System (ITS) enables the regional exchanges to attract significant volume in NYSE stocks. On the other hand, it is not clear that lower commission costs and higher trading volume are a good thing.[6] For one thing, the total costs of the service are probably now higher—lower per transaction, but there are many more transactions. The issuers always had the power to move their listings to trading arrangements that did involve lower commissions, but there was never any sign that they expressed any demand for such arrangements. The finance literature strongly suggests that it is the rare short-term trader indeed who can make trading decisions that are profitable, which suggests that most short-term trades make no contri-

[5] The best discussion and evaluation is Norman S. Poser, Restructuring the Stock Markets: A Critical Look at the SEC's National Market System, 56 NYU L. Rev. 583 (1981) [hereinafter: Poser]. Poser views the NMS initiative as badly flawed. Its ambiguity is demonstrated, however, by the fact that Jonathan R. Macey & David Haddock, Shirking the SEC: The Failure of the National Market System, 1985 Univ. of Ill. L. Rev. 315, characterize the NMS as a deregulatory initiative, and criticize the SEC for not moving ahead.

[6] For the arguments that there is 'too much' trading in contemporary U.S. markets, see Lynn A Stout, Are Stock Markets Costly Casinos? Disagreement, Market Failure and Securities Regulation, 81 Va L Rev 611 (1995), and Paul G Mahoney, Is there a Cure for 'Excessive' Trading?, 81 Va L Rev 713 (1995).

bution towards moving prices in the right direction. As Norman Poser, among others, pointed out long ago, the competition from the regional exchanges does not seem to generate competition in price discovery.[7] The dealers on the regional exchanges simply mimic the quotes of the NYSE specialist, and then attract order flow by other means. Interestingly enough, it now appears that the dealer competition on the much touted multi market maker structure of the NASDAQ has a similar character.[8]

It is possible to offer a simple political explanation for the regional market trading volume made possible by the ITS. It is that the federal securities regulators and regulation cannot obtain support in the geographically dispersed US Congress unless it offers benefits to persons located outside New York. Before the 'big bang' the regionals attracted volume through give-ups designed to evade the NYSE minimum commission structure. After the 'big bang' they lost this volume, but were given the ITS instead.[9]

But whatever the success or failure of these initiatives, they are very much a feature of US security regulation, and continue to be copied and admired around the world.

CONCLUSION: COMPETITION AND THE OBJECTIVES OF SECURITY REGULATION

Competition between markets has a different effect depending on which of these different types of objectives is at stake. Those regulatory objectives which I have grouped as Exchange objectives are well-served by competition. They all involve a trade-off between improved quality and cost, and the best way to find the trade-off which best meets the needs of the users of securities markets is to offer them a choice of markets, and let them choose. Because fraud has always been conducted on an international scale, and can be more easily carried out internationally today than ever because of lowered transportation and communication costs, fraud enforcement requires international cooperation. However, since there is no clear right and effective mix of sanctions, preventive strategies, and enforcement approaches, there is no case for a uniform approach. It is possible that some countries fall below an acceptable minimum standard, and if so their firms and markets should not be accepted into the international securities trading system.

[7] Poser, supra note 5, at 925.

[8] See William G Christie & Paul H Schultz, Why Do NASDAQ Market Makers Avoid Odd-Eight Quotes?, 49 Journal of Finance 1813 and 1841 (1994).

[9] This feature of U.S. regulation and subsidy programs appears elsewhere. For instance, AMTRAK (the national corporation that provides inter-city passenger rail transportation), in order to obtain its subsidy, provides long distance trains that are particularly uneconomic. If it shrunk its system to the short-haul, high density and more profitable corridors, mostly on the coasts, it would not have enough support to get any subsidy at all.

The market design initiatives, however, are threatened by competition. If, on the one hand, the regulation simply requires what the market would provide anyway it has no point. If, however, it requires something that the markets would not otherwise provide because the users do not value it enough to pay for it, the existence of competition will undermine the initiative. The regulators can successfully dictate the structure of the market only if they succeed in suppressing regulatory competition, and the classic way to suppress competition is to agree with your competitors not to compete.

14

Approaches to Market Regulation

JAMES H. CHEEK, III

INTRODUCTION

The Current Environment for Capital Market Regulation

The 20th century has seen radical changes in global financial markets and these changes are relentless as we approach the 21st century. Rapid technological development, innovative hybrid financial products, new automated trading systems, and concentration of investment power within institutions are late 20th century phenomena that have led to a true globalization of financial markets, with a record level of cross-border investment and trading. Firms providing financial services and products are increasingly operating and offering their services and products in multiple countries with the result that investors are increasingly willing and able to channel their capital across national boundaries and borrowers and securities issuers are increasingly seeking sources of funds across the same national boundaries. The ease of capital flow alone places tensions on historical approaches to capital market regulation and rekindles the debate over regulatory competition giving new life to the concern regarding an international 'race to the bottom' in the market for securities regulation.

It is impossible to overstate the impact of technological progress on the global securities markets. Technology has made possible computerized markets that instantaneously link traders without regard to their physical location or institutional affiliation. Technology also makes possible the use of novel forms of market-clearing mechanisms, such as the large-scale single price auctions conducted by the fully computerized Arizona Stock Exchange. Market entrants continue to find ways to leap-frog existing market structures and regulatory constraints by introducing services and products that take advantage of the latest technological developments. Global securities markets and regulatory forces in those markets must anticipate and respond to technological changes, preserving the positive benefits of market regulation, whether it be domestically or internationally focused.

Closely related to the challenges presented by technological change are the increasing pressures created by developments in the technology of finance. Markets have demanded and financial product gurus have created new financial instruments and trading techniques which challenge old regulatory concepts and fail to fit traditional definitions and regulatory constraints. No single issue has dominated the agendas of capital market regulators in the last several years more than the perceived systemic risk in the global financial markets caused by the creation and trading of financial derivatives. These new financial instruments reduce the costs of bringing borrowers and savers together and increase their opportunities to manage risk but at the same time dramatically accelerate the market ripple effect of financial market changes. Such broad risks to the global capital markets created by financial derivative products and bold new technological developments have led to unparalleled efforts to forge close, cooperative relationships among the regulators of the world's capital markets.[1]

An additional factor forcing global regulators to rethink their regulatory approach is the fact that institutional investors increasingly dominate the global securities markets. In particular, the U.S. system of market regulation which was designed to protect the small, individual investor must adjust to current market realities where in the U.S. individual investors hold less than half of the value of all publicly traded equity securities and account for less than 25% of the market trading volume of equity securities.[2] Institutional investors generally need less regulatory protection and demand liquid but honest markets without costly regulatory impediments to capital raising and trading activities. If regulatory systems do not adjust to the increased institutionalization of global securities markets, such investors are likely to search for congenial markets that are not subject to institutionally troublesome regulatory constraints.

With all of these dynamic developments influencing global securities markets and regulators, it is important to reflect on existing regulatory approaches to the financial markets in order to consider whether there is any single or unified approach which can best meet the challenges of the 21st century global securities markets.

[1] These efforts range from the comprehensive review of the global over-the-counter derivative market published in 1993 by the Group of Thirty, a group of international financial services executives and former senior regulators, to be recent May 1995 Windsor Conference of 16 international regulators sponsored by the U.S.'s CFTC and the U.K.'s SIB which was designed to improve regulatory crisis management of the global derivatives markets in the wake of the collapse of Barings plc. See 'Futures Regulators Agree to Cooperate Globally', *Wall St. J.* (May 18, 1995) and 'Derivatives: Practices and Principles', *Global Derivatives Study Group* (1993).

[2] Latest statistics show that individuals at the end of 1994 owned 48.2% of the U.S. equity markets compared to 51.8% held by institutions. 'Ownership Statistics of U.S. Markets', *Federal Reserve Board* (1995). See generally Brancato & Gaugham, *Institutional Investors and Capital Markets* (1991).

HISTORIC APPROACHES TO MARKET REGULATION

Securities market regulation generally developed when capital markets were largely domestic or national in scope, a circumstance long since past. National regulators today feel the pressure of dealing with cross-border transactions as they have never felt before and there is an increasing plea from those regulators that market regulation should be harmonized internationally to avoid international regulatory arbitrage and to minimize the risk of regulatory failure which could have systemic implications for the global securities markets. The following section of this Chapter will analyze the differences in some of the current regulatory approaches.

The U.S. Regulatory System

The U.S. regulatory system for its securities markets adopted over 60 years ago focuses on creating a regulatory structure which results in fully informed and honest markets.[3] The system working through an internet of seven different statutes[4] results in the regulation of the distribution of securities, a mandatory corporate disclosure system for publicly traded companies, the regulation of securities professionals, the regulation of investment companies, the regulation of trading markets, the regulation of takeovers, acquisitions and shareholder solicitations, and the regulation of insider trading. In addition, the U.S. regulatory system contains enforcement and liability provisions which provide the policing mechanism for the U.S. securities markets.[5] Each state in the U.S. also has a system of securities

[3] The two principal U.S. statutes are the Securities Act of 1933 and the Securities Exchange Act of 1934. The stated purpose of the 1933 Act is 'to provide full and fair disclosure of the character of securities sold . . . and to prevent frauds in the sale thereof . . .' The stated purpose of the 1934 Act is 'to provide regulation of securities exchanges and of over-the-counter markets . . . to prevent inequitable and unfair practices on such exchanges and markets . . .' The U.S. legislative scheme followed the legislative examples set much earlier in England in the Bubble Act of 1720, the Companies Act of 1844 and the Directors' Liability Act of 1890. See generally Loss & Seligman, *Fundamentals of Securities Regulation* (1995).

[4] The seven statutes are the Securities Act of 1933, the Securities Exchange Act of 1934, the Public Utility Holding Company Act of 1935, the Trust Indenture Act of 1939, the Investment Company Act of 1940, the Investment Advisers Act of 1940 and the Securities Investor Protection Act of 1970. In 1980 a ten year project to consolidate these statutes in a new modern single piece of legislation was concluded with the publication of the Federal Securities Code. American Law Institute, *Federal Securities Code* (1980) The Code was never adopted into legislation but many of its concepts have been implemented by regulations adopted by the SEC. More recently in 1995, a new comprehensive legislative effort to revise the U.S. regulatory system was introduced by Congressman Jack Fields. The bill called the 'Capital Markets Deregulation and Liberalization Act of 1995' proposes sweeping changes, including preemption of state securities laws and sheltering brokers from liability for sales to institutional investors, and is unlikely to be adopted.

[5] Legislation has been passed in the U.S. House of Representatives and Senate which significantly limits securities class actions. See *Private Securities Litigation Reform Act*, S.240 (passed June 28, 1995); *Securities Litigation Reform Act*, H.R. 1058 (March 8, 1995).

regulation which shares similar goals and uses similar regulatory techniques as U.S. federal legislation but has less of an impact due to budgetary and federal preemptive constraints.

The Securities and Exchange Commission has the principal job of implementing and enforcing the U.S. regulatory scheme. It is fair to say that while the regulatory scheme has been viewed as strict and formalistic, in recent times the Commission has taken a flexible approach to regulation in an effort to deal with evolving market issues. The Commission however has its own domestic coordination challenges as there are other federal agencies which have regulatory jurisdiction over certain aspects of the securities markets, including the Federal Reserve Board, the Department of Treasury, the Department of Labor, the Commodities Future Trading Commission, the Office of the Comptroller of the Currency, the Federal Deposit Insurance Corporation, the Securities Investor Protection Corporation, and the Pension Benefit Guaranty Corporation. Such regulatory fragmentation has led to some overlapping and inconsistent regulation and to proposals that federal financial regulation be consolidated in a single cabinet-level department within the executive branch of the government so that regulatory policies can be coordinated along functional lines across financial products, services and markets.[6] While attracting some support, it is unlikely that a single regulatory body will be created and the U.S. regulatory system will continue to have its own need for coordination among regulatory policy makers or domestic regulatory competition may erode the ability of the U.S. system to effectively interact globally.[7]

In reaction to this need for coordinated U.S. regulatory policy in face of international competitive pressures, the CFTC and the SEC in particular have made significant efforts in recent months to coordinate and provide flexible regulation to address the needs of the global securities markets. As described in a later portion of this Chapter, adjustments have been made to historic U.S. regulatory requirements to facilitate cross-border securities transactions and the CFTC has played a major role in forging a coordinated global regulatory policy regarding derivatives. In addition, the Working Group on Financial Markets, consisting of the Chairman of the Federal Reserve Board, the Secretary of Treasury, and the Chairs of the Securities and Exchange Commission and the CFTC, have provided an institutional structure in the U.S. for financial market regulatory cooperation. Thus, even though legislative uniformity is lacking in the U.S. and there exist some nat-

[6] The principal proponent of such a consolidation of financial regulation has been the Chicago Mercantile Exchange. See 'Model for Federal Financial Regulation', *Chicago Mercantile Exchange (1993)*.

[7] There continues to be a legislative proposal to merge the CFTC and the SEC but it is unlikely to be adopted. See H.R. 718, *The Markets and Trading Reorganization and Reform Act* (1995). See generally Coffee, 'Competition versus Consolidation: The Significance of Organizational Structure in Financial and Securities Regulation', 50 *Bus. Law*. 447 (1995).

ural instincts of regulatory competition, international competitive pressures work toward the building of a consistent and coordinated U.S. regulatory policy as applied to matters important to the global securities markets.

The U.K. Self-Regulatory System

The United Kingdom has long had a system of securities regulation with a minimal statutory base and with the Stock Exchange being the most influential source of regulation. Within the last ten years changes in this regulatory system have pushed it closer to the U.S. model with the enactment of the Financial Services Act 1986, as amended most recently by the Public Offers of Securities Regulation 1995, and the creation of the Securities and Investments Board which authorizes the self-regulatory organizations that make and enforce rules with respect to their members' activities in the financial services industry. Significant differences in regulatory approach however continue to exist between the U.S. and the U.K. systems.[8] The United Kingdom relies more heavily on self-regulation under a fragmented system of self-regulatory organizations that make and enforce rules with respect to their members' activities. Nevertheless, the goal of seeking a well informed and honest market place does result in a prospectus being prepared and filed and in restrictions on insider trading. Generally speaking over the years, regulatory changes have been designed to produce more detailed information and provide for broader dissemination of information tending toward the U.S. model. The U.K. system also has a number of provisions which streamline the offering process for seasoned issuers and secondary trades, an increasing trend in the U.S. system. Consistent with U.S. regulatory philosophy, the U.K. requires companies to file periodic information and to disclose material developments in order to keep the market place fully informed. As the regulatory approaches have moved closer together in certain basic areas, the U.K. and U.S. regulators have forged a number of joint initiatives between themselves as well as other national regulators in such countries as Switzerland, France and Japan. These initiatives originally framed as memoranda of understandings started as information sharing and enforcement cooperation agreements but in more recent times have attacked more specific market issues such as derivatives trading[9] and investment adviser regulation.[10] Thus while national regulatory differences clearly

[8] See Large, *Financial Services Regulation—Making the Two-Tier System Work* (1993).

[9] The Windsor Declaration issued in May 1995 was the product of cooperative effort by the CFTC and SIB to coordinate regulatory policy of global futures regulators in the wake of the Barings plc collapse.

[10] In May 1995, the SEC and the U.K. Investment Management Regulatory Organization issued a Joint Declaration on Cooperation and Supervision of Cross-Border Investment Management Activity. This declaration was made within the framework of the 1991 MOU among the SEC, the CFTC, SIB, and the U.K. Department of Trade and Industry. See

remain, global securities market issues have demanded and resulted in a higher level of bilateral U.S.–U.K. regulatory cooperation and joint global leadership being provided by the U.S. and the U.K. regulators.

Other Selected Market Regulatory Approaches

Such diverse countries as Japan, Russia and China have in recent times moved away from an informal, consultive style of securities regulation and have moved toward a more formal statutorily based system of regulation. In June 1991, Japan suffered from the disclosure that several securities firms had reimbursed their institutional clients for losses in the securities markets. This scandal exposed a weak regulatory system which was characterized by informality, private input and negotiation. As a result of the scandal, in 1992 the Securities and Exchange Surveillance Commission was formed with responsibility for supervising the securities markets to ensure fair markets. Nevertheless this 'SEC' continues to be subject to the Ministry of Finance and has limited enforcement powers, and thus its effectiveness is still an open question.[11]

As Russia attempts to become a capitalistic society, mechanisms have been borrowed from the West to build a regulatory market structure. The Russian Federation Commission on Securities and Exchanges has been given new powers and the Statute on Joint Stock Societies and regulations issued by the Ministry of Finance thereunder have established a primary offering mechanism based on disclosure concepts. The system is very rudimentary but does indicate a tendency toward accepting Western regulatory structures in developing and stabilizing a securities market system.[12]

Similarly in China, a uniform system of securities regulation has been emerging in recent times. Scandals in the financial markets have led to the establishment of the State Council Securities Commission and the China Securities Regulatory Commission and in 1993 the SCSC promulgated regulations on issuing and trading shares which now govern all securities issued in China. Again while the system is relatively embryonic, its general regulatory approach relies upon Western principles of fairness and full disclosure[13] and includes insider trading sanctions[14] as well as continuous disclosure requirements.

generally Greene, 'International Securities Law Enforcement: Recent Advances on Assistance and Cooperation.' 27 *Vand. J. of Transnational Law* 635 (1995).

[11] See Milhaupt, 'Managing the Market: The Ministry of Finance and Securities Regulation in Japan', 30 *Stan. J. of Int'l. Law* 423 (1995).

[12] See Brown, 'Order from Disorder: The Development of the Russian Securities Markets', 4 *Univ. of Penn. J. of Int'l. Bus. Law* 509 (1995).

[13] See Tarbutton, 'China—A National Regulatory Framework for the PRC's Stock Market Begins to Emerge', 2 *Ga. J. of Int'l. and Comp. Law* 411 (1995).

[14] There is clearly an evolving consensus among global market regulators that insider trading should be regulated notwithstanding the fact that business customs in many countries

Another evidence of the shift of decentralized regulatory approaches in non-U.S. markets was the adoption in 1995 by Switzerland of a new comprehensive securities law. The Federal Stock Exchange Law adopted in March 1995 and scheduled to take effect April 1, 1996 is the first law to regulate the Swiss securities markets and coincides with a nationwide electronic exchange taking the place of regional exchanges formerly regulated by authorities in Swiss cantons. The legislation covers all aspects of securities trading but primarily focuses on rules relating to disclosure, trading activities and takeovers. The new legislation principally aims to boost the liquidity and transparency of the Swiss securities markets which will be regulated by an internal self-regulatory body set up by the Swiss Stock Exchange and under the ultimate regulatory responsibility of the Swiss Banking Commission. This example again shows movement toward principles embodied in the U.S. regulatory system but with extreme reluctance to place an independent regulatory authority such as the Securities and Exchange Commission firmly in control of market regulation.[15]

The foregoing developments are set forth in a brief general way as examples of the changes being created in national regulatory approaches which were developed for domestic markets which are being forced to compete globally for investment activity. The international markets themselves as opposed to specific national policies are requiring that markets have a more coordinated, a more formal, statutorily based model, market regulatory system. These examples of recent changes indicate however that even as competitive developments push for changes regulatory systems will continue to be influenced by governmental and political domestic considerations and traditions and it is unlikely that a single, truly harmonious international regulatory approach will emerge from these developments.

International Coordinating Organizations

There are a number of organizations which seek to achieve harmonious international securities regulation. Among these organizations are the European Commission, the International Organization of Securities Commissions (IOSCO), the International Federation of Stock Exchanges, the Group of 30, and the International Councils of Securities Dealers and Self-Regulatory Organizations. In addition, international economic organizations such as the Organization for Economic Cooperation and Development

consider profits from insider trading to be an insider prerequisite. Global recognition of the need for insider trading sanctions arises not from an acceptance of immorality of such trading but from a practical recognition that institutional investors insist on fair markets. Even Germany has made insider trading a criminal offence and recently achieved its first conviction involving sales by the controlling Krones A.G. family in advance of poor financial performance disclosure. See 'Germany Has First Insider Conviction', *N.Y. Times* (Aug. 19, 1995).

[15] See Studer, 'New Swiss Law May Improve Investing Climate, Despite Concerns About Fairness and Oversight', *Wall St. J.* (April 17, 1995).

and the United Nations Commission of Transnational Corporations have from time to time sought to provide international direction relating to global securities market matters.

Even though the European Union (EU) has adopted a number of disclosure directives[16] borrowing from the U.S. and the U.K. regulatory systems, IOSCO has become the most important of these organizations attempting to harmonize international securities regulation. IOSCO however suffers from the lack of binding authority over its members who frequently experience difficulty in reaching consensus. Yet it remains the principal forum currently available to discuss and consider coordination of international regulatory standards and currently has an agenda which focuses on harmonization of disclosure and accounting requirements applicable in cross-border offerings as well as a major project on capital adequacy concerns. In recent months IOSCO has worked closely with the Basle Commission on Banking Supervision to develop a common minimum framework for assessing the risk of derivatives activity of banks and securities firms. The report, prepared before the Barings collapse, has been a positive development in providing a framework for coordinated regulation and was in May 1995 endorsed by the SEC and the CFTC.

Disclosure standards as a result of IOSCO and EU efforts are coming closer together around the world and thereby improving the quality of information in the world securities markets. Even in the disclosure area, however, there remain considerable differences, particularly as to applicable accounting principles and auditing standards. Efforts have been made over the years to harmonize accounting standards and auditing procedures. In addition to IOSCO, global coordination in this area is sought by the International Accounting Standards Committee which represents close to 100 professional accounting bodies in almost 50 countries. Because the IASC has no official status, its standards are essentially recommendations and it as a whole has made little progress in achieving international harmonization.[17] But more progress has been made in recent times and international momentum is building. In a recent development, the SEC has

[16] The directives are intended to develop a supranational securities law from Europe's common market, and include the Listing Particulars Directive, the Interim Reports Directive, the Prospectus Directive, the Major Shareholders Directive, and the Insider Trading Directive. Instead of mandatory strict regulatory constraints, the directives seek to establish common minimum standards. See Warren, 'Global Harmonization of Securities Laws: The Achievements of the European Communities', 31 *Harv. Int'l. L.J.* 185 (1990).

[17] An example of a typical project using IASC standards was a recent joint research study report issued by the FASB, the Canadian Institute of Public Accountants and the Mexican Institute of Public Accountants. The report highlights the differences in each country's standards and reviews the statements and standards issued by the IASC. In addition, in 1995 the IASC decided on formats for reporting financial information for product-based business segments and geographic segments. In doing so, the IASC moved closer to U.S. GAAP standards in this area.

moved away from its absolute insistence that pure U.S. accounting standards be followed in order for foreign issuers to offer and list securities in the United States.[18] Current trends are suggestive that eventually home country accounting standards as modified by certain IASC standards may be used in place of the United States GAAP in qualified cross-border securities offerings, but any enunciated international accounting principles are likely to continue to be sufficiently general in nature to permit accommodation for domestic cultural and economic differences.

Considerable progress through these international organizations and the leadership efforts of U.S. and U.K. regulators has been made on the surface toward common regulatory approaches.[19] There is in place in the EU countries, the United States, Japan, Australia and Canada, a disclosure scheme relating to the listing of securities and in many cases disclosures in the offering of securities is supplemented by a scheme of continuous disclosure. Insider trading is generally unlawful and several countries regulate takeovers. Investment companies are universally regulated and broker-dealers are regulated in most countries. Yet more consistent and systemic efforts to produce coordinated policy is needed for 21st century securities markets. In that light it is encouraging to see the structured and formalistic regulatory approach of the U.S. being modified to reduce some of its strict constraints which have impeded historic efforts at building a coordinated international regulatory approach to meet the systemic challenges existing in tomorrow's global securities markets.

GOALS OF A REGULATORY SYSTEM

It is a maxim that efficient operation of the capital markets is critical to a national economy. Without investor confidence, an economy cannot raise

[18] Chairman Levitt has testified that the SEC is committed to developing international accounting and disclosure standards acceptable in all jurisdictions and is working with IOSCO and IASC to develop mutually acceptable standards for companies engaged in cross-border offerings and listings. Levitt, *Testimony Concerning International Markets and Individual Investors before the Committee on Banking, Housing and Urban Affairs*, U.S. Senate (Sept. 28, 1994). As an example of this commitment, the SEC has allowed foreign issuers to use the international cash flow standard sanctioned by IOSCO and the IASC without a reconciliation to U.S. GAAP. See Sec. Act Rel. No. 33-7053 (April 1994). More recently the SEC has accepted the IASC Standard No. 22 relating to business combinations, abandoning the requirement for foreign issuers to reconcile differences attributable to the method of accounting for a business acquisition and amortization period of related goodwill. See Sec. Act Rel. No. 33-7120 (Dec. 1994).

[19] Even U.S. corporate governance standards are making their way into U.K. and European corporate regulatory environments, principally through the efforts of the Cadbury Committee (the Committee on the Financial Aspects of Corporate Governance) in establishing the Model Code of Best Practices. See 'Corporate Governance is Bringing Change to the Boardroom of Europe', *Wall St. J.* (July 12, 1995).

capital, sustain economic growth or give individuals a means to provide for their long term financial needs. Investors demand liquid, transparent, and well informed markets. They demand markets with low transaction costs and high integrity. It is these very goals that a regulatory system applicable to transnational securities offerings and markets must seek and it is also these very demands which are at work to force closer harmonization of different regulatory approaches. The challenge is to apply these goals to dramatic new market structures and products.

While debates continue to rage in the United States regarding whether one agency should regulate the financial markets in the United States,[20] the greater and more significant debate continues to be whether the global securities markets are best benefited by a harmonization scheme or by a competitive scheme of national securities regulation. It is a fact that the former plenary power of national regulatory structures with responsibility for local markets or trading exchanges is threatened by the widening of international markets. Participants in global securities markets can easily evade national regulatory structures if they are burdensome by transacting business in an out-of-jurisdiction market or exchange with less burdensome constraints. Previously separate and autonomous national regulatory systems are increasingly conscious of each other and the potential for snaring transactional volume by reducing their regulatory burden. The resulting pressures have created movement toward commonality of regulatory systems without sacrificing wholly their national structures and the last part of this paper demonstrates the movement by the SEC in recent months away from its strict application of domestic U.S. standards to global securities market issues.

Without question there are segments of securities regulation which are more in need of and adaptable to harmonious regulation than others. Those that go to the heart of global regulatory needs to provide liquid, efficient, well informed and fair markets are the ones most apt for coordinated regulation. Any resulting harmonization arrangements are likely to have multiple unspecified details that will leave plenty of room for competitive manoeuvring. For example, the Basle Committee of Banking Supervision, after consultation with IOSCO, issued an Accord on minimal capital standards for commercial banks which only specifies broad categories of risk standards but leaves many definitions and details unspecified and most importantly is silent on the details of the accounting system that should be the basis of the calculation of capital levels.[21] This flexibility gives national

[20] See note 6 *supra*.

[21] This Accord was never fully accepted by IOSCO's Technical Committee even though it recommended that the international community agree upon internationally acceptable minimum capital standards. See 'Disagreement Plagues Committee Discussions on Harmonized International Capital Standards', *Int'l. Sec. Reg. Rep.* (July 17, 1992); GAO, *Securities Markets: Challenges to harmonizing International Capital Standards Remain* (1992). Some

regulatory regimes wide room for competitive manipulation and over time the erosion of harmonization policies such as the Accord could be substantial. Strong economic, political and moral commitments by the international regulatory community will be necessary to make any harmonization arrangements work.

THE NEED FOR REGULATORY FLEXIBILITY

The reality of the political and economic domestic instincts coupled with the demands of fluid, transnational securities markets heightens the need for global regulators to adopt flexible regulatory policies. The U.S. system historically has been the most strict and formalistic but as the balance of this Chapter demonstrates sea changes are underway in the U.S. system and global regulators should take note and move their own systems closer to a harmonized international regulatory model. Even though the U.S. regulatory system is based on statutes drafted over 60 years ago, and periodic efforts are made at total legislative reform, the current legislative scheme is likely to remain in place and it is only through the skills of the SEC to flexibly use administrative rulemaking and interpretive powers that the statutory scheme can accommodate the needs of the 21st century capital markets. The SEC recently has made a number of significant deregulatory steps, including some which reduce the constraints on foreign issuers raising capital in the United States and listing their securities on U.S. trading markets as well as the constraints restricting U.S. investors from purchasing shares of foreign companies. Yet even more can be and should be done.[22]

Over the last two years, the SEC has adopted a number of deregulatory initiatives designed to modify impediments to cross-border transactions. For example, the SEC has expanded access to short-form registration statements for foreign private issuers,[23] extended unallocated shelf registration statements for foreign issuers,[24] expanded the utilization of multijurisdictional disclosure statements accepting home country disclosure systems,[25] made accommodations for modifying certain U.S. GAAP financial reporting requirements,[26] and granted exemptions from Rule 10b-6 for certain distributions by foreign issuers.[27]

progress however has been made recently. See 'IOSCO Endorses Value-At-Risk Models for Figuring Capital Adequacy', 27 *Sec. Reg. L. Rpt.* 1222 (July 21, 1995).

[22] For specific further suggestions for modification, see Greene, 'Hegemony or Deference: U.S. Disclosure Requirements in the International Capital Markets', 50 *Bus. Law.* 413 (1995).

[23] See Sec. Act. Rel. No. 33-7053 (Apr. 19, 1994).

[24] Id.

[25] See Sec. Act Rel. No. 33-7004 (June 28, 1993). See generally Quigley, 'The Multijurisdictional Disclosure System', 28 *Sec. & Com. Reg.* 117 (June 28, 1995).

[26] See Sec. Act Rel. No. 33-7056 (Apr. 19, 1994). See also Sec. Act Rel. No. 33-7054 (Apr. 19, 1994); Sec. Act Rel. No. 7055 (Apr. 19, 1994); Sec. Act. Rel. No. 7053 (Apr. 19, 1994).

[27] See Sec. Act Rel. No. 33-7021 (Oxt. 6, 1993); Sec. Act Rel. No. 7028 (Nov. 3, 1993).

One major example of U.S. regulatory flexibility created by adept rule-making is found in Rule 144A. Rule 144A has no territorial limitations and permits secondary trading of securities among qualified institutional buyers wherever situated.[28] In essence, it provides a liquid and fluid trading market among institutional investors free of the regulatory constraints of the U.S. securities laws. Furthermore Regulation S adopted under the U.S. statutory scheme permits U.S. investors to increase their investments in foreign securities.[29] Regulation S removes the threat of extraterritorial reach of the 1933 Act registration provision for most offshore securities distributions, permitting U.S. investors to purchase them provided that the transaction takes place offshore and there are no directed selling efforts in the United States. Regulation S, however, does not specifically deal with when and where and under what circumstances a foreign purchaser which acquires a security pursuant to Regulation S can, after the end of the applicable restricted period (currently 40 days), sell the security to a U.S. person or within the U.S securities markets.[30] It is interesting to note that prospectuses prepared for Rule 144A transactions generally conform to U.S. disclosure requirements with the notable exception of the accounting presentations which generally present financial statements prepared on home country accounting principles with some general discussion of material differences between U.S. GAAP and the accounting principles but rarely a reconciliation. Neither the investors nor the pricing of the issues related to the offering are affected by this presentation. The Rule 144A practice is thus an excellent example of U.S. regulatory flexibility and market conditions combining to move formerly stringent domestic disclosure standards created for individual investors into the 21st century of the global securities markets.

On the domestic front, the SEC has moved recently to ease burdens on capital raising,[31] and to simplify disclosures including the use of abbreviated financial information in annual reports, prospectuses and proxy state-

[28] See Sec. Act Rel. No. 33-6862 (Apr. 23, 1990). See generally Steinberg, 'Regulation S and Rule 144A: Creating a Workable Fiction in an Expanding Global Securities Market', 29 *Int'l. Lawyer* 43 (1995); Rovinescu and Thieffry, supra, pp. 51–7.

[29] See Sec. Act Rel. No. 33-6863 (Apr. 24, 1990).

[30] Recently the SEC issued an interpretive release regarding certain 'problematic practices' which have developed under Regulation S to avoid U.S. registration by parking securities offshore with little or no economic risk and with a clear intent to return the securities to the U.S. market. In addition to its interpretive comments, the SEC asked for comments whether Regulation S needed to be amended to deal with suspected abuse, but the usefulness of the flexibility currently provided by Regulation S will likely rule the day. See Sec. Act Rel. No. 33-7190 (June 27, 1995).

[31] See Sec. Act Rel. No. 33-7187 (June 27, 1995) (shortening the Rule 144 holding period for restricted securities to one year); Sec. Act Rel. No. 33-7188 (June 27, 1995) (permitting broad solicitation of offers before the filing of a prospectus); Sec. Act Rel. No. 33-7185 (June 27, 1995) (providing new exemptions for limited offerings).

ments.[32] In addition, an SEC Advisory Committee on the Capital Formation and Regulatory Processes chaired by Commissioner Wallman is hard at work to totally replace the current 1933 Act's system of registering securities with a system of registering companies, thereby removing in U.S. domestic markets many of the old regulatory constraints on domestic capital raising and secondary trading.

On the foreign front, in December 1994 the SEC adopted rules to simplify certain registration reporting requirements for foreign companies.[33] In particular, one initiative gives foreign companies greater flexibility in choosing the currency to be used in the presentation of their financial statements. In addition, the new rule eliminates duplicative record keeping for foreign registrants with operations in a country with a 'hyperinflationary' economy. Another rule change streamlines reconciliation requirements for foreign companies accounting for business combinations and significantly reduces their record keeping burden.

These changes in the last two years by the SEC reflect the flexibility and willingness which the Commission has to approach global capital market issues. This flexibility provides the opportunity to bridge different regulatory approaches to global securities markets through increased multilateral and bilateral discussions. No one nation can claim the global securities markets and it is clear that the domestic markets of any one nation are inextricably linked to the global securities markets. The dynamics of multilateral and bilateral discussions coupled with flexible domestic regulation are not likely to result in a single harmonious international regulatory system or a single global securities commission but in multiple regulatory systems which co-exist with a more common set of regulatory principles. Only through such a coordinated and consistent international regulatory network can global securities markets of the 21st century continue to develop and thrive with minimal systemic risks.

[32] See Sec. Act Rel. No. 33-7183 (June 27, 1995) (allowing abbreviated financial statements); Sec. Act Rel No. 33-7189 (June 27, 1995) (simplifying acquisition financial statement requirements).

[33] See Sec. Act Rel. No. 33-7117 (Dec. 13, 1994); Sec. Act Rel. No. 33-7118 (Dec. 13, 1994); Sec. Act Rel. No. 33-7119 (Dec. 13, 1994); Sec. Act Rel. No. 33-7120 (Dec. 13, 1994).

15

Tackling Systemic Risk on Markets: Barings and Beyond

ANDREW M. WHITTAKER

INTRODUCTION AND BACKGROUND

Introduction

In these comments, I plan to focus on one particular area of regulatory endeavour—protection against systemic risk affecting markets—and how it is being addressed as part of the follow-up to the Barings case. This will help us to consider how far what is being done internationally in that context can be described under the headings 'co-operation' and 'convergence', and how far it could be said to indicate something more, which might be described, perhaps rather grandly, as the beginnings of the emergence of a world regulatory order.

Business Background

First, it will be helpful to look at the business background. The global financial markets are changing very rapidly. Key trends from the viewpoint of market regulation are:

- increasing internationalisation of investor involvement (especially US and German pension funds);
- increasing interchangeability of products, so trading strategies can be achieved through derivatives as well as equities;
- increasing complexity of investment products and trading, particularly cross-border;
- concentration of trading among a small group of multinational firms;
- development of risk management techniques and the trading of risk;
- a greater reliance on technology to trade and to manage risk;
- entrepreneurialism and risk-taking in uncertain environments;
- increasing use of screen-based trading systems to extend marketplaces beyond a single jurisdiction;

- increasing interconnectedness of marketplaces (e.g. through linkages and trading of competing products);
- increased pressure on established markets to respond competitively to these developments; and
- the significance of emerging markets.

All these trends are features of, and could be summed up in the word, 'globalisation'.

Regulatory Background

Against this globalisation of business, the regulatory structure can be starkly contrasted.

First, regulation is organised sectorally, with separate regulatory structures for banking business, securities business and insurance business. This is not the case in all countries, but it is the case in a very significant number worldwide. Further, various international organisations of regulators, Basle for the banking regulators, IOSCO, the International Organisation of Securities Commissions, for the securities regulators, and the International Association of Insurance Supervisors, for the insurance regulators, are similarly divided. Although there has been constructive international work between Basle and IOSCO, and among insurance supervisors, with increasing contact among them now formalised in a 'Tripartite Group', this is still at very early stages.

Secondly, regulation is mainly national, while business is international. In this respect, regulation follows the pattern set by legal systems generally. As with the territorial limitations of legal systems, those of regulatory systems both cause impediments to international business and impede the effectiveness of regulatory action in a case involving more than one jurisdiction.

It should be noted, of course, that the European Community is an exception. Its single market directives on banking, insurance and, particularly, investment services could be said to create a regional regulatory structure, with a part-harmonised legal and regulatory infrastructure, but raising its own issues.

Finally, regulation is multi-tiered, with both operators of exchanges and their supervisors having significant roles. The exchange authorities also, of course, combine their regulatory responsibilities with competitive commercial activities.

SYSTEMIC RISK AND MARKET REGULATION

Objectives of Market Regulation

Before looking at specific concerns about systemic risk affecting markets, I want to make a few points about the objectives of market regulation. There are in my view three possible objects for market regulation:

- first, protection of investors against abuse (for example, by front running their orders);
- second, promotion of market integrity, in the sense of the reliability of the price formation process and the market's freedom from manipulation; and
- third, protection against systemic risk.

Protection of investors is the traditional concern of securities regulators, along with the promotion of market integrity (in which the competition authorities also play their part). Protection against systemic risk has largely been the concern of banking regulators, and their work has concentrated on the prudential regulation of market participants. The interests of securities and indeed banking regulators in the systemic risk issues affecting what may be termed 'trading infrastructures'—market and clearing and settlement systems—is fairly new but of growing significance. It is not market participant regulation, or regulation of conduct, but 'infrastructure regulation', designed to provide a secure platform and systems on which industry can operate.

Systemic Risk Affecting Markets

Let us now move on to consider what systemic risk issues are presented by the infrastructure—what is meant by 'systemic risk affecting markets'.

By 'systemic risk affecting markets', I mean risks related to markets (including their related clearing and settlement arrangements) which have systemic implications. These risks could be categorised as:

- *contagion risk*, that a default by one market participant or user will lead to defaults by others;
- *user confidence risk*, that there is a sudden and significant loss of confidence in the market by its users;.
- *systems risk*, that a market's own dealing settlement or clearing systems will break down;
- *operational risk*, that a market's operational effectiveness is impeded, for example, by the process of sorting out a default and resuming business as usual;

- *clearing guarantee risk*, that the resources available to back a clearing house guarantee prove to be inadequate;
- *settlement process risk*, that longer settlement periods will increase the scale of losses incurred in a default;
- *market risk*, that market prices will change dramatically or be highly volatile, possibly also affecting prices on other markets; and
- *legal risk*, that the legal infrastructure fails to support the market's operations.

But in addition to the risks presented by markets, markets are key in the fight *against* systemic risk because:

- their multilateral nature increases the potential scale of domino effects;
- their infrastructure role allows independent day to day commercially driven monitoring of exposures;
- their officially recognised status (where applicable), allows effective action to be taken to limit domino effects;
- clearing house guarantees provide user confidence but concentrate risk and necessitate effective risk management by the clearing house;
- a loss of confidence in one market, or other systemic problems there, can spread directly to other markets, even without the default of a member or user.

So let us look at the techniques which can be used to tackle these issues which globalisation means we need to address internationally, as well as within our own jurisdictions.

CO-OPERATION AND CONVERGENCE

In the regulatory world, progress internationally has largely been based on the two themes: co-operation and convergence, though with some significant role too for mutual recognition. Let us consider how these two regulatory techniques can deal with the issues presented by globalisation of the financial markets.

Progress in Co-operation and Convergence

Co-operation means working together to achieve a common goal or helping another to achieve his own goal. In the regulatory world, co-operation is better developed domestically across sectors and internationally within a given sector. International co-operation across sectoral boundaries is less well developed, though there are positive signs, as noted above.

In practice, for example, co-operation between securities regulators generally works well because:

- they share similar goals, experiences and attitudes;
- a regulator giving co-operation today may gain directly from doing so, in resolving an issue which also affects him, or may need co-operation himself tomorrow;
- there are, increasingly, good personal contacts among regulators world-wide, largely through the work of the International Organisation of Securities Commissions. All IOSCO members commit themselves to mutual co-operation, and uncooperative regulators put their membership at risk.

Convergence, in contrast, means the process of applying increasingly similar rules to a given situation in different jurisdictions, and is closely related to harmonisation or approximation of laws, which may, however, allow for harmonisation of minimum standards only, with considerable differences in the actual requirements applying.

Convergence may be attempted:

- as a precondition for market access;
- in the interests of efficiency of operations or supervision; or
- to create a level playing field.

Its most developed forms can be seen in the single market harmonisation scheme in the EU and in the capital adequacy agreements of Basle.

Limitations of Co-operation and Convergence

Regulatory co-operation has its limitations:

- it is generally case-related and post-hoc, arising in an investigation, enforcement, or firefighting context; and
- it needs to take place against a background of legal powers and privileges which allow co-operation to take place and effective action to result from it.

Convergence too has its limitations:

- it is often hard to achieve, particularly where a wide range of issues arise (e.g., the European experience in contrast to Basle);
- it risks treating unlike things alike in the interests of a level playing field (e.g., as some would say, treating trading risks in the same way in a bank as in a securities house, even though the nature of their relationship to their capital providers is very different);
- it may result in a regime that is more suited to developed markets than to emerging or vice versa; and
- it may be over-rigid and dirigiste, impeding innovation (for example, in the use of proprietary risk assessment models as part of the assessment of capital adequacy).

Even taken together, co-operation among national regulators and convergence of national requirements may fail to deal adequately with the globalisation of risk and the interconnectedness of markets, for four reasons.

First, they fail to address *regulatory jurisdiction*. This is emerging as a problem in the process of implementing the Investment Services Directive: if an investor in country A requests a firm in country B to effect a transaction on an exchange in country C, which country's rules apply? At present, there is no single answer, and no common view as how to find an answer.

Second, they do not provide the *international structure and systems* needed to deal with issues on a continuing basis.

Third, they allow *gaps* between regulatory regimes: client money may be protected in each of two regulatory regimes, but at risk as it passes between them.

Fourth, they do not fully recognise the need, arising from the interconnectedness and mutual dependence of markets, to tackle issues from the *perspective* of their potential impact on global, as distinct from national, systemic safety.

So even in theory, I believe that effective regulation requires something rather different from mere co-operation and attempts at convergence.

IMPACT OF THE BARINGS CASE

Issues Raised

Now let us move from theory to fact. The collapse of Barings in February 1995 raised a range of issues relating to systemic risk on markets. In particular, relating to:

- the ability for large positions to be built up on a single market in the belief that the trading concerned involves riskless arbitrage between two markets trading the same contract, or each is fully hedged by positions on the other market;
- the operation of exchange default procedures and their consistency with national law: for example, whether margin moneys held in Japan for Barings could be transferred with client positions they had been supplied to secure;
- the impact on the market price of the contracts concerned (and on the market generally) of knowledge of the need for a forced close-out of Barings positions; and
- the need for effective crisis-management arrangements to be put in place internationally, however basic these might inevitably need to be.

The nature of the risks Barings has revealed is in my view leading to a significant refocusing of regulatory effort, with a concentration on areas of potential systemic risk, rather than customer protection or market integrity, whether relating to markets themselves or to the supervision of market participants. By demonstrating the seriousness of the issues at stake, Barings has galvanised government, regulatory, market and industry action. Just as, in the past, significant national events, from the South Sea Bubble onwards, have led to national regulatory responses, so the Barings case is leading to an international regulatory response. It has presented the world's securities regulators with a global problem, which needs to be tackled on a multinational, multi-tier and sometimes cross-sectoral basis. And it needs to be tackled by more than the conventional techniques of co-operation and convergence. Systemic problems need systemic solutions.

The Developing Reponse to Barings

The starting point of the post-Barings regulatory response was a speech given by Mary Schapiro, Chairman of the Commodity Futures Trading Commission, at the Annual Futures Industry Association Conference in Boca Raton in March 1995. In it, she announced:

> 'I am pleased to tell you this morning that the CFTC and the Securities and Investments Board of the United Kingdom are proposing to convene a meeting of the futures market regulators from the world's major markets. This group will develop an agenda of market and customer protection initiatives, building upon existing international relationships, in order to:
>
> - enhance communication among international regulators and market authorities during a financial crisis;
> - identify legal and practical impediments to containing the spillover effects of financial disruptions at specific firms or in specific markets;
> - foster protection of customer funds wherever located—at the intermediary, the custodian, and the market;
> - promote national bankruptcy laws that forestall liquidity crises by not freezing the margins and positions of solvent customers within insolvent firms; and
> - improve mechanisms for detecting and addressing concentrations of positions held in multiple markets that threaten the financial integrity of the markets.
>
> It is my hope that this group can suggest both unilateral and multilateral actions that regulators can undertake toward achieving each of these ends. We hope that IOSCO, representing more than seventy nations, will provide a forum for communication and implementation of these actions. The Barings failure gives us a unique opportunity to ensure that our house is in order and to work with our colleagues around the world to achieve the best possible regulatory standards for our markets.'

Following this initiative, representatives of regulatory bodies from 16 countries responsible for supervising the activities of the world's major futures and options markets met on 16 and 17 May 1995 at Windsor. The 'Windsor Declaration' which resulted from this meeting indicates that the authorities present, building on previous work on international regulatory co-operation, agreed that they would support mechanisms:

- to improve prompt communication of information relevant to material exposures and other regulatory concerns;
- to review the adequacy of existing arrangements to minimise the risk of loss through insolvency or misappropriation and enhance them as appropriate;
- to promote appropriate national provisions and market procedures that facilitate the prompt liquidation and/or transfer of positions, funds and assets, from failing members of futures exchanges; and
- to support measures to enhance emergency procedures and co-operation among market authorities and regulators.

In reaching these areas of general agreement, those present also acknowledged that specific work was needed in a range of different areas. The Windsor Declaration was indeed an 'agenda' for action.

In parallel with this work by securities commissions, industry representatives were equally aware of the need for action. As a result, the Futures Industry Association, which represents the US futures industry, set up a 'Global Task Force', with representatives from exchanges and market participants around the world, which published in June 1995 a set of Financial Integrity Recommendations for futures and options markets and market participants. These 60 recommendations show the same set of concerns as those in the Windsor Declaration, and also include recommendations for customers about the way in which they use futures and options in their businesses. It is therefore unsurprising that the IOSCO Technical Committee, in considering follow-up work to the Windsor declaration, agreed that it should move forward in contact with the relevant industry organisations.

Finally, Finance Ministers from the Group of Ten industrialised nations, meeting at Halifax in mid-June 1995, agreed:

'Closer international co-operation in the regulation and supervision of financial institutions and markets is essential to safeguard the financial system and prevent an erosion of prudential standards. We urge:

- a deepening of co-operation among regulators and supervisory agencies to ensure an effective and integrated approach, on a global basis, to developing and enhancing the safeguards, standards, transparency and systems necessary to monitor and contain risks;
- continued encouragement to countries to remove capital market restrictions, coupled with strengthened policy advice from international financial institutions on the appropriate supervisory structures; and

- Finance ministers to commission studies and analysis from the international organisations responsible for banking and securities regulations and to report on the adequacy of current arrangements, together with proposals for improvement where necessary, at the next Summit.'

So there can be no doubt about the significance of the issues, or the need to resolve them.

Key Areas of Work (as identified at Windsor)

The key areas of work affecting markets which are being done post-Barings concern:

- co-operation between market authorities;
- protection of customer positions and funds/assets default procedures; and
- regulatory co-operation in emergencies.

Let me illustrate the significance of this work by picking on just one area—the treatment of large exposures within what is termed 'co-operation between market authorities'. (An example might be a market's exposure to the solvency of its member as a result of a large position held by that member on the market.) In this area, those present at Windsor agreed to promote 'active surveillance within each jurisdiction of large exposures by market authorities and/or regulators as appropriate'. They also agreed that further work should be undertaken to consider 'mechanisms whereby large exposure and other relevant information is and could be shared on a bilateral or multilateral basis among regulators and markets'.

This work is being carried forward in the IOSCO working group concerned with regulation of secondary markets. It is still at an early stage, and it is not yet possible to predict exactly what may result. But the possibility is that it will at least involve some form of shared understanding among market authorities or regulators that when they are worried about the size of an exposure to them, they will be able to verify with other markets claims that that exposure is hedged, or is otherwise not a risk position. These pieces of work are not being done, and could not satisfactorily be done, bilaterally with individual firms or markets. They are being done on a collaborative basis, involving all the major markets. This may be one element only, but it would be one element in the establishment of a structure, or system, designed to combat systemic risk affecting markets.

CONCLUSIONS

The conclusion I want to leave with you is one of optimism tempered with realism. The Barings case is a test case for international regulators. It has revealed a need for international action, which has been widely recognised and led to an ongoing agenda. It has changed the focus of securities regulation, making it more international, and more aware of the systemic risk issues affecting markets in particular.

An effective response will involve an ongoing system of safeguards, with markets and regulators working together in a cohesive way, which could fairly be described as the beginning of an international regulatory order. But while this is an ambitious goal, we must recognise—and in my view consciously aim—that an international regulatory structure needs to be qualitatively different from national regulatory structures. It must apply a principle of 'subsidiarity', so that what *can* be done nationally, *is* done nationally. It must be strong yet flexible. And, in order to be achievable, it must be targeted on what is essential in the common interest of us all—in other words, on systemic risk.

16

Cooperation and Convergence: The View from Brussels

CHRISTOPHER CRUICKSHANK

The European Union (EU) is a good example of convergence in the sense that the 15 Member States (MS) have agreed a very close degree of integration between their respective economies, in the areas of capital movement, export of goods, provision of services and movement of persons.

The financial sector is of course a vital component of this economic integration. We have worked hard over the last few years to create convergence in financial services, helped by the complete liberalisation of capital movements, which we have had since 1990. European legislation now provides for freedom to do cross-border business in the insurance, banking and securities sectors, whether on the basis of branches set up in host countries or on the basis of freedom of services.

Although convergence within Europe has been and continues to be a major goal this does not mean that the European market is closed in on itself. A few years ago some commentators saw in our internal market programme the risk that a 'fortress Europe' would result. I believe that experience now shows that this view was quite unjustified.

Capital movements freedom applies just as much to transfers between EU MS and other countries as it does to transfers between MS. The EU territory is open to the setting up of subsidiary companies owned by non-member state parents, which once incorporated in a EU MS have the same freedoms as locally-owned firms to provide financial services and set up branches in other MS. In other words such companies also have the benefits of the 'European passport'.

What the Commission would like to see is an equally open and liberal policy applied in other world markets. We are very pleased therefore with the outcome of the GATS negotiations in Geneva last July, where the EU negotiators were able to persuade countries like Japan and Korea to maintain their offers of most favoured nation (MFN) status despite a US preference for a more limited approach. We now have a valuable interim agreement which will last until 1997, and which we hope will be the basis for yet further progress.

Turning now more specifically to our legislation in the securities markets field, we have focused our efforts on two types of player in these markets, i.e. issuers of securities on the one hand and intermediaries, or investment firms, on the other.

As far as *issuers* are concerned, they should be able to tap the entire EU pool of savings, as far as possible with the same conditions and ease that they can tap pools of savings in their domestic markets.

We have made reasonable progress in opening up the European domestic markets to issuers of securities, considerably helped by the fact that capital movements have been completely liberalised. This allows issuers to make public offers in all MS and to become listed on stock exchanges there as well.

In particular, common standards have been agreed for public offer prospectuses i.e. prospectuses that have to be published when securities are sold to the public for the first time. This legislation is based on the principle of mutual recognition. This means that a public offer prospectus that has been approved in one MS can be used for simultaneous public offers of securities on several different domestic markets.

We would like to see greater use made of this facility. In the past a good number of privatizations have been limited to investors residing in a single MS. We feel that such offers should be open to investors from all MS, which would have the added advantage in promoting the liquidity of secondary trading in the securities in question.

We also have as a long term objective mutual recognition of disclosure documents, such as public offer prospectuses, as between the EU countries and other countries in the world having major capital markets. This would represent convergence on a truly international level.

In this respect, the Commission is following closely the discussions that are taking place in the International Organisation of Securities Commissions (IOSCO) on world-wide disclosure standards. Agreement on international accounting standards would enable the EU to enter into negotiations with countries outside the EU, aimed at securing mutual recognition of public offer and listing prospectuses, based on agreed international accounting standards.

We therefore welcomed the July 1995 agreement between IOSCO and IASC (International Accounting Standards Committee) to work together towards a comprehensive set of international accounting standards by the end of 1999.

We believe that companies should only be required to prepare one set of consolidated accounts. We plan to examine the possibility for European companies with an international vocation to prepare their consolidated accounts on the basis of international accounting standards, without however changing the directives on the annual accounts of companies.

As regards *securities intermediaries* the main obstacle that confronted us was to remove the barriers for intermediaries such as brokers, dealers and portfolio managers, to operate on a EU-wide basis. For this, we have followed the model of the single licence laid down in the Second Banking Coordination Directive. We believe that it would be unfair and unacceptable for banks to be able to operate in a securities market on the basis of a single licence but for non-bank investment intermediaries to be left out of this process. Consequently, the Investment Services Directive provides a European passport, or a single licence, for non-bank intermediaries to carry out a wide range of securities related activities.

This directive contains an additional feature, which is to liberalise and open up membership in the EU not only of stock exchanges but of derivatives markets as well. Once a firm has been authorised in its home MS, and whether it is a bank or a non-bank, it must then be considered as eligible for membership of the stock or futures exchange in the host MS.

The effect of this is that no MS will in future be able to maintain a statutory 'numerus clausus' in its stock exchange rules. Moreover the directive makes it possible to be a member of any stock exchange in the EU on an electronic basis without any physical presence in the country of the market itself. This should encourage a high degree of competition between stock exchanges and between derivative markets in the EU, with resulting improvements in the efficiency and liquidity of markets.

As regards the important problem of capital adequacy, we shall be keeping close contact with the ongoing work of the Basle-based Committee of Banking Supervision, and shall if necessary and appropriate put forward proposals to adjust the Capital Adequacy Directive (CAD) in the light of new recommendations made by the Committee. We consider that it is most important to ensure that convergence applies in this important area, and that the trading activities of EU based banks and investment firms are not put at a competitive disadvantage compared to their rivals based elsewhere.

The Basle Committee published in April 1995 proposals to enable widespread use by institutions of value-at-risk models in the measurement and control of market risks with a view to calculating capital requirements. Once the outcome of the consultation process in Basle is known, we will need in Brussels to initiate work on amending the CAD. We have indicated that models can be used even at the moment provided that they are approved by the supervisors and provided that the amount of regulatory capital does not fall below the minimum level set by the CAD.

Because the CAD applies to both credit institutions and investment firms this will mean that EU investment firms will also be able to make extensive use of value-at-risk models for capital adequacy purposes.

In this context a number of US securities firms under the name of the 'Derivatives Policy Group' have put forward a proposal on the use of models in the measurement of OTC derivative risks. We have found that there is much similarity here with the approach being developed in Basle and I understand that the IOSCO working groups have had the opportunity to examine them. It seems to me that there is once again a chance that international groupings of banking and securities supervisors can converge in terms of measuring the risk inherent in securities business. I do hope this chance will be seized. As I said earlier, we have benefited from finding a combined regime for banks and securities firms at the EU level, and it would be good to think that something similar could be produced internationally.

Cooperation between securities supervisors is an essential feature of our financial services legislation. Each of our directives provides for cooperation between the supervisors of the firm's home MS and those in the host countries where it is doing business. This cooperation takes the form of exchanges of information, protected by a professional secrecy regime. In many cases these cooperation arrangements have been given greater focus by the conclusion of bilateral agreements between supervisors known as 'memoranda of understanding'.

We welcome these closer ties between supervisors. Our own contribution to cooperation takes the form of inviting supervisors to regular meetings of an ad hoc committee, the role of which is to advise the Commission on policy issues and to discuss matters of common interest. We have recently submitted a proposal for a new directive to the Council and the European Parliament designed to formalise this committee and to put it onto the same basis as the Banking Advisory Committee. It would then be known as the 'Securities Committee', which in addition to an advisory role would have limited powers to make technical adaptation to existing legislation.

Although we have done much to create convergence in the EU the most important step still lies ahead of us. This is of course the introduction of a single currency. In addition to the considerable benefits to trade in manufactured goods that would result, truly integrated financial services markets would for the first time be possible.

In the securities field, trading of securities in the EU tends at the moment to be split up into several separate markets, each trading in its own domestic currency. This means that there is no single pool of capital that can be mobilised in the EU but rather several smaller pools. Investors investing in other currencies accept not only a price risk but also a currency risk.

A single currency would for the first time make possible a truly integrated securities market. We very much hope that the UK will in due time join with other MS in this common enterprise. We believe that this would be of inestimable benefit to financial service providers based in the City of London, whose undoubted expertise means that they are uniquely well placed to take advantage of the new perspectives that are opening up.

17

Liability of Derivatives Dealers

HAL S. SCOTT

The OTC derivatives market is huge. The 1995 International Swaps and Derivatives Association (ISDA) survey indicates that there was $11.5 trillion in contracts outstanding at the end of 1994. This activity has produced, by some accounts, at least 30 multimillion dollar derivative suits in the United States by customers against major securities firms that advised them about derivatives or entered into derivatives transactions with them in the 1990s. *Gibson Greetings v. Bankers Trust Co.*,[1] involved a claim for $32 million in compensatory damages and *Proctor & Gamble v. Bankers Trust Co.*,[2] involved a claim for $195 million. *Gibson* was settled for approximately $14 million in 1994. The real blockbuster was *Orange County Investment Pool v. Merrill Lynch & Co.*,[3] in which Orange County sued for $3 billion in damages.

Although there is great variety in the derivative transactions behind the different litigations, many of the transactions were swaps reflecting bets that interest rates would stay constant during 1993 and 1994. The *P&G* and *Gibson* derivatives were complex interest rate swaps where either a rise in short term or long term rates would very quickly put the parties in the red. Orange County involved structured notes called inverse floaters which represented a direct bet that interest rates would stay constant or decline.

The complaints in these litigations are based on a combination of common law and statutory claims that can be broken down into four main categories: ultra vires, fraud, suitability and contract. This Chapter examines each theory, as well as the exposure of dealers to regulatory sanctions.

ULTRA VIRES

The basic ultra vires claim is that the customer corporation was prohibited by law from engaging in a particular transaction. For example, Orange County claims that the transactions it entered into with Merrill Lynch were

[1] CV No. C-1-94-620 (S.D. Ohio, filed September 12, 1994).

[2] CV No. C-1-94 735 (S.D. Ohio, filed October 27, 1994).

[3] Ch. 9 Case No. SA 94-22272-JR, Adv. No. SA 94-1045-JR (C.D.B.R. Cal., filed January 12, 1995).

prohibited by the California Constitution because they required Orange County to become indebted in excess of Orange County's income and revenue for the year. Similarly, in *Lehman Bros. Commercial Corp. v. China International United Petroleum and Chemicals Co., Ltd.* ('*UNIPEC*'),[4] UNIPEC claims that its foreign exchange swaps were in violation of Chinese laws prohibiting all persons, except those approved by the State Administration of Exchange Control, from engaging in foreign exchange transactions.

The possibility of ultra vires swap contracts was a risk well known since the English case of *Hazell v. Hammersmith*,[5] where the House of Lords decided that thousands of interest rate swaps entered into by local authorities with banks were ultra vires and therefore void. The resulting mark-to-market losses to the banks have been estimated to be in excess of £500 million.[6]

In U.S. corporate law, the ultra vires defense to contract liability has limited application.[7] Corporate charters are now written in very broad terms and, where they are more limited, courts will allow apparent or inherent authority to trump the lack of actual authority. Courts are particularly reluctant to apply the doctrine when it is only invoked to avoid the losing side of a contractual bet and would not have been invoked if the bet had been profitable. As a matter of economic analysis, these limitations on the doctrine make sense. Generally, it would be cheaper for corporate owners to monitor their agents' compliance with a corporate charter than it would be for third parties contracting with the corporation.

If the Orange County contracts were subjected to this analysis, it might be quite difficult to hold the swap contracts ultra vires. The Treasurer of Orange County quite likely had apparent authority to enter into the contracts even if he did not have actual authority. And clearly the County is seeking to avoid unprofitable contracts which it might well have profited on. Economically, it would seem a lot cheaper for the State or the County to monitor contractual compliance with the State constitution than it would be for the derivative dealer, particularly where the capacity issue involves novel or difficult issues of interpretation of the enabling statutes or constitution.[8] The problem is not

[4] No. 94-CIV-8304 (S.D.N.Y., filed November 15, 1994).

[5] [1992] 2 AC 1.

[6] This is the amount the municipalities owed the banks on the contracts. In an attempt to reduce their losses, the banks sought to recover in restitution an estimated £125 million they had already paid on the void contracts.

[7] *See* R. Clark, *Corporate Law* §16.1 at 676 (1986).

[8] There is a serious question as to whether the contracts violated the California constitutional debt limitations. Apparently, Orange County entered into reverse repos with Merrill Lynch, using structured notes as well as regular instruments as collateral, to obtain the funds to finance the purchase of more structured notes. One could well argue that it was the reverse repos rather than investments in structured notes which exceeded any debt limitations. And the Treasurer had obtained an opinion of the California Attorney General that Orange County had authority to enter into reverse repos. On the other hand, the use of the structured notes as collateral for the reverse repo loans permit an argument that the structured notes were an integral part of the borrowing.

simply solved by obtaining a covenant of capacity from a counterparty. Such covenant would not likely be binding absent capacity.

Of course, Orange County is not a private corporation. One could well argue that the validity of the ultra vires defense should be different in the public contracts area because it is seeking to protect the public fisc for the benefit of taxpayers. On the other hand, why should one private firm rather than the public as a whole bear the loss for imprudent actions of public agents?

FRAUD

The fraud claims arise either out of common law or statutory law related to securities and commodities, the Securities Act of 1933, the Securities Exchange Act of 1934 (together the 'Securities Laws') or the Commodity Exchange Act. As the common law generally imposes no duty to reveal all material information, plaintiffs have a strong incentive to fit the derivative transaction in question into coverage of the Securities Laws or the Commodity Exchange Act. Coverage under these laws hinges on whether certain derivatives are deemed securities or commodities, a matter as yet undecided by the courts.

However, as a result of the *Gibson Greetings* case, the CFTC and the SEC both initiated investigations of Bankers Trust that resulted in consent orders whereby Bankers Trust agreed to pay a $10 million fine.[9] Both the SEC and CFTC concluded that Bankers Trust had committed fraud in the sale of certain derivatives. In fact, the SEC concluded that two of the twelve types of derivative transactions involving swaps were securities,[10] and the CFTC concluded that all twelve derivatives were some type of commodity option or future contract. Subsequent to the SEC order, P&G amended its complaint to include causes of action based on violations of the Securities Laws.

[9] *See In re BT Securities Corp.*, Rel Nos. 33-7124, 34-35136, 3-8579, Fed. Sec. L. Rep. (CCH) [1994–1995 Decisions] 85,477 (December 22, 1994).

[10] The term 'security' within the meaning of 3(a)(10) of the 1934 Act is: 'any note, stock, treasury stock, bond, debenture, certificate of interest or participation in any profit-sharing agreement or in any oil, gas, or other mineral royalty or lease, any collateral-trust certificate, preorganization certificate or subscription, transferable share, investment contract, voting-trust certificate, certificate of deposit, for a security, any put, call, straddle, option, or privilege on any security, certificate of deposit, or group or index of securities (including any interest therein or based on the value thereof), or any put, call, straddle, option, or privilege entered into on a national securities exchange relating to foreign currency, or in general, any instrument commonly known as a 'security'; or any certificate of interest or participation in, temporary or interim certificate for, receipt for, or warrant or right to subscribe to or purchase, any of the foregoing; but shall not include currency or any note, draft, bill of exchange, or banker's acceptance which has a maturity at the time of issuance of not exceeding nine months, exclusive of days of grace, or any renewal thereof the maturity of which is like-wise limited.' 15 U.S.C. §78c(a)(10).

It is still unclear which derivatives are deemed to be securities. The SEC order appears to take the position that swaps which can be characterized as options on securities, or indexes of securities, are securities. Thus, the two derivatives that the SEC deemed to be securities were interest rate swaps whose value was determined in reference to certain T-bill rates. However, the definition of 'security' in the 1934 Act is extremely broad and might cover all derivatives. As the Supreme Court stated recently in *Reves v. Ernst & Young*,[11] Congress enacted a definition of 'security' that was 'sufficiently broad to encompass virtually any instrument that might be sold as an investment.'

Assuming that a derivative is considered a security, the dealer in such a security would have an obligation to disclose material information about the security to a buyer. A major difficulty is encountered in determining what is material information with respect to a particular derivative. This issue has been addressed in a number of forums.

With respect to accounting, SFAS 119 *Disclosure about Derivative Financial Instruments and Fair Value of Financial Instruments* (October 1994)[12] requires the disclosure of the following information either in the body of the financial statements or in the accompanying footnotes:

- the amounts, nature, and terms of each class of derivatives, including differentiation between instruments held or issued for purposes of trading and purposes other than trading;
- the average, maximum, and minimum aggregate fair values during the reporting period of each class of derivatives held or issued for trading purposes, with differentiation between assets and liabilities;
- the net gains or losses arising from derivatives trading activities during the reporting period and where those net gains or losses are reported in the income statement;
- a description of the entity's objective for each class of derivatives held or issued for purposes other than trading and how these instruments are reported in financial statements; and
- a description of anticipated transactions for which the risks are hedged with derivatives, including the expected time frame for the transactions, the amount of related hedging gains and losses that are explicitly deferred, and the transactions or other events that result in recognition of the deferred gains and losses.

The SFAS encourages but does not require disclosure of quantitative information about interest rate risk or other markets risks of derivatives that is

[11] 494 U.S. 56, 61 (1990).

[12] Some of the requirements of SFAS 119 already applied to swaps under two prior statements, FASB Statement No. 105, *Disclosure of Information about Financial Instruments with Off-Balance Sheet Risk and Financial Instruments with Concentrations of Credit Risk* (March 1990) and FASB Statement No. 107, *Disclosures about Fair Value of Financial Instruments* (December 1991).

consistent with the way the entity manages those risks. It also encourages such disclosures about other assets and liabilities. These accounting standards are designed for 'public' disclosure in financial statements rather than for 'private' disclosure to an investor, the principal concern of this Chapter. However, derivative dealers might well be liable for failing to make adequate disclosure in their financial statements, and public disclosure obligations offers at least a starting point for thinking about the private disclosure issue.

The Bank for International Settlements (BIS), through the Working Group of the Euro-currency Standing Committee of the Central Banks of the Group of Ten countries, has put forward a discussion paper on *Public Disclosure of Market and Credit Risks by Financial Intermediaries* (September 1994). The paper is known as the Fisher Report, after the Chairman of the group, Peter R. Fisher, Executive Vice President of the Federal Reserve Bank of New York. The Report recommends that all financial intermediaries should move in the direction of publicly disclosing periodic quantitative information which expresses, in summary form, the estimates relied upon by the firm's management of:

- the market risks in the relevant portfolio or portfolios, as well as the firm's actual performance in managing the market risks in these portfolios;
- the counterparty credit risks arising from its trading and risk management activities, including current and potential future credit exposure as well as counterparty credit worthiness, in a form which permits evaluation of the firm's performance in managing credit risk.

The Report envisions disclosure of 'value-at-risk' analysis of derivatives portfolios for market risks. This is an analysis which gives statistical estimates of losses or gains over a given holding period, at a given confidence level. The Report suggests that what might be disclosed, as an example, would be the high, low, and average value-at-risk for holding periods of one-day, and two-weeks, that occurred during the reporting period. The Report, however, does not suggest mandating any particular method of calculating market risk.

As for credit risks, basic information would consist of current credit exposure (net replacement values when close-out netting arrangements are in place, otherwise gross replacement values), broken down by credit quality class, and/or counterparty type. It might also include further breakdowns by maturity, estimates of future credit exposure, and measures of losses over the reporting period. Again, no particular form of disclosure is envisioned.

Central bankers' concerns about disclosure are different from those of accountants. FASB is interested in the ability of anyone (analysts and counterparties, as well as investors) to evaluate firms with derivatives. The central bankers are concerned that markets have information in order to price the instruments, and that monetary authorities have sufficient information to formulate monetary policy. They are also concerned that counterparties have accurate information because this may reduce systemic risk, possible chain reaction bankruptcies. While these concerns are related, they are different and produce different formulations of disclosure standards.

One recent effort has touched on disclosure from the dealer—investor perspective.[13] Representatives from various dealer groups, including the International Swaps and Derivatives Association, on August 17, 1995 issued 'Principles and Practices for Wholesale Financial Market Transactions ('the Principles').' The preparation of the Principles was coordinated by the Federal Reserve Bank of New York. The Principles do not mandate any disclosure. Section 4.2.2 entitled 'Reliance on Investment Advice' provides that a 'Participant *may* communicate to its counterparty economic or market information relating to Transactions and trade or hedging ideas or suggestions. All such communications (whether written or oral) should be accurate and not intentionally misleading.'[14] Section 4.2.3 entitled 'Transaction Information' puts the onus on the investor in obtaining information. It provides that:

> A Participant should either ask questions and request additional information or seek independent professional advice when it does not have a full understanding of either the risks involved in a Transaction or the fit between a Transaction and its desired risk profile. A counterparty should answer such questions and respond to such requests for additional information in good faith, and the information provided should be accurate and not intentionally misleading. A participant should expect that, if it does not expressly ask questions or request additional information with respect to a transaction, its counterparty will assume that the Participant understands the transaction and has all the information it needs for its decision-making process.

The Principles seem to adopt a common law fraud approach under which disclosure is voluntary and only actionable when inaccurate or intentionally misleading, as contrasted with the Securities law approach in which disclosure is mandatory, and the failure to disclose material information is actionable. Also, there is some difficulty in making an investor responsible for not asking the right question. How does one know what he doesn't know? The SEC plans to formulate its approach to this issue in a Draft Concept Release scheduled for release in 1995.

OTC derivatives are different from most other securities (including exchange-traded derivatives like futures and options) in one important respect—they are generally offered to and often designed for a particular

[13] See also, Institute of International Finance, 'A Preliminary Framework For Public Disclosure of Derivatives Activities and Related Credit Exposures (1994).

[14] Emphasis added.

customer, not the general investing public. This has at least one important consequence. Disclosure needs can be judged in the context of particular investors. Disclosure needed by the Treasurer of P&G could well be different from that needed by less sophisticated investors. Where securities are generally offered to a wide range of investors it is not feasible to tailor disclosure requirements to particular investors, whereas it is feasible for OTC derivatives.[15] In effect, the disclosure issue tends to merge with the suitability issue discussed below.

SUITABILITY

Suitability claims appear in two forms: the pure suitability claim and the disclosure suitability claim. In the pure suitability claim the plaintiff claims that the defendant violated his duty to recommend and sell only suitable investments. In order to recover, the plaintiff must prove that the investments were unsuitable, the defendant had a duty not to recommend or sell unsuitable investments, the defendant acted with some level of intent, and that the plaintiff reasonably relied on the defendant's recommendation in purchasing the security.[16] Plaintiffs have pointed to four different sources of rules that can create the duty to recommend or sell only suitable investments: the common law fiduciary duty, Rule 10b-5 of the 1934 Act, the New York Stock Exchange's (NYSE) Know Your Customer Rule, and the National Association of Securities Dealers' (NASD) Suitability Rule.

In *P&G* and *Gibson Greetings*, plaintiffs tried to show that the derivative dealers assumed the role of advisor to the plaintiff and thus assumed fiduciary duties. Other plaintiffs have supplemented this argument with appeal to the NYSE's Know Your Customer Rule[17] and the NASD Suitability Rule.[18] It is currently unclear whether a private right of action exists under

[15] Of course, if one generally thinks that mandatory disclosure obligations should be kept to a minimum, one would favour less disclosure for derivatives as well. See F. Easterbrook and D. Fischel, *The Economic Structure of Corporate Law* 276-314 (1991).

[16] See e.g. *Brown v. E.F. Hutton, et. al.*, 991 F.2d 1020 (2nd Cir. 1993); *Tiernan v. Blyth, Eastman, Dillon & Co.*, 719 F.2d 1 (1st Cir. 1983); *Clark v. John Lamula Investors, Inc.*, 583 F.2d 594 (2nd Cir. 1978).

[17] Every member organization is required through a general partner, a principle executive officer or a person or person designated under the provisions of Rule 342(b)(1) to (1) use due diligence to learn the essential facts relative to every customer, every order, every cash or margin account accepted or carried by such organization and every person holding power of attorney over any account accepted or carried by such organization. (2) Supervise diligently all accounts handled by registered representatives of the organization . . .' CCH New York Stock Exchange Guide, sec. 2405

[18] In recommending to a customer the purchase, sale or exchange of any security, a member shall have reasonable grounds for believing that the recommendation is suitable for such customer upon the basis of the facts, if any, disclosed by such customer as to his other security holdings and as to his financial situation and needs.' CCH NASD Manual, sec. 2152 (Art. III, sec. 2).

these two rules, but it appears that violations of the rules can at least be a factor in determining whether dealers have committed fraud under Rule 10b-5 by selling unsuitable investments. Dealers may have a defense that the plaintiff either knew, or by reasonable investigation could have known, that the investments were unsuitable.

The central issue in this area is whether a large sophisticated investor should have a suitability claim. While this may seem dubious, the City of San Jose effectively utilized a 10b-5 suitability claim to win a jury verdict against multiple brokerage firms.[19]

A plaintiff's sophistication alone is generally not dispositive of whether a given investment is suitable. An investment bet with a 100-1 payoff would not appear suitable for a sophisticated pensioner with limited resources. Courts rather determine suitability based on the investment objectives of the plaintiff.[20] If a defendant recommends a speculative investment to an investor that he knows is pursuing conservative investment goals, one might conclude it was done with fraudulent intent. However, one might argue that sophistication is quite relevant in this context. If the sophisticated pensioner accepts the risky bet, perhaps he has changed his investment objectives.

Sophistication is clearly relevant to the issue of reasonable reliance. If the plaintiff knew or could have known that the investment was unsuitable to his investment objectives, there is a strong argument that he should not be allowed to recover.

The disclosure suitability claim is a mixture of a pure suitability claim and a fraud claim. The complaint is that the dealer committed fraud not by recommending or selling an unsuitable security, but by doing so without disclosing that the investment was unsuitable. The sophisticated investor is likely to argue that he reasonably relied on the recommendation given what he was told, but would not have done so if he knew all the facts. The disclosure suitability claim could properly be applied to a sophisticated investor since even a sophisticated investor would be unable to judge the suitability of an investment to his risk preferences without knowing the material risks of the investment.

The Principles also deal with the suitability issue. Section 4.2.2. provides:

> Absent a written agreement or an applicable law, rule or regulation that expressly imposes affirmative obligations to the contrary, a counterparty receiving . . . communications should assume that the Participant is acting at arm's length for its own account and that such communications are not recommendations or investment advise on which the counterparty may rely.

Only if an investor informs a dealer that it wishes to rely on its advice, the

[19] *City of San Jose v. Paine Weber*, No. C 84-20601, Order Denying Motion for New Trial (N.D. Cal. 1991).

[20] See *Lefkowitz v. Smith Barney, Harris Upham & Co.*, 804 F.2d 154, 155 (1st Cir. 1986); *Tiernan, supra* at 5.

dealer agrees to do business on that basis and the investor gives the dealer information about his financial situation, will the dealer incur any responsibility for recommending suitable investments.

The drafters explicitly rejected an 'alternative approach' that would require a dealer to determine the suitability of an investment recommendation. Their commentary states, 'the alternative approach would undermine the finality of agreed Transactions, and create tremendous uncertainty regarding the economic risk position of participants.'[21]

In March 1995 six major securities firms, in cooperation with the SEC and CFTC, agreed to adopt a *Framework for Voluntary Oversight* ('Voluntary Framework') under which the firms would undertake to have certain management controls, submit quantitative reports covering credit risk exposures, evaluate risk relative to capital and adopt guidelines for dealing with non-professional counterparties to derivatives contracts. While the Voluntary Framework, like the Principles, generally takes an arm's length approach, it goes significantly further in placing affirmative obligations on dealers. In 'Counterparty Relationships,' II.C (Nature of Relations), it states:[22]

> In cases where existing transaction documentation does not expressly address the nature of the relationship between the professional intermediary and its nonprofessional counterparty and the professional intermediary becomes aware that the nonprofessional counterparty believes incorrectly that the professional intermediary has assumed advisory or similar responsibilities towards the nonprofessional counterparty with respect to a prospective OTC derivative transaction, the professional intermediary should take steps to clarify the nature of the relationship.

It goes on to provide in II.E:

> *Specific Transaction Proposals.* In circumstances where a professional intermediary, at the express request of a nonprofessional counterparty, formulates a specific OTC derivative transaction proposal that is tailored to particular transactional objectives specified by the counterparty, the professional intermediary should formulate the transaction proposal in good faith based on the information and objectives specified by the counterparty and subject to the terms of the parties' contractual arrangement.

And II. F further provides:

> *Special Situations.* In circumstances where a nonprofessional counterparty has expressly requested assistance in evaluating an OTC derivative transaction in which

[21] The Principles, at 7.

[22] The drafters use two key terms throughout, 'professional intermediary' (a dealer) and 'nonprofessional counterparty.' Although it is not entirely clear, nonprofessional counterparty seems to refer to any counterparty who is not a professional intermediary. Thus, it would include the treasurers of corporations. This terminology, which implicitly recognizes the possible disparity in knowledge between professional intermediaries and sophisticated investors, is in contrast to the terminology of the 'Principles' where everyone is a 'Participant.'

the payment formula is particularly complex or which includes a significant leverage component, the professional intermediary should offer to provide additional information, such as scenario, sensitivity or other analyses, to the nonprofessional counterparty or should recommend that the counterparty obtain professional advice.

The Voluntary Framework clearly imposes more obligations on dealers than does the Principles.[23] This partially reflects the different orientation of the regulators involved. The first concern of the SEC in the Voluntary Framework would be to protect investors whereas the first concern of the Federal Reserve Bank of New York in the Principles would be to protect the safety and soundness of banks by limiting their liability. One significant difficulty in this area arises from the proliferation of suitability rules. While none of the private rules are binding, they could well be invoked or cited by courts.

CONTRACT

There are two main types of contract claims. The first is that an investor is not bound by his investment agreement. For example, UNIPEC argues that it was not bound by its agreement because it was made by an agent with no authority to bind the corporation, and Gibson argued that a swap with Bankers Trust was not binding because it was made under economic duress in a situation of financial emergency. UNIPEC's argument is a first cousin to the ultra vires argument examined earlier. Although UNIPEC does not claim the corporation had no power to enter into the contract, it does claim that the particular agent who entered into the contract had no corporate authority. While it remains to be seen whether the agent had apparent authority even if he lacked actual authority, obviously the claim that an agent acted beyond his authority is a standard one and should not be surprising in the derivatives context.

The second type of claim is that the contract should embody certain prior oral understandings reached between the parties or, if it does not, that there was no meeting of the minds and thus no contract at all. P&G claims that it never agreed to Bankers Trust's secret and proprietary early lock-in pricing model as a term of its derivative transactions. UNIPEC claims that it had an oral agreement with Lehman Brothers to close out all transactions if they reached a net debt position of $5 million (later raised to $8 million). Again, this is just a standard contract claim. Obviously if derivatives dealers breach their contracts they may be held liable. The implications of

[23] Section 5 of the Principles, 'Considerations Relating to Relationships Between Participants' discusses more affirmative obligations. However, such obligations are introduced with the phrase 'A Participant may wish to . . . [do various things].'

this claim is that the key characteristics of the instruments may have to be documented and agreed in writing.[24]

REGULATORY ACTIONS

The SEC and CFTC actions show that derivatives dealers are exposed to federal agency actions, based on the concerns of these agencies with investor protection. Bank dealers are also exposed to actions by bank regulators. A written Agreement between the Federal Reserve Bank of New York and Bankers Trust of December 5, 1994 ('the Agreement'),[25] focuses on Bankers Trust's leveraged derivatives (LDT) business.[26] The Fed's concern is that bank holding companies under its supervision will be damaged by allegations and recoveries based on claims of fraud. Therefore, the remedial measures required by the Agreement require greater disclosure of risks to customers, greater transparency of pricing and better control over the actions of people involved in marketing and selling derivatives.

For example, the Fed's order requires that Bankers Trust shall conduct its LDT Business in a manner which seeks to reasonably ensure that each LDT customer has the capability to understand the nature and material terms, conditions, and risks of any LDT entered into with the customer. It further provides that Bankers Trust shall distribute to each customer written term sheets and sensitivity analyses designed to illustrate a broad range of outcomes and distribution of risks at maturity. Bankers Trust must constantly update its customers as to risks. The Agreement also provides that Bankers Trust will update its customer as to the value of positions entered into. It is unclear to what extent the practices set forth in the Agreement will be applied to the derivatives business of other banks.

CONCLUSION

Derivatives dealers face serious threats of liability to sophisticated investors under the various theories of liability examined herein. From the normal

[24] This is suggested by the Voluntary Framework, II.F. Such documentation is not part of ISDA standard documentation because it is too transaction-specific.

[25] Fed. Banking L. Rep. (CCH) [Current] 90,332.

[26] 'For purposes of this Agreement the leveraged derivative transaction business is intended to encompass derivative transactions (I) where a market move of two standard deviations in the first month would lead to a reduction in value to the counterparty of the lower of 15 percent of the notional amount or $10 million, and (ii) for notes or transactions with a final exchange of principal, where counterparty principal (rather than coupon) is at risk at maturity, and (iii) for coupon swaps, where the coupon can drop to zero (or below) or exceed twice the market rate for that market at maturity, and (iv) for spread trades that include an explicit leverage factor, where a spread is defined as the difference in the yield between two asset classes.'

perspective of the securities laws, this might appear routine; dealers are just being held accountable for how they sell new investment products, and securities laws have always been applied to sophisticated investors (albeit somewhat differently than to unsophisticated investors). And there is nothing much new about the doctrine of ultra vires or holding parties to contractual obligations. But since many securities dealers are banks, and since significant legal exposures could affect their safety and soundness, there may be a concern about applying normal rules in this situation. The solution to this problem, in my opinion, is not to change the standards, but to make them clearer. Currently, there is much confusion as to what needs to be disclosed with respect to particular derivatives, and what the proper suitability standards should be. Hopefully, these issues will soon be addressed by the SEC.

There is a significant need to improve the documentation of derivatives transactions; they cannot be documented like standard securities trades.[27] The documents cover such matters as:

- the relationship of the parties, e.g. is the dealer acting as an advisor or merely a seller;
- the investment objectives of the customer and the suitability of the derivative given such objectives;
- the material properties of the derivative (this could be tailored for individual products against a standard baseline for 'plain vanilla' products); and
- any ongoing reporting duties of the dealer with regard to the value or properties of the product.

[27] *See* T. Plews, 'Fighting the fear factor in documenting derivatives,' *European Financial Services Law* (August/September 1995).

Index